The Eschatological Person

VERITAS
Series Introduction

"... the truth will set you free" (John 8:32)

In much contemporary discourse, Pilate's question has been taken to mark the absolute boundary of human thought. Beyond this boundary, it is often suggested, is an intellectual hinterland into which we must not venture. This terrain is an agnosticism of thought: because truth cannot be possessed, it must not be spoken. Thus, it is argued that the defenders of "truth" in our day are often traffickers in ideology, merchants of counterfeits, or anti-liberal. They are, because it is somewhat taken for granted that Nietzsche's word is final: truth is the domain of tyranny.

Is this indeed the case, or might another vision of truth offer itself? The ancient Greeks named the love of wisdom as *philia*, or friendship. The one who would become wise, they argued, would be a "friend of truth." For both philosophy and theology might be conceived as schools in the friendship of truth, as a kind of relation. For like friendship, truth is as much discovered as it is made. If truth is then so elusive, if its domain is *terra incognita*, perhaps this is because it arrives to us—unannounced—as gift, as a person, and not some thing.

The aim of the Veritas book series is to publish incisive and original current scholarly work that inhabits "the between" and "the beyond" of theology and philosophy. These volumes will all share a common aspiration to transcend the institutional divorce in which these two disciplines often find themselves, and to engage questions of pressing concern to both philosophers and theologians in such a way as to reinvigorate both disciplines with a kind of interdisciplinary desire, often so absent in contemporary academe. In a word, these volumes represent collective efforts in the befriending of truth, doing so beyond the simulacra of pretend tolerance, the violent, yet insipid reasoning of liberalism that asks with Pilate, "What is truth?"—expecting a consensus of non-commitment; one that encourages the commodification of the mind, now sedated by the civil service of career, ministered by the frightened patrons of position.

The series will therefore consist of two "wings": (1) original monographs; and (2) essay collections on a range of topics in theology and philosophy. The latter will principally be the products of the annual conferences of the Centre of Theology and Philosophy (www.theologyphilosophycentre.co.uk).

Conor Cunningham and Eric Austin Lee, *Series editors*

The Eschatological Person

Alexander Schmemann and Joseph Ratzinger in Dialogue

ANDREW T. J. KAETHLER

Foreword by D. Vincent Twomey

CASCADE *Books* · Eugene, Oregon

THE ESCHATOLOGICAL PERSON
Alexander Schmemann and Joseph Ratzinger in Dialogue

Veritas Series

Copyright © 2022 Andrew T. J. Kaethler. All rights reserved. Except for brief quotations in critical publications or reviews, no part of this book may be reproduced in any manner without prior written permission from the publisher. Write: Permissions, Wipf and Stock Publishers, 199 W. 8th Ave., Suite 3, Eugene, OR 97401.

Cascade Books
An Imprint of Wipf and Stock Publishers
199 W. 8th Ave., Suite 3
Eugene, OR 97401

www.wipfandstock.com

PAPERBACK ISBN: 978-1-6667-3371-6
HARDCOVER ISBN: 978-1-6667-2861-3
EBOOK ISBN: 978-1-6667-2862-0

Cataloguing-in-Publication data:

Names: Kaethler, Andrew T. J., author. | Twomey, Vincent, foreword.

Title: The eschatological person : Alexander Schmemann and Joseph Ratzinger in dialogue / Andrew T. J. Kaethler ; foreword by D. Vincent Twomey.

Description: Eugene, OR : Cascade Books, 2022 | Series: Veritas | Includes bibliographical references and index.

Identifiers: ISBN 978-1-6667-3371-6 (paperback) | ISBN 978-1-6667-2861-3 (hardcover) | ISBN 978-1-6667-2862-0 (ebook)

Subjects: LCSH: Eschatology. | Theological anthropology—Christianity—History of doctrines—20th century. | Schmemann, Alexander, 1921–. | Benedict XVI, Pope, 1927–.

Classification: BT701.3 K34 2022 (paperback) | BT701.3 K34 (ebook)

07/08/22

With one exception, Bible quotations are from the Catholic Edition of the Revised Standard Version of the Bible, copyright © 1965, 1966 National Council of the Churches of Christ in the United States of America. Used by permission. All rights reserved worldwide.

First Cor 15:28 follows the translation used by Schmemann and Ratzinger, the New Revised Standard Version Bible: Catholic Edition, copyright © 1989, 1993 National Council of the Churches of Christ in the United States of America. Used by permission. All rights reserved worldwide.

All italics are original to the quotations, unless otherwise indicated.

To Mom and Dad,
who challenged me to reach out beyond myself.

In the Christian teaching man is always a *person* and thus not only a "microcosm" reflecting the whole world, but also a unique bearer of its destiny and a potential "king of creation." The whole world is given—in a unique way—to each person and thus in each person it is "saved" or "perishes."

—Alexander Schmemann

One can consider the personal as the really real, the stronger and higher form of reality, which does not reduce the biological and mechanical to mere appearance, but draws them into itself and thus opens them up to a new dimension.

—Joseph Ratzinger

Life in its true sense is not something we have exclusively in or from ourselves: it is a relationship. And life in its totality is a relationship with him who is the source of life. If we are in relation with him who does not die, who is Life itself and Love itself, then we are in life. Then we "live."

—Pope Benedict XVI

Contents

Acknowledgments ix

Foreword by D. Vincent Twomey xi

Introduction xvii

1. Schmemann: Eschatology as Context 1
2. Schmemann and Personhood: Eucharistic Beings 34
3. Ratzinger: Eschatology as Christology 78
4. Ratzinger and Personhood: "Beyond the Self" 137
5. Conclusion: A Matter of Time 184

Bibliography 199

Index 209

Acknowledgments

First and foremost, I am deeply grateful for my wife, Alene. Without her support, love, spiritual and nutritional nourishment, friendship, and encouragement none of this would have been possible. Charlotte, Paige, Lewis, Alasdair, Madeline, and Elizabeth, thank you for daily reminding me that there are more important things in life than academics, i.e., you, my family!

The topic of relationality arose out of relationality, out of friendship that was ignited at a conference I attended in Durham. Much argument, banter, beer, and bread was shared with Sotiris Mitralexis, Norm Klassen, and Fr. Isidoros Katsos, inspiring the theological musings that fed directly into my work as a PhD student at the University of St Andrews. In St Andrews, the dialogue continued with Loe-Joo Tan, Keith Jagger, John-Harmen Valk, and David Baird. I am grateful to David not only for his dialogue and friendship but also for tangibly representing and continuing the Catholic conversation/conversion that was being stirred up in print by Joseph Ratzinger. As this book began its life as a doctoral thesis, I must thank my PhD supervisor Alan Torrance. If it were not for him, I would not have added Ratzinger as the other interlocutor in my project. I am also thankful for Alan's intellectual perceptivity, pastoral encouragement, and his optimistic *Lebenskraft*. I am grateful for the comments and encouragement given by the examiners of my thesis, Fergus Kerr and Vincent Twomey.

Much thanks to Norm Klassen for reading through and commenting on this work when it was still in its PhD form. I am also thankful for Norm's and Jens Zimmerman's support and advice on a number of the related articles that preceded this monograph. I am grateful for the friendship and intellectual inspiration of Jared Schumacher who willingly dialogues with anyone, for Fr. Vincent Twomey's ongoing encouragement and mentorship, and for Conor Cunningham's interest in including this book in his series.

Some of the material in this book was previously published in academic journals and in an edited volume. I appreciate the permission for republication by the following journals: *Modern Theology*, *Mitteilungen Institut Papst Benedikt XVI*, and *Logos: A Journal of Catholic Thought and Culture*; and by Wipf and Stock for allowing me to republish material from my chapter in Eric Austin Lee and Samuel Kimbriel's edited volume, *The Resounding Soul: Reflections on the Metaphysics and Vivacity of the Human Person*.

Over the last five years, I have repeatedly taught a course at Catholic Pacific College based on Ratzinger's *Introduction to Christianity*. This provided the opportunity to continue to steep myself in Ratzinger's relational ontology and also enabled me to share Ratzinger's fantastic and profound insights with my students—thanks for letting me gush about all things Ratzingerian! I am grateful for these students and to have shared in their excitement as they, too, discovered and encountered the God who *is* love because he *is* relation.

Foreword

JOSEPH RATZINGER'S BOOK *ESCHATOLOGY: Death and Eternal Life* was about to be published in 1977, when he received a letter from Pope Paul VI at the end of the summer semester appointing him archbishop of Munich and Freising. His election was the last thing the born-academic wanted. As he said years later in an interview,[1] he was at the time primed to write his *magnum opus* on dogmatic theology, having completed eight fruitful years on the Regensburg Faculty of Theology. There, he had finally found a congenial home after his spectacular journey through the major German universities during some of the most tumultuous years in the history of theology: before, during, and after the Second Vatican Council. His *Eschatology* was not a part of that major project. It was something less ambitious, namely his one and only contribution to the *Kleine katholische Dogmatik*, a pocketbook-size series on dogmatic theology that he had planned with his colleague Johann Auer. But it was the fruit of some twenty years of teaching and reflecting on the subject.

In the same interview, he frankly confessed that his only ambition in life was to make an original contribution as a theologian in response to the intellectual and existential challenges of our times. Such would no longer be possible as archbishop of Munich, one of the biggest dioceses in Europe. And yet, it is no exaggeration to say that his small book, *Eschatology: Death and Eternal Life*, is precisely that: an original answer to some of the most existentially explosive issues in both church and politics today. He considered this—for all its conciseness—"his best-executed work."[2] He wrote it during a sabbatical semester in 1976. It is indeed dense and profound but also highly controversial. On publication, it gave rise immediately to a virulent debate among his fellow German theologians.

1. Seewald, *Benedict XVI*, 2:97.
2. Seewald, *Benedict XVI*, 2:88.

He had questioned some of their fundamental assumptions.

To quote the title of chapter 1, those assumptions amounted to the effective denial of the essence of Christianity. The tract on eschatology, which dealt primarily with the "Four Last Things" (death, judgment, heaven, and hell), was no longer taken seriously by theologians—and consequently was ignored in preaching. At the pastoral level, prayer for the repose of the souls of the dead was seen as redundant. When the "Four Last Things" were touched on, it was only to criticize their theological underpinning. In a sense, this was understandable, since in the earlier manuals of dogmatic theology, they had been treated in a narrow, individualistic way, being effectively summed up as "saving one's soul." Ratzinger was acutely aware that his eschatology, rooted as it is in Scripture (as interpreted in the light of the church's living Tradition), was radically countercultural.

As Ratzinger wrote in an introduction to the sixth edition in 1990, the book was written in the first place against the background of the emergence of the new theologies of hope, which soon mutated into different forms of "political theology." In effect, theologians had transformed hope of eternal life into hope for a better future in this world; their theologies of hope would find their most radical expression in the various liberation theologies. One more lasting effect was the preoccupation of missionaries with peace, justice, and the integrity of creation, to the exclusion of the deeper concern for eternal salvation. Contemporary secular politics was (and still is) dominated by various forms of utopianism, i.e., attempts to create the kingdom of God here on earth in the not-too-distant (but, in fact, never-to-be-realized) future. In the words of the political philosopher Eric Voegelin, the divergent forms of secular politics can be described as nothing other than various forms of the immanentization of the eschaton.[3] As we know from the history of the twentieth century, instead of paradise on earth, they ended up creating hell on earth. In fact, both the new theologies of hope and the dominant understanding of politics today (and not just progressivism or neo-Marxism) share the same intellectual roots, which both Ratzinger and Voegelin trace back to the mystic Joachim of Fiore (1135–1202). As a result, the various theologies of hope, and their related political theologies produced by Catholic and Protestant theologians, found an immediate resonance with the broader public, to the detriment of both Christian living and political life.

---

3. See Voegelin, *New Science of Politics*, 107–62.

In the second place, Ratzinger recalls that, in the wake of Vatican II, the crisis with regard to Tradition had become virulent in the Catholic Church. The immediate result was the attempt to reconstruct faith directly from Scripture itself but without recourse to Tradition. Accordingly, it was claimed that the notion of the "immortality of the soul" had to be rejected as a "Platonism" that, in the church's theology and praxis over the centuries, had superimposed itself on the original biblical faith in the resurrection. "Together with an extraordinary philosophy of a timelessness that reigned beyond death, it was then explained that the resurrection takes place at the moment of death. This theory soon found its way into the language of preaching, so that in many places the liturgy of praying for a dead person was designated as 'a celebration of the resurrection.'"[4]

Both these trends in theology raised fundamental issues that affect not just theology but society at large and the everyday lives of Christians. In theology, these included the question of the interpretation of Scripture and the role of Tradition (and so of the church's authority) in that task. The central issue, however, was the meaning of being a person situated in time and destined for eternity. This raised the question of the meaning of salvation itself and so of divine worship. What was at stake was the meaning of Christ's own death and resurrection, the very core of our faith. Profound philosophical questions were involved in all of these theological issues, but above all, the nature of time and eternity, the coherence of the body-soul dualism, and the place of metaphysics in the modern approach to theology in terms of salvation history. At the existential level (and so at the pastoral level) the issues included the meaning of what it is to be a person in community, of death and eternal life, of divine worship and how it relates to politics. In sum: what does it mean to be a Christian?

The theological tracts on eschatology and ecclesiology had been the two topics Ratzinger had dealt with most often during his career as a professor of dogmatic theology. He explored the various issues in different contexts in his voluminous publications as an academic. He would continue to develop them as archbishop, as cardinal prefect of the Congregation for the Doctrine of the Faith, and as Pope Benedict XVI.

The author of this important book focuses on two of the most central issues of all: the human person and time. In the first place, how does one's understanding of eschatology shape one's conception of temporality; and secondly, what bearing does an answer to that question have on

---

4. Benedict XVI, *Tod und Ewiges Leben*, 12 (author's translation).

an understanding of what it is to be a person? In sum: what does it mean to be a person in time? To answer this question, Kaethler compares the answers given by one of the major, modern Russian Orthodox theologians, Alexander Schmemann, to those given by Ratzinger.

The choice of Protopresbyter Schmemann (1921–1983) is significant for several reasons. He was the long-term dean at St. Vladimir's Orthodox Theological Seminary, New York, renowned among other things for its liturgical theology, as well as adjunct professor on several universities and theology faculties. Father Schmemann was not only an expert in the Eastern theological tradition but was also well versed in Catholic theology. While studying at the St. Sergius Orthodox Theological Institute in Paris, he became familiar with the theology of a number of the prominent French Catholic theologians, such as Jean Daniélou. More importantly, as Schmemann once wrote, eschatology was the driving force of all his theology. One could say the same about Ratzinger. And finally, like Ratzinger, for Schmemann, the Divine Liturgy was a primary focus of his theology both as a source and as a goal. Knowing Ratzinger's appreciation of the Eastern theological tradition and his close personal relations with so many Orthodox theologians, it is indeed likely that they met in person at the Second Vatican Council, where Schmemann was one of the Orthodox observers. (Ratzinger refers to one of Schmemann's works in a commentary on a text taken from *Lumen Gentium*, the Council's Dogmatic Constitution on the Church.)[5]

What does it mean to be a person in time? This fundamental question raises the further question as to the relationship between ontology and history, specifically salvation history, and thus eschatology. This book examines how Schmemann's and Ratzinger's different understanding of eschatology shapes their respective notions of personhood. Influenced by the rise of philosophical personalism in the early twentieth century, both authors find personalism (understood in terms of a relational ontology) a fitting means for expressing what it means to be a person in time. Both authors are allowed to speak for themselves. The result is an illuminating and a constructive dialogue. Their agreement and their differences emerge from the writer's presentation of their respective theologies in such a way as to highlight existential implications of each approach for the Christian attitude to life.

---

5. Ratzinger, "Konzilsaussagen über die Mission" (Conciliar Statements about Mission; with reference to Schmemann's contribution in *La primauté de Pierre dans l'Église orthodoxe*, by N. Afanassieff et al.), 27.

Schmemann's writings have not been subject to the appreciation or critical analysis they deserve. This book is a welcome contribution to both, offering the reader an insight into the richness of his liturgical theology and stimulating further research. By way of contrast, though Ratzinger's theology was generally ignored during his long tenure as prefect of the Congregation for the Doctrine of the Faith, it has in recent years been increasingly the subject of critical analysis by younger theologians. This welcome publication is a serious contribution to the evaluation of both thinkers—but it is also a stimulus to contemporary theologians to take up the challenges implicit in their respective theologies, a challenge made more urgent by the theological task to achieve church unity based on the truth.

I happened to be present in his lecture hall at the University of Regensburg to witness the occasion when, in December 1974, Professor Joseph Ratzinger was conferred with the *Golden Cross of Mount Athos* by Metropolitan Damaskinos Papandreou. The honor was in recognition of the way Ratzinger had long encouraged ecumenical dialogue but also for the support he gave to various Orthodox students, as well as for his involvement in establishing the Orthodox Center at Chambésy, Geneva. Years later, reflecting on the honor given to him on that day, he wrote that he did not consider it "an honour in the usual sense but rather as a permanent task to respond to the spiritual heritage of Mount Athos, to the call to unity, with all the force and with that humility which behooves the passion for unity, in other words, the patience of waiting, patience that does not want to do of itself what only God can give."[6]

D. Vincent Twomey

---

6. Ratzinger, "Grußwort," 10–11.

Introduction

The truth is that only in the mystery of the incarnate Word does the mystery of man take on light. For Adam, the first man, was a figure of Him Who was to come, namely Christ the Lord.

—*Gaudium et Spes*

"O Lord, what is man that thou dost regard him or the son of man that thou dost think of him? Man is like a breath, his days are like a passing shadow" (Ps 144:3–4). Quoting Ludwig Feuerbach, Alexander Schmemann pithily replies that "Man is what he eats"[1] and argues that Feuerbach's link between food and human identity matches the biblical conception of the human person. According to Schmemann, we first see the link between food and human identity in Genesis with Adam and Eve eating the forbidden fruit and finally in the Gospels with the Last Supper. The human person is the creature who communes with God sacramentally through the created order; through this sacramental engagement, the human person is brought into relation with all things. With this relational image of the human person, Schmemann sets out the argument for his sacramental vision of reality and argues that, ironically, while Feuerbach is correct, his conclusions are wrong, because his image of the person excludes God.

In agreement with Schmemann, Joseph Ratzinger makes clear that "we do not speak rightly about man unless we also speak about God. But we cannot speak rightly about God unless God himself tells us who

---

1. Schmemann, *For Life of World*, 11.

he is."² The human person remains shrouded in mystery without God's self-disclosure in the person of Jesus Christ. Like us, Jesus lived in a particular time and location. To affirm the incarnation, therefore, is to affirm that God entered into time. As a result, temporality has its place in the midst of our ontological questions of what it means to be human. In other words, it is not enough to ask what it means to be a human person. We must ask what it means to be a person in time. In Christian theology, moreover, questions about temporality inevitably lead to eschatology. Eschatology provides meaning and direction to temporality, revealing its true nature. Therefore, the aforementioned question of time and personhood is transformed, leading to the question that shapes this present work: how does eschatology shape personhood in the theologies of Schmemann and Ratzinger?

As seen in the work of the twentieth-century continental existentialist philosophers, the question of personhood and time has considerable ethical implications.³ Shifting away from traditional definitions of the human person that are based on metaphysical notions of substance, these philosophers construed temporality as the fundamental reality that pertains to the human person: we are beings in time. As a result, new questions arose, particularly: can we speak of what it means to be a human person (assuming an essentialist approach), or can we speak only of particular persons (implying an anti-essentialist one)? Sartre famously stressed, "Existence precedes essence."⁴ Likewise, Martin Heidegger argues that "the 'essence' of *Da-sein* lies in its existence. The characteristics to be found in this being are thus not objectively present 'attributes' of an objectively present being which has such and such an 'outward appearance,' but rather possible ways for it to be, and only this. The thatness of this being is primarily being."⁵ As a result of his prioritizing of existence

---

2. Ratzinger, *Gospel, Catechesis, Catechism*, 14.

3. "In his [Heidegger's] first great book, *Being and Time*—and there you have historicism right in the title, don't you?—Heidegger describes man as a being towards death. He says that human beings, insofar as they are conscious, are the beings who at every moment of their lives know they are going to die. Death is a temporal event and he is saying, I think with enormous clarity, that the centre of the modern world is choice, anxiety about death, and extreme individualism. All thought arises from the concrete, dynamic situation of the individual. This is what he says in *Being and Time*, and what I have called historicism" (Cayley, *George Grant in Conversation*, 124).

4. Sartre, *Existentialism and Humanism*, 26. In this translation, it reads "existence comes before essence."

5. Heidegger, *Being and Time*, 29.

over essence, Heidegger had difficulty closing down on ethical claims. We see this clearly in his response to the ethics of technology, where he suggests that we should have a comportment of both yes and no—*die Gelassenheit zu den Dingen* (releasement toward things).[6] It could even be argued that the fact that he joined the Nazi party is indicative of the ethical import of his conception of beings in time.[7] How we understand being and time shapes the way we perceive identity, truth, and, in turn, justice.

Theologically, as long as we seek to know and worship God, the question of personhood persists:

> A consideration of human nature and destiny is a necessary component of any theological account of the Christian Gospel. Because—and only because—the Christian Gospel concerns the ways and works of the triune God, it necessarily concerns the human creature whom God calls into being, saves and perfects. . . . Christian theology does not have to choose between God and humankind, or to abandon both; passion for God is necessarily passion for humanity.[8]

Over the last century, theology has had to rethink its approach, if not contextualize it. The subjective turn and the notion of person as a "self-conscious free center of action"[9] eroded the ancient language of substance and, along with it, the ontological understanding of person. In consequence, the Trinity became unintelligible, "for the one divine nature evidently excludes three consciousnesses."[10] In the twentieth century, the notion of personalism arose with the likes of Martin Buber, Franz Rosenzweig, and Ferdinand Ebner. This opened the doors to a new approach that, unlike the notion of the self-conscious individual, could be reconciled with the trinitarian account of personhood—one being in three persons. Both Schmemann and Ratzinger find personalism (relational ontology) a fitting means for expressing what it means to be a person in time.[11]

---

6. Heidegger, *Discourse on Thinking*, 54.

7. George Grant claims that "this [Heidegger's affiliation with the Nazis] is much more than a historical question about Europe in the 1930s. If one uses it as an oyster knife to open up his brilliance, the whole question of the destiny of modernity can be revealed" (Schmidt, *George Grant in Process*, 66).

8. Webster, "Human Person," 223.

9. Kasper, *God of Jesus Christ*, 285.

10. Kasper, *God of Jesus Christ*, 287.

11. Kasper highlights Ratzinger as a theologian who "in particular has made his

Why bring Schmemann and Ratzinger into dialogue on the subject of personhood and eschatology? This project initially began with Schmemann in mind. Eschatology permeates almost all of his work, and there is minimal critical engagement on his thought, none in regard to eschatology and personhood. In addition, I saw this as an ecumenical opportunity to further the hopes set forth by John Zizioulas, who notes in *Being as Communion: Studies in Personhood and the Church* that theological anthropology "provokes and invites contemporary theology to work with a view to a synthesis between the two theologies, Eastern and Western."[12] Theological anthropology is fertile ground for ecumenical dialogue. Ratzinger entered into the project as the Western counterpart to Schmemann, and his erudition and theological insight radically transformed the enterprise, not to mention my life. Ratzinger has written extensively on eschatology and on the nature of personhood, and like Schmemann, he has a relational ontology, making him an appropriate dialogue partner.

Schmemann and Ratzinger are contemporaries. Schmemann was born in 1921 in Estonia, and his family, along with many other Russian émigrés, fled from the Russian Empire when Schmemann was a young child. They settled in Paris. Here he received his education and was ordained an Orthodox priest (1946). In 1951, he departed to America to join the faculty at St. Vladimir's Seminary in New York, where he remained until his death in 1983.[13] Ratzinger was born in Bavaria, Germany, in 1927. He was ordained in 1951 and became a doctor of theology in 1953. For the next twenty-plus years, he worked as a professor in various German universities[14] until his election and consecration as archbishop of Munich and Freising in 1977. He remained in Munich until he was appointed prefect for the Sacred Congregation for the Doctrine of the Faith (CDF) by Pope John Paul II in 1981. Ratzinger served the church as prefect until he was elected pope in 2005.[15] In 2013, he resigned as

---

own these insights" (Kasper, *God of Jesus Christ*, 290).

12. Zizioulas, *Being as Communion*, 26.

13. For more biographical information, see Meyendorff, "Life Worth Living"; J. Schmemann, *My Journey*. A full-length biography has not been written.

14. "University of Bonn (1959–1963), the University of Münster (1963–1966), the University of Tübingen (1966–1969), and the University of Regensburg (1969–1977)" (Rowland, *Ratzinger's Faith*, 1).

15. See Ratzinger, *Milestones*; Nichols, *Thought of Benedict XVI*; Rowland, *Ratzinger's Faith*.

pope and dedicated his remaining years to prayer.[16] Although I have not discovered any documentation to prove it, it is possible that Ratzinger and Schmemann met at the Second Vatican Council. Schmemann was an Orthodox observer at the Council, while Ratzinger was a *peritus* to Cardinal Frings of Cologne.

This study engages with all of Schmemann's work (a much smaller corpus than Ratzinger's), including his journals. Due to the limitation of space and because this monograph engages in constructive systematic theology as opposed to historical theology, I focus primarily on the work that Ratzinger produced after his *Habilitationsschrift*. My study excludes documents that he wrote as prefect of the CDF and as Pope Benedict XVI. This monograph is interested in the particular theology of Ratzinger, not the expression of the offices he held.[17] Although various secondary sources are employed, my concern throughout has been to prioritize primary texts rather than secondary interpretations and expositions.[18]

Schmemann and Ratzinger have distinct approaches to eschatology and personhood, and thus the *modus operandi* of each thinker needed to independently determine what concepts required to be expounded. Therefore, I have not attempted to impose Schmemann's construct onto Ratzinger's, or the inverse. I let each speak for himself, and in so doing, an informative and constructive dialogue naturally occurs.

Outline

Chapter 1 explores Schmemann's understanding of eschatology and temporality. This brings Schmemann's christocentrism to the surface; Christ is the kingdom. According to Schmemann, time must be conceived teleologically, and since Christ entered into and overcame that form of death

---

16. For more biographical information, see Guerriero, *Benedict XVI*; Seewald, *Benedict XVI*.

17. Arguably, the three *Jesus of Nazareth* volumes that he published during his pontificate reflect his own reflections on the person of Christ and not his official position. This is why he published them under the name Joseph Ratzinger and not Pope Benedict XVI. Although my research focused on what he wrote prior to these volumes, I interact with aspects of this work in a number of footnotes.

18. Most of the secondary sources on Schmemann verge on hagiography. See Plekon, "World as Sacrament." In regard to Ratzinger, since he was elected pope, more secondary sources have been published, although many of these, particularly the works written in English, are biographical in nature. See Corkery, *Joseph Ratzinger's Theological Ideas*, 11.

that constitutes the end of time, Christ becomes the new "end of time," that is, the culmination in which the totality of our temporality is to be viewed. This is conceived, moreover, in terms of event language. Christ's life (establishing the kingdom), death (facing all that is counter to the kingdom), and resurrection (overcoming death) are the final events of history. History has concluded with Christ. In the meantime, our present reality belongs to the "old" aeon, which finds its meaning in the "new" aeon, in which Christ sits at the right hand of the Father.

Chapter 2 brings together Schmemann's notion of eschatology (and hence temporality), thanksgiving, and personhood, all of which intersect in liturgical remembrance. The Eucharist, the heart of liturgical remembrance, is the passage that takes us beyond temporality to the person of Christ who awaits us in the "new" aeon. According to Schmemann, this encounter is absolutely vital, for humans are endowed with personhood by God, the God who names and remembers us. The only appropriate response to God is gratitude, to offer everything—the world and its temporality—*up* to God in thanksgiving. This means, for Schmemann, that human personhood is priestly in character.

Turning to Ratzinger, chapter 3 corresponds to chapter 1. Like Schmemann's, Ratzinger's eschatology highlights his Christocentrism: Christ is the kingdom. For Ratzinger, Christology absorbs eschatology, and therefore, his eschatology is fundamentally relational rather than chronological. As a result of his relational focus, the eschatological priority of the kingdom is tethered to the "last things" (*eschata*). Moreover, temporality is envisaged relationally, which means that temporality is an essential element of human identity—even death itself will not separate us from the temporal. While history is understood as already complete, according to Schmemann, for Ratzinger, history remains open-ended until God is all in all (1 Cor 15:28). Following St. Augustine, Ratzinger's conception of the human experience of time is more complex and nuanced than Schmemann's. Time reflects eternity: past and future are not separated from the present. With this view of temporality, Ratzinger avoids Schmemann's dualism of the "old" and "new" aeon; Schmemann's inability to account for evil; and finally, Schmemann's view of the church as detached from history.

Chapter 4 examines Ratzinger's notion of personhood and temporality. His Christology lays the groundwork for the relationality of both the cosmos (our context) and personhood. For Ratzinger, the fullness of personhood is experienced only in the transcending of the self. It is in what amounts to a dying to self that true identity is established. The "I" only *is* in relation, in the I-Thou-We structure of relationship. Such relationality, Ratzinger suggests, binds us to temporality because of the temporal "before and afters" of relationships. It is with this in mind that Ratzinger configures his conception of the soul and also, therefore, his interpretation of the "last things"—what happens in death.

In chapter 5, I explicate both the shared affinities and the differences between Ratzinger and Schmemann. Both theologians present a relational view of personhood, but they part ways with respect to their interpretations of the implications of eschatology for temporality. I conclude that Ratzinger offers a more consistent and developed view of relationality than Schmemann, in that Ratzinger's concept of relationality consistently permeates personhood, eschatology, and temporality. By comparison, Schmemann's view, I shall suggest, is relationally inconsistent and leads ultimately to the denigration of temporality.

1

Schmemann: Eschatology as Context

For, in the last analysis, everything depends on one thing: can we, do we "earnestly desire," with our whole being and in spite of all our insufficiency, fallenness, betrayal and laziness, to receive the words of this prayer as our own, desire them as our own? "Hallowed be Thy name. Thy kingdom come, Thy will be done, on earth as it is in heaven."

—ALEXANDER SCHMEMANN

THE EUCHARIST AND ESCHATOLOGY are the two leitmotifs of Schmemann's theology. If the Eucharist constitutes the heart of Christianity which pumps life through dying veins then eschatology provides the eyes that detect fallen creation and proleptically transform this perception into a vision of the kingdom come. To take this analogy further, the heart not only sustains life but is the poet's place of feeling. The eye not only sees but is the window to the soul. Living, seeing, and feeling precede knowing, even knowing oneself. Of course, this illustration breaks apart if we push it too far; nonetheless, it provides an image that helps make sense of Schmemann's liturgical emphases.

This chapter is divided into three parts. The first part examines Schmemann's understanding of eschatology and how it makes sense of the Christian story. The second part considers the relationship between eschatology and sacrament, how eschatology shapes the way we understand the world. Finally, the third part explores Schmemann's conception of the relationship between eschatology and time. To return to the image given above, one cannot see without the action of the heart; therefore, I have integrated Schmemann's conception of the Eucharist, perfect thanksgiving, throughout the three parts of this chapter, as well as in the following chapter.

Beginnings and Endings

Thus eschatology, being the essential term of reference of the Christian faith itself, permeates the whole of Christian theology and indeed makes possible theology itself, i.e. the transformation of our human and hopelessly limited words into *theoprepeis logoi*, "words adequate to God," truly expressive of the eternally transcendent divine truth.[1]

Prone to grand generalizations, especially regarding Western thought, Schmemann argues that misconstrued eschatology is the fatal flaw of Western theology; it lost the symbolic vision of the fathers, and, as a result, it has lost sight of the true reality of the world. Accordingly, eschatology has become a science of prediction concerning the last days or is speculation about judgment and the afterlife. In short, eschatology has become the last chapter, if not the appendix of systematic theology.[2] In contrast to this claim, Schmemann posits that for the story of salvation history, the last chapter is integral to the first, and both chapters, as bookends, provide the theological lens for all that falls in between. Paradise is what unites beginning and end, and it is what gives the church her Christian vision:

> Paradise is the primordial state of man and all creation, our state before the fall, before our "banishment from paradise," and our state upon our salvation by Christ, the eternal life that was promised by God and in Christ is already granted, already opened to man. Paradise in other words is the *beginning* and

---

1. Schmemann, "Problem of Church's Presence," 9.

2. Schmemann argues that "by limiting eschatology to the last chapter of all, we have deprived all the other chapters of the eschatological character that they ought to have" (Schmemann, *Liturgy and Tradition*, 95).

the *end*, to which is oriented and through which is defined and determined the entire life of man and in him of all creation.[3]

The title of Robert Louis Wilken's sixth chapter in *The Spirit of Early Christian Thought* sums it up pithily, "The End Given in the Beginning."[4] Yet, it also works the other way, to which we shall return in the section that follows.

Eschatology for Schmemann is not a theory, nor is it speculation of the "last days." Eschatology is the very tenor of Orthodox theology. It is "a dimension, a coefficient of the entire theological enterprise, shaping and permeating the whole Christian faith as its dynamic inspiration and motivation."[5] It is a way of seeing and participating that recognizes that all creation is destined for what Schmemann calls the "fulfilment of the divine economy."[6] This vision is liturgical and sacramental, a relationship that Schmemann held tightly together. On one hand, as an Orthodox liturgical theologian, Schmemann needed to have a robust sacramentality. Without it liturgy is reduced to mere smells and bells. On the other hand, he needed a deep understanding of liturgy in order to keep sacramentalism from sliding into pantheism. Liturgy and sacrament are eschatologically informed, and both, so to speak, remind each other of this orientation. Schmemann writes,

> A sacrament is both cosmic and eschatological. It refers at the same time to God's world as he first created it and to its fulfilment in the kingdom of God. It is cosmic in that it embraces all of creation, it returns it to God as God's own. . . . It is to the same degree eschatological, oriented toward the kingdom which is to come.[7]

In regard to liturgy, Schmemann contends that "liturgical theology has as its proper domain or 'object' eschatology itself, which is revealed in its fullness through the liturgy."[8] We could say that liturgy is a reminder that sacraments are more than cosmical, and sacraments remind us that liturgy's orientation to the kingdom is in relation to the cosmos. However, the two are so intertwined for Schmemann that to speak of the liturgical is to

---

3. Schmemann, *Eucharist*, 23.
4. Wilken, *Spirit of Early Christian*, 136.
5. Schmemann, *Church, World, Mission*, 28.
6. Schmemann, *Eucharist*, 34.
7. Schmemann, *Eucharist*, 34.
8. Schmemann, *Liturgy and Tradition*, 143.

speak of the sacramental and vice versa. To have a sacramental Christian vision is to see eschatologically. This also sheds light on why "Sacrament of the Kingdom" is the subtitle to Schmemann's magnum opus *The Eucharist*. The kingdom, the end, the eschaton is what one experiences in the liturgy. Steeped in the liturgy, the participant's vision becomes eschatological, and the world is seen sacramentally.

The Eschatological Structure of *The Eucharist*

Posthumously published four years after his death, *The Eucharist* represents the summation of Schmemann's work. The structure of the book reveals the broad landscape of Schmemann's theology, highlights his indebtedness to the divine liturgy, and reveals his double-sided hermeneutical key: eschatology and thanksgiving. Each chapter, excluding chapter 2 ("The Sacrament of the Kingdom") and chapter 9 ("The Sacrament of Thanksgiving"), corresponds specifically and chronologically to the various sections of *The Divine Liturgy of St John Chrysostom*. Chapter 2 is puzzlingly based on the first line of the divine liturgy ("Blessed is *the kingdom of the Father and the Son and the Holy Spirit, now and forever and to the ages of ages. Amen*").[9] To be clear, chapter 2, not chapter 1, as one would expect, revolves around the opening line of the liturgy. Yet, introducing chapter 5, Schmemann recounts what has occurred up to this point in the liturgy, and there is no mention of the kingdom: "The first part of the liturgy, which, as we have seen, consists of the assembly as the Church [ch. 1], the entrance [ch. 3] and the sacrament of the word [ch. 4]."[10] To spell out the obvious, the kingdom is not a "section" of the liturgy in the same way, for example, that the sacrament of the entrance is. Therefore, Schmemann's placing of "The Sacrament of the Assembly" and "The Sacrament of the Kingdom" (chs. 1 and 2) side by side, rather than beginning with a chapter on the kingdom, is theologically motivated.

From a linear perspective, would it not make more sense to conclude the book with a chapter on the sacrament of the kingdom? This is made clearer by looking at what Schmemann writes about the temple: "The temple is experienced and perceived as *sobor*, as the gathering together of heaven and earth and all creation in Christ—which constitutes

---

9. Chrysostom, "Divine Liturgy" (italics added).
10. Schmemann, *Eucharist*, 81.

the essence and purpose of the Church."[11] To speak of heaven for Schmemann is to speak eschatologically, and, certainly, "earth" and "creation" suggests something of the beginning. Thus, placed back-to-back, the chapters (1 and 2) image the church, in which heaven and earth come together and the end (Christ) makes sense of the beginning.[12] Chapter 2 clearly propounds that if the assembly as the church is "the *beginning* of the eucharistic celebration, its first and fundamental condition, then its *end* and completion is the Church's entrance into heaven, her fulfilment at the table of Christ, in his kingdom."[13] Schmemann argues that it is imperative to spell out the end immediately following the beginning, for it reveals the unity of the Eucharist and its essence as movement and ascent. In other words, eschatology is necessary to understand the beginning, and both are necessary to understand the Christian life as passage. The rest of the book passes through the various sacramental stages of the liturgy and reaches completion with chapter 12, "The Sacrament of Communion." The book, its structure following the divine liturgy, concludes with the joyous encounter of the kingdom; it ends where, in a sense, it began.[14] With the kingdom set before us, the final chapter reflects back and reveals the kingdom in our midst: "We have seen the true light! We have received the heavenly Spirit! We have found the true faith! Worshipping the undivided Trinity, who has saved us."[15] On the final page of *The Eucharist*, Schmemann concludes by once again uniting the beginning and the end:

> All is clear. All is simple and bright. Such fulness fills everything. Such joy permeates everything. Such love radiates through everything. We are again in the *beginning*, where our ascent to the table of Christ, in his kingdom, began. We depart into life, in order to witness and to fulfil our calling. Each has his own, but it is also our common ministry, common liturgy—"in the communion of the Holy Spirit." "Lord, it is good that we are here!"[16]

---

11. Schmemann, *Eucharist*, 19.
12. Schmemann, *For Life of World*, 29.
13. Schmemann, *Eucharist*, 27.
14. This structural pattern can also be seen in Schmemann's earlier work *For the Life of the World*.
15. Schmemann, *Eucharist*, 244.
16. Schmemann, *Eucharist*, 245.

There are two interrelated senses of *beginning* in this quote, hence Schmemann's use of italics. First, beginning refers to the liturgical pattern in which the church assembles, its first liturgical act. Second, it refers to the cosmic level, a return to what it *was* to be and in Christ what it *will* be. The two senses reveal each other: liturgy (an eschatological act) as epiphany reveals the underlying reality of the cosmos, and the cosmos of our everyday encounter eschatologically mirrors liturgy. This is proclaimed in the last line of *The Eucharist*, which echoes the first chapter of Genesis. In short, through the liturgical passage, the parishioner enters paradise;[17] by ascending (being *lifted up*) to the banquet table of Christ, the participant is enabled upon "return" to "this world" to recognize the world's eschatological potential: God will be all in all.[18]

How does chapter 9, "The Sacrament of Thanksgiving," fit in Schmemann's scheme? Like chapter 2, chapter 9 holds theological privilege. Similar to eschatology, thanksgiving is at the heart of the Christian life and is central to our personhood, a theme to which we shall repeatedly return. Furthermore, the Eucharist is the apogee and the end of liturgy. As explicated later in this chapter, it is its end, structurally and theologically. Finally, thanksgiving is central to liturgy because of its relationship to paradise and therefore to eschatology. According to Schmemann, "thanksgiving is the experience of paradise."[19] Like eschatology, thanksgiving is overarching. Therefore, it is apparent that, because of its overarching subject, chapter 9, like chapter 2, is an exception to the structure of *The Eucharist*.

Clearly, the composition of *The Eucharist* reflects Schmemann's theological approach. The form matches the content, and what it reveals is the centrality of eschatology and thanksgiving. The title and subtitle of the book discloses this: Eucharist means thanksgiving, and eschatology concerns and constitutes our whole orientation to the kingdom.

---

17. "The whole liturgy is to be seen as the sacrament of the Kingdom of God" (Schmemann, *Liturgy and Tradition*, 95).

18. "That God may be all in all" (1 Cor 15:28) and "our life is hid with Christ in God" (Col 3:3) are the two most quoted verses in Schmemann's corpus.

19. Schmemann, *Eucharist*, 174.

The End as the New Beginning

> Last lecture this year: "The Eucharist and Eschatology." My whole heart is there.[20]

We have seen that, for Schmemann, eschatology is central to theology. It is the lens through which we should view the world, and it enables us to understand the beginning. As a result, we are enabled to perceive the complete narrative in the perspective God intends. Furthermore, it is intimately related to thanksgiving. Eschatology does not concern merely the "last things." One question remains: what does Schmemann's eschatology reveal about the world?

As life itself, Christ came to restore the world and "the fragmentary life of the world was gathered into His life; He was the heart beat of the world and the world killed Him. But in that murder the world itself died. It lost its last chance to become the paradise God created it to be."[21] Once again following the pattern set out by Adam and Eve, humanity rejected God's gift of life, his Son, and because of this rejection the stain of death remains on "this world." That is not to say that we should not care for the world. The world can be improved, but it cannot reach the end for which it was intended: paradise. By rejecting Christ, this world condemned itself. Natural joy and satisfaction cannot be attained, for "in the world in which Christ died, 'natural life' has been brought to its end."[22] The implications of the world's deicide is irreversible.[23] Yet, this is not the last word.

Theology begins at the cross but ends with Christ's resurrection and ascension—the true last words. Christianity proclaims joy, a "new all-embracing joy, and with this joy it transformed the End into a Beginning.

---

20. Schmemann, *Journals*, 165.
21. Schmemann, *For Life of World*, 23.
22. Schmemann, *For Life of World*, 24.

23. This is an interesting claim that seems to suggest that Christ's crucifixion was God's reactionary measure. It also highlights Schmemann's dualistic notion of time, which is explicated later in this chapter. In contrast, Ratzinger repeatedly emphasizes that throughout John's Gospel and the Synoptic Gospels, Jesus is shown to be preparing his disciples for his final historical act of obedience, a necessary act to fulfill his mission. Looking at Caiaphas's prophetic utterance in the Gospel of John (11:49–52), Ratzinger concludes that "the Temple of stone must be destroyed, so that the new one, the New Covenant with its new style of worship, can come. Yet at the same time, this means that Jesus himself *must* endure the crucifixion, so that, after his Resurrection, he may become the new Temple" (Ratzinger, *Jesus of Nazareth*, 170).

Without the proclamation of this joy Christianity is incomprehensible."[24] Schmemann turns to the Gospel of Luke and highlights that it begins (2:10) and ends with joy (24:52)—a microcosm of the pattern of salvation history. In the former passage, the angel proclaims that he brings "good news of a great joy"; and in the latter passage, Christ's followers are full of joy after receiving Christ's blessing: "And they worshiped him, and returned to Jerusalem with great joy." After Christ's ascension, it is in the Eucharist that we encounter the joy of the Lord. However, this is no ordinary joy. It is eschatological joy, for "the 'assembly as the Church' is above all the joy of the regenerated and renewed creation, the gathering of the world, in contrast to its fall into sin and death."[25] Hid with Christ in God (Col 3:3), the church perceives the world as it will be when God is all in all (1 Cor 15:28). Put differently, through the Eucharist, we recognize the world's latent sacramentality.[26] The eschatological vision comes out of, and at the same time enables participation in, the work of Christ. Christians gather together to *"fulfill the Church*, and that means to make present the One in whom all things are at their *end*, and all things are at their *beginning.*"[27] Creation finds its fulfillment in Christ, who is the *telos* of all reality. At the same time, the *telos* is the new beginning. It is life seen as transfigured joy.

Baptism is the key, both symbolically and experientially. Prior to baptism, the catechumen encounters Christ, but, as Schmemann articulates, "to enter into the joy of His presence, to be with Him, meant a conversion to another reality."[28] There is nothing in and of this world that reveals this, and therefore we must die to this world. Baptism is the sacramental experience of dying in Christ to this world. What emerges from the baptismal waters is a new creation, a kingdom being, rather than a human who is wed to this world.[29] With new eyes, each Christian is enabled to see beyond the immediacy of this world. Eschatology is not so much about perceiving the future as it is proleptically perceiving Christ and his kingdom in the midst of this world.

---

24. Schmemann, *For Life of World*, 24.
25. Schmemann, *Eucharist*, 53.
26. Schmemann, *Journals*, 20.
27. Schmemann, *For Life of World*, 27.
28. Schmemann, *For Life of World*, 28.
29. See Schmemann, *Church, World, Mission*, 138.

For Schmemann, eschatology is the lens without which we fail to see the Christian story in its proper perspective. To be a Christian is to be oriented to the kingdom.[30] Without the *telos* of the kingdom, the beginning of the Christian story remains opaque and *a fortiori*; so does the present. The liturgy reveals this eschatological dimension, and Schmemann highlights this in the structure of *The Eucharist*. Alongside eschatology sits the overarching notion of thanksgiving, which Schmemann connects with both paradise and the Eucharist. Finally, Schmemann's eschatology highlights the disparity between this world and the kingdom, and the need to die to this world in order to participate in Christ's kingdom. It is through this baptismal death that one is enabled to see eschatologically with kingdom eyes and discern the eschatological symbolism of the world.

Eschatological Symbolism

Schmemann's all-pervading eschatology is balanced with a well-developed symbolism. For example, over 70 percent of chapter 2 in *The Eucharist*, "The Sacrament of the Kingdom," is concerned with expounding the corruption of symbolism and its proper eschatological nature, a theme he repeatedly articulates. Schmemann argues that, without eschatological symbolism, the world becomes an end in itself, or it becomes radically separated from God. In both cases, the world loses all sense of meaning, and the world becomes "grace-proof."[31] In this section, we shall look at Schmemann's approach to the following three notions: (1) the nature of symbolism and its relation to theology, (2) the distinction between symbol and sacrament, and (3) the epistemological role of eschatological symbolism for making sense of the world.

The Theological Nature of Symbol

In *For the Life of the World*, Schmemann opaquely expresses his conception of symbol in the following way: "The relationship between the sign in the symbol (A) and that which it 'signifies' (B) is neither a merely semantic one (A *means* B), nor causal (A *is the cause of* B), nor representative (A *represents* B). We called this relationship an *epiphany*."[32] A symbol

---

30. Schmemann, *Liturgy and Life*, 88.
31. Schmemann, "Worship in Secular Age," 13.
32. Schmemann, *For Life of World*, 141.

has a certain irreducible and irreplaceable quality. For example, it is not like an allegory, in which the reader can discard the concrete image once the immaterial concept has been understood. The symbol itself has value, for it consists of the reality to which it points. The whole of *a* expresses *b*, although not necessarily the whole of *b*, and it does so without losing its own ontological reality.[33] To put it in different terms, a symbol is a concrete reality that participates in an even greater concrete reality; in fact, its very being subsists via that greater reality, namely God. All of this would remain meaningless if left at the level of semiotics—simply one way of describing signification—but by moving into the realm of ontology, it brings the structure of the world into question. Better yet, the symbolic ontology envisioned by Schmemann bears upon the way we recognize the relationship between God and the world. Schmemann's understanding of particular symbols rests upon his understanding of the world's symbolic structure:

> The world is symbolic—"signum rei sacrae" [sign of something sacred]—in virtue of its being created by God; to be "symbolical" belongs thus to its ontology, the symbol being not only the way to perceive and understand reality, a means of cognition, but also a means of participation. It is then the "natural" symbolism of the world—one can almost say its "sacramentality"—that makes the sacrament *possible* and constitutes the key to its understanding and apprehension.[34]

An understanding of symbol rests on one's theological method/vision.[35] In an article on "Symbols and Symbolism in the Byzantine Liturgy," Schmemann makes this point and brings to the fore the different understanding of the terms *symbol*, *represents*, and *signifies* in the vocabulary of Saint Maximus the Confessor and Germanus of Constantinople. According to Schmemann, Germanus is largely responsible for illustrative symbol, in which symbol is easily identified with the signified (e.g., red wine is illustratively identifiable as blood); whereas Maximus roots symbol in mystery, primarily the *mysterion* (the sacraments of the church). The *mysterion* is both "the very content of faith, the knowledge of the divine mystery revealed in Christ, and the saving power communicated through

---

33. Schmemann, *For Life of World*, 141–42.
34. Schmemann, *For Life of World*, 139.
35. Schmemann, *For Life of World*, 138–39.

and in the Church."³⁶ This duality of presence and action that is central to Maximus's theology and theological method works itself out into his concept of symbol, in which symbol "is thus the very reality of that which it symbolises. By representing, or signifying, that reality it makes it present, truly represents it."³⁷ It is unfortunate that Schmemann does not set out Germanus's theological method, for the contrast between the two methods would make Schmemann's point stronger. Nonetheless, it is clear that understanding symbol is part of the theological endeavor, and its definition does not precede but flows out of one's theological vision.

For Schmemann, theology precedes semiotics, but not simply theology—rather, liturgical theology. The heart of liturgical theology is summarized in the Latin phrase *lex orandi lex credendi*. Doxology is the first and foundational act of Christian life, and all theological knowledge should grow out of and lead back to this.³⁸ David Fagerberg astutely points out that, for Schmemann, "the liturgy is not an object to observe, or a resource to quarry from, or a milieu to work out of; liturgy is the condition for theology."³⁹ This symbolical or sacramental view (Schmemann uses *sacramental* and *symbolical* interchangeably)⁴⁰ finds its being in the reality of the incarnation as experienced in faith through the liturgy of the church. In fact, Jesus is the symbol of symbols; Schmemann rhetorically asks, "Was it not said by Christ Himself that the one who sees Him sees the Father, the one who is in Him has the communion of the Holy Spirit, the one who is in Him has already—here and now—eternal life?"⁴¹ When the church, both East and West, lost sight of her liturgical footing, she stumbled and fell away from the sacramental world structure. As a result, the sacramental and eschatological basis of theology was lost in the fog of metaphysical inquiry. The transformation of the elements became the new focus, and this shift blocked out the context, i.e., liturgy.⁴²

Symbol and faith are intricately linked, "for faith is 'the evidence of things unseen' (Heb 11:1), the knowledge that there is another reality

36. Schmemann, *Liturgy and Tradition*, 122.
37. Schmemann, *Liturgy and Tradition*, 123.
38. Schmemann, *For Life of World*, 141.
39. Fagerberg, *Theologia Prima*, 77.
40. "This experience—in which we find also the *institutional* structure of the Church, her hierarchy, canons, liturgy, etc.—was *sacramental, symbolical* by its very nature" (Schmemann, *Eucharist*, 35).
41. Schmemann, *For Life of World*, 148.
42. See Schmemann, *Liturgy and Tradition*, 11–20.

different from the 'empirical' one, and that this reality can be entered, can be communicated, can in truth become 'the most real of realities.'"[43] Symbols make visible the invisible and effable the ineffable.[44] It is only through symbol that the invisible and the ineffable can be verbalized; we cannot speak of what we have not seen, and "because it is not of 'this world' [it] is given to us—in 'this world'—in symbols."[45] Faith is both an encounter and a desire, and symbols act "epiphanically," revealing both cognitively and experientially, seeing and tasting; hence, the appropriate language of "participation" rather than "reflection." Unlike abstract knowing, "faith certainly is contact and a thirst for contact, embodiment and a thirst for embodiment: it is the manifestation, the presence, the operation of one reality within the other. All of this *is* the symbol (from συμβάλλω, 'unite,' 'hold together')."[46] It is with this account of symbol that Schmemann makes sense of the world, of matter.

"Man is what he eats."[47] This sentence encapsulates the theme of *For the Life of the World* (life) and its backdrop (world as sacrament). Schmemann poses the question, what life do we mean when we state that Christ died for the life of the world? Spiritual life? Physical life? The answer is neither. Where spiritual life is everything, gnosticism thrives. Food is reduced to spiritual food, and this spiritual food simply enables one to endure the secular physical world. It pits the spiritual against the physical world, and the physical world is all but irrelevant. On the other hand, those who elevate the physical life, the activists (caught up in the social gospel), ignore contemplation, prayer, and fasts. Here, "one eats and drinks, one fights for freedom and justice in order to be *alive*, to have the *fullness of life*. But what is it? What is the life of life itself? . . . At some ultimate point, within some ultimate analysis, we inescapably discover that in and by itself action has no meaning."[48] For Schmemann, the answer is simple: "Man is what he eats." The world was made to feed humankind. God meets us in this tangible material realm. This is where and how he establishes communion: the world is symbol.[49]

43. Schmemann, *Eucharist*, 39.
44. Schmemann, *For Life of World*, 141.
45. Schmemann, *Church, World, Mission*, 24.
46. Schmemann, *Eucharist*, 39. See Schmemann, *For Life of World*, 151.
47. Schmemann, *For Life of World*, 11.
48. Schmemann, *For Life of World*, 13.
49. Schmemann, *For Life of World*, 14.

In the same book, Schmemann points out that the writer of Genesis intentionally centered the fall on food. The forbidden fruit was unlike all other fruit in the garden; it was not a gift given by God. By eating the fruit, Adam and Eve did not commune with God, for it was not given by God. The end of the fruit went no further than the fruit itself; it was not symbolical/sacramental. The fruit is an image of the world loved for its own sake, and "eating it is the image of life understood as an end in itself."[50] Through this act, the human person's ontological status as priest was ruptured. The human person is to be *homo adorans*, "the one for whom worship is the essential act which both 'posits' his humanity and fulfills it."[51] And ontologically, as priest, he is to worship God by offering back to God the gifts that were given to him—a constant receiving and giving back.[52] This reciprocity has been broken because the world "has fallen away from the awareness that God is all in all."[53] We have lost sight of the sacramentality of the world.

The symbolic worldview naturally recognizes that God is all in all. Christ died for the life of the world, not just for the soul. The world is not a battlefield, in which the supernatural is opposed to the natural. Schmemann asserts that it is our great sin that we have maintained this divide.[54] Accordingly, "the only real fall of man is his noneucharistic life in a noneucharistic world. The fall is not that he preferred world to God, distorted the balance between the spiritual and material, but that he made the world *material*, whereas he was to have transformed it into 'life in God,' filled with meaning and spirit."[55] The good news is that "in Christ, life—life in all its totality—was returned to man, given again as sacrament and communion, made Eucharist."[56] It is this vision that must be recaptured from the church fathers. To see the world as sacramental is to see the world as symbolical, hence symbols are seen as realities.

---

50. Schmemann, *For Life of World*, 16.
51. Schmemann, "Worship in Secular Age," 4.
52. Schmemann, *Church, World, Mission*, 223.
53. Schmemann, *For Life of World*, 16.
54. Schmemann purports that the true Christian dichotomy concerns the "old" and the "new."
55. Schmemann, *For Life of World*, 18.
56. Schmemann, *For Life of World*, 20.

Eschatological Ascent: From Symbol to Sacrament

And so, everything in the liturgy is *real*, but it is a reality not of "this world" and not in its fallen and splintered time, but in the assembled new time.[57]

Previously, it was noted that Schmemann uses *sacramental* and *symbolical* interchangeably. Although poetic and beautiful, his writing is often in need of semantic hygiene, and this is certainly an example. There is an important distinction between symbol and sacrament that is easily overlooked because of Schmemann's indiscriminate use of both words. In order to clarify, we shall turn to Schmemann's conception of liturgy, church, and world, all three of which he refers to as both symbol and sacrament. What do liturgy, church, and world hold in common, making it possible for Schmemann to speak of them as both symbol and sacrament? Liturgy, church, and world are passages, passovers, movement toward fulfillment in Christ; all three are eschatologically bound and in relation to the Eucharist.[58] The world is a symbol in its incomplete state of becoming. It is sacrament, because there can be no bread and wine without the world,[59] and thus, in one sense, it is the first sacrament.[60]

The church is symbol that is transformed by the eucharistic meal into a sacrament for the world. Schmemann explains it in the following way:

> The nature of the institution can be termed *sacramental*, and this means not only a given or static inter-dependence between the visible and the invisible, nature and grace, the material and the spiritual, but also, and primarily, the dynamic essence of the Church as passage from the old into the new, from this world into the world to come, from the kingdom of nature into the Kingdom of Grace.[61]

The church is the presence and communication of the kingdom.[62] For the world, it becomes a passage to the kingdom, and, in this role, it becomes sacrament.

---

57. Schmemann, *Eucharist*, 223.
58. Schmemann, *Eucharist*, 35.
59. Schmemann, *For Life of World*, 139–40.
60. See Noble, "From Sacramentality of Church."
61. Schmemann, "Ecclesiological Notes," 36–37.
62. Schmemann, *Liturgy and Tradition*, 95.

In "Symbols and Symbolism in the Byzantine Liturgy," Schmemann examines symbolism in St. Maximus's mystagogical commentaries. Here, liturgy is a symbol, and this is understood only in light of the *mysterion*.[63] Liturgy so perceived reveals that a particular symbol is "not of this or that particular event or person, but precisely of the whole *mysterion* as its revelation and saving grace."[64] Similar to the sacramentality of the world, liturgy is sacramental, in that it is the context that enables Christians to see properly. In *The Eucharist*, Schmemann likens liturgy to a man walking in absolute darkness with a flashlight in a familiar and beautiful building. The flashlight illuminates the various rooms and halls and identifies the building in its wholeness and unity.[65] Liturgy is served on earth but accomplished in heaven; hence, in the illustration, the building is hidden from plain sight. Schmemann posits, "We do not *repeat* and we do not *represent*—we *ascend* into the mystery of salvation and new life."[66] The whole liturgy is an *epiklesis*. Here, the symbols of the liturgy are transformed through the work of the Holy Spirit and take on the reality to which they point. In this transformation, "each rite is transformed by the Holy Spirit into *that which it is*, a 'real symbol' of what it manifests."[67] Yet, this process of transformation remains invisible to the natural eye and is "certified only by faith."[68]

Liturgy, from the Greek word *leitourgia*, means "a service performed on behalf of a community and for its benefit."[69] The service or the goal of liturgy is the church herself, and the church is the presence and mark of the kingdom. Schmemann writes, "In a sense the Church is indeed a *liturgical institution*, i.e. an institution whose *leitourgia* is to fulfill itself as the Body of Christ and a new creation."[70] When the liturgy—through the Eucharist—makes the church the body of Christ, the church is transformed from institution to sacrament. Likewise, as passage and movement toward Eucharist, the liturgy becomes sacrament, the sacrament

---

63. Schmemann also refers to liturgy as an icon (Schmemann, *Church, World, Mission*, 132).

64. Schmemann, *Liturgy and Tradition*, 123.

65. Schmemann, *Eucharist*, 222.

66. Schmemann, *Eucharist*, 221.

67. Schmemann, *Eucharist*, 223.

68. Schmemann, *Eucharist*, 222.

69. Schmemann, *Liturgy and Tradition*, 79.

70. Schmemann, *Liturgy and Tradition*, 79.

of the church.[71] World, liturgy, and church are interdependent symbols that come to fruition—reaching their apogee as sacrament—in the Eucharist.[72] It is important to note that the passage toward the altar and the Eucharist is an *ascent*; the participant is "lifted" to the heavenly altar. This is why it is called a passage.

The Eucharist is unique among all the sacraments. It is the sacrament of sacraments,[73] "the symbol of the kingdom par excellence, the one that fulfills all other symbols—the Lord's day, baptism, Pascha, etc.—as well as all of Christian life 'hid with Christ in God.'"[74] The Eucharist is "fully *realised* symbol."[75] It brings all other symbols into unity and transforms them into sacraments. It is telling that in *The Eucharist*, Schmemann calls the Eucharist the sacrament of: assembly, the kingdom, entrance, the word, the faithful, offering, unity, anaphora, thanksgiving, remembrance, the Holy Spirit, and communion.[76]

Both symbol and sacrament bring "things" together. A sacramental/symbolical worldview is one in which the natural and supernatural are brought together (supernatural is seen as "natural in an extraordinary degree"),[77] or, more accurately, it is where the old and the new come together. A sacrament is a symbol fulfilled; symbols such as liturgy are transformed into sacraments. Schmemann posits that in the words of Christ at the Last Supper—"do *this* in remembrance of me"—the *this*—the meal, the thanksgiving—is already sacramental, not sacrament but sacramental. "The institution means that by being referred to Christ, 'filled' with Christ, the symbol is fulfilled and becomes *sacrament*."[78] Hence, the Eucharist is the most complete symbol, the fullest sacrament, fully cosmic and fully eschatological.

The things of this world are symbols with or without our participation, but they cannot be recognized as such,[79] nor can they become sacrament for us, without our eschatological participation in Christ. Symbols

---

71. Schmemann, *Church, World, Mission*, 22.
72. See Schmemann, *For Life of World*, 151.
73. Schmemann, *Eucharist*, 36.
74. Schmemann, *Eucharist*, 43.
75. Schmemann, *Eucharist*, 44.
76. Each chapter in *The Eucharist* is titled accordingly.
77. Schmemann, *Church, World, Mission*, 223.
78. Schmemann, *For Life of World*, 140.
79. Schmemann, *For Life of World*, 140.

are a gift, but they can never be sacrament without being offered back to God in gratitude, which completes the participatory action God initiated. This is why the Eucharist is the sacrament par excellence; it is Christ's life, and, along with it, the entire cosmos (via incarnation), perfectly offered to God. As Christians, the Eucharist is our thanksgiving, as we are joined with Christ in his complete and perfect offering. It is no wonder that Schmemann's final words given from the *ambo* (he died a few weeks later) were words of thanksgiving, prefaced with: "Everyone capable of thanksgiving is capable of salvation and eternal joy."[80] The first step for a Christian is gratitude in response to the gifts given, and, with this step, she receives, offers back, and fulfills her priestly role.[81]

In summary, according to Schmemann, a symbol is a latent sacrament that is transformed into sacrament through Christ who is perfect thanksgiving.[82] This recognition on the part of the Christian is based in faith and known eschatologically. That is, we are able to recognize the sacramentality of the world only when we are hid with Christ in God (Col 3:3).

Cosmic and Eschatological Union: Making Sense of the World

In contradistinction to the Latin view of sacraments, which Schmemann caricatures as a panacea for the wounds of sin, Schmemann argues that the Orthodox ecclesial experience reveals the sacraments as revelatory:

> A sacrament is understood primarily as a revelation of the genuine *nature* of creation, of the world, which, however much it has fallen as "this world" will remain God's world, awaiting salvation, redemption, healing and transfiguration in a new earth and a new heaven. In other words, in the Orthodox experience a sacrament is primarily a revelation of the *sacramentality* of

---

80. Schmemann, "Final Words."

81. "And in this thanksgiving, praise, and joy, we once again become genuine human beings" (Schmemann, *Church Year*, 64).

82. Mathai Kadavil misses this important point (the movement, the becoming, the transformation of symbol into sacrament) in his article on Schmemann's eschatological symbolism. He writes, "We can see that the essential particularity of eschatological symbolism is that in it there is no distinction between the sign and the signified" (Kadavil, "Sacramental-Liturgical Theology," 116). Oddly, while Kadavil adequately summarizes much of Schmemann's sacramental vision, he misses the whole point of the "eschatological" in "eschatological symbolism." The symbol partakes and points but awaits its fulfillment, when God will be all in all.

creation itself for the world was created and given to man for conversion of creaturely life into participation in divine life.[83]

The sacraments of the church reveal for what creation was intended and foreshadow what creation will become. For example, the waters of baptism regenerate in the way that water was always intended to regenerate. All creation "was originally summoned and destined for the fulfillment of the divine economy—'then God will be all in all.'"[84]

In "The World as Sacrament," Schmemann explains why eschatological symbolism is necessary for making sense of the world. His argument is based on the two paradoxical yet parallel Christian accounts of the world given to us in Scripture and tradition: the world is good, or the world is bad. Both accounts must be taken into consideration and held in tension. In the first sense, God loves and cares about the world. It is the object of his affection: "For God so loved the world that he gave his only Son" (John 3:16). In the second sense, the world is seen as a prison from which one must be freed. The world competes with God for our affections: worship of God or worship of matter.

Like a pendulum, the church swings back and forth between the two extremes. The first sense is necessary, for "there can be no Christianity where the world is not seen as an object of divine love."[85] At the same time, the Christian ascetic tradition has shown that we need to "leave" the world in order to develop a healthy detachment, which helps us recognize that freedom is found in Christ and not in materialism.[86] The first sense taken to the extreme leads to a religious-less Christianity, in which God gets in the way of our world-saving endeavors, whereas the second sense easily leads to gnosticism and neglect for creation.

How can we hold these two senses together? Schmemann argues that we can do this only if we see "ourselves and our whole created environment in sacramental terms."[87] The more we think in this manner, the more we are aware that this world passes away, and that this world has meaning only in Christ's coming in glory. This connects with the second sense of the world and reminds us that a sacramental correspondence

83. Schmemann, *Eucharist*, 33–34.
84. Schmemann, *Eucharist*, 34.
85. Schmemann, *Church, World, Mission*, 219.
86. For a profound reflection on asceticism by a scholar who has been influenced by Schmemann, see Fagerberg, *On Liturgical Asceticism*.
87. Schmemann, *Church, World, Mission*, 220.

always points beyond. In other words, the world is not an end in itself. Nonetheless, it is the space wherein God communicates his love:

> We might do better to think of that practical daily world as something incomprehensible and unmanageable unless and until we can approach it sacramentally through Christ. Nature and the world are otherwise beyond our grasp; time also, time that carries all things away in a meaningless flux, causing men to despair unless they see in it the pattern of God's action, reflected in the liturgical year, the necessary road to the New Jerusalem.[88]

The symbolical perspective that Schmemann posits is cosmic, in that it reveals something about the world. It is eschatological, in that it reveals the world is not yet what it is to be.[89] According to Schmemann's logic, by prioritizing the eschatological, the cosmic vision is restored. Yet, if this is reversed, it is not possible to have "the holy materialism ('God so loved the world . . .') upon which Christian spirituality ought to be based."[90]

To summarize this section, according to Schmemann, eschatological symbolism is foundational; it is a "a coefficient of the entire theological enterprise."[91] Experienced and known in worship, the symbol is a foretaste of the reality that is beyond. Even at the eucharistic table, we return to this life with our thirst piqued, not quenched:

> However *real* a symbol may be, however successfully it may communicate to us that other reality, its function is not to quench our thirst but to intensify it: "Grant us that we may more perfectly partake of Thee in the never ending day of Thy Kingdom." It is not that this or that part of "this world"—space, time, or matter—be made *sacred*, but rather that everything in it be seen and comprehended as expectation and thirst for its complete spiritualization: "that God may be all in all."[92]

---

88. Schmemann, *Church, World, Mission*, 226.

89. "This [the eschatological perspective] means also that it is precisely her knowledge and constant partaking of the 'end' that *relates* the Church to the world, creates that correlation between the *now* and the *not yet* which is the very essence of her message to the world and also the only source of the 'victory that overcomes the world.' Apocalypticism, on the other hand, is truly a heresy, for it is the rejection of Christian eschatology, its replacement with Manichean dualism, the abandonment of that tension between being 'in the world' and yet 'not of the world' which is constitutive of the Church and of her life" (Schmemann, *Church, World, Mission*, 10).

90. Schmemann, *Church, World, Mission*, 221.

91. Schmemann, *Church, World, Mission*, 28.

92. Schmemann, *Eucharist*, 39.

Although a symbol brings together disparate realities, it also highlights the vast disparity between the symbol itself and the signified to which it invariably points. Even the Eucharist, the sacrament of sacraments, still remains a symbol, albeit the symbol par excellence, that will be fulfilled in the consummation of God's kingdom. It is the Eucharist that enables the worshiping church to see both the cosmic and the eschatological nature of the world. The Eucharist is not an ultimate end; it is a means: "The fulfillment of the Eucharist is in the communion and transformation of man for which it is given."[93] This is why, argues Schmemann, there is no adoration of the Holy Gifts in the Orthodox Church. Writing about the waters of baptism, Schmemann articulates that the consecrated water is "to be that which all matter is meant to be: a means to an end, which is man's deification—knowledge of God and communion with God."[94] This logic can also be applied to the bread and wine of the Eucharist. Schmemann's teleological emphasis shapes his whole project, and, as we shall see, this brings him into conflict with Ratzinger's theological approach.

Eschatology and Time: Liturgical Dualism

The Future is not an aspect of time, but time is the future's work-in-progress.[95]

We have seen thus far the import of eschatology for understanding the Christian narrative and what eschatology reveals about the world's symbolical structure. The rest of this chapter explicates how eschatology, according to Schmemann, shapes time and history. Eschatology and temporality are natural bedfellows; if eschatology has cosmic implications, as seen above, then all forms of extension (space and time) and life are affected. This raises a number of questions. In what way does eschatology shape temporality? Does it affect time and history by renouncing the import of both? Schmemann has a teleological and anagogical account of the relationship between the time of the world and eschatology, and he sets up this relationship in three ways. First, he solidifies the relationship between Judaic worship and early Christian worship. Second, Schmemann demonstrates that the Christian view of time is founded in the Hebrew view of time. Third, he connects (not conflates) the Eucharist with the worship inherited from the synagogue. These three ways form

---

93. Schmemann, *Of Water and Spirit*, 50.
94. Schmemann, *Of Water and Spirit*, 50.
95. Knight, *Eschatological Economy*, 18.

and maintain what Schmemann calls liturgical dualism. Finally, in light of liturgical dualism, Schmemann argues that Christ redeemed time by entering into death.

Judaic-Christian Worship: Liturgical Dualism

In the second chapter of *Introduction to Liturgical Theology*, Schmemann makes three important points. First, he argues that the liturgy of time stems back to the church's beginning, to her Judaic roots.[96] Second, he argues that the liturgy of time is dualistic; it is not subsumed by the Eucharist but is correlative with it. Third, following from the first two points, he concludes that eschatology is not world-renouncing. Why are these three points important? They provide the backbone to Schmemann's understanding of time and its relation to the kingdom. In what follows, I set out Schmemann's argument for liturgical dualism, dealing with the first two points. The following section—"Eschatologically Transparent Time"—considers the third point.

Schmemann argues that there is a genetic link between the Christian cult and the liturgical tradition of Judaism. Liberal theology has obscured this link, purporting that the post-apostolic church is formed, in large measure, by Hellenism, rather than by Judaism.[97] The organized catholic church of the second century is portrayed as having undergone a vast transformation, and its sacramentalism is perceived as a negative symptom of Hellenism. As shown by historical liturgics, such a view displays a gross ignorance of liturgical history.[98] The other trend, represented by Gregory Dix (1901–1952), recognizes the Judaic-Christian link; but Dix argues that the link was severed after the destruction of the temple in AD 70.[99] Contrary to liberal theology and Dix, Schmemann argues that there has always been a close connection between Christian and Hebrew liturgy, and, regardless of the differences, their worship is of the same type.[100] For example,

---

96. The liturgy of time (the *ordo*) includes the annual and weekly cycle of time and the daily hours of prayer.
97. Schmemann, *Introduction to Liturgical Theology*, 53–54.
98. Schmemann, *Introduction to Liturgical Theology*, 54–55.
99. Schmemann, *Introduction to Liturgical Theology*, 64.
100. Schmemann, *Introduction to Liturgical Theology*, 55.

if such things as the blessing of the name of God, praise, confession of sins, intercession and finally the glorifying of God for His work in history—as elements set in a definite order and relationship—if these constitute the normal structure of the prayer of the synagogue, it is to be noted that the same elements, in the same order and relationship, make up the structure of early Christian prayer.[101]

This shows that the *charismas* of the early church were practiced within an *ordo*. The synagogue worship practiced by the apostles set the norm for Christian worship.

At the same time, Schmemann argues that there is another motif that runs alongside the integrated Judaic-Christian worship. Christ set up a new cult and instituted new practices. Schmemann maintains that "the religious community which He formed in His disciples was not only united by His teaching, but also had its own 'rule of prayer' (Luke 11:1) and its own cultic assemblies."[102] Nevertheless, what is new for the early Christians is not merely form (e.g., Eucharist and baptism);[103] basically, the Jewish form remained intact as the structure of Christian worship. The newness stems from the content: the Messiah *has* come. The "old" cult prophesies the *coming* of the Messiah and his kingdom, while the "new" cult witnesses that the Messiah *has come* and inaugurated his kingdom. As prophesy, the old cult needed to be fulfilled by witness. The new form, Eucharist and baptism, testify to the radical newness of the Christian content that was imparted into the old. For the early church, both sacraments are rooted and fulfilled in Christ, and only in Christ. Schmemann argues that, for the new cult, there is no other content than Christ, his coming, and "the work He accomplished. The disciples understood this cult as the *parousia*, the presence of Christ. In it they 'proclaimed the death of the Lord and confessed His resurrection.' Outside the faith in Christ as Messiah, outside the faith in His *parousia* in the Church, it has no meaning."[104]

Rooted in Christ, baptism and Eucharist set the early Christians apart from other Hebrews. Baptism initiated the convert into the Christian community, and, as part of the community, the convert regularly partook of the Eucharist and prayed the common prayers. These worship

---

101. Schmemann, *Introduction to Liturgical Theology*, 55.
102. Schmemann, *Introduction to Liturgical Theology*, 58.
103. Even these find their roots in Judaism.
104. Schmemann, *Introduction to Liturgical Theology*, 63.

practices were of greater importance than the Hebrew practices because the early Christians understood themselves as something new. Nonetheless, Christian practices did not entail a discarding of the old practices. The old practices were considered enriched and fulfilled by the new; this is liturgical dualism. In Schmemann's own words, liturgical dualism "is a participation in the old cult and at the same time the presence—from the very beginning—of the cult of the new."[105] Liturgical dualism "constitutes the original basis for Christian worship, its first 'norm.'"[106] After the destruction of the temple, the two practices of synagogue and Eucharist were brought together: the *synaxis* (assembly)—which preserved the synagogue structure—and the Eucharist came together to form the eucharistic assembly. Today, we can still see the synagogical character in the *preanaphora* (what precedes the eucharistic prayer). What is vitally important for Schmemann is that, although the Eucharist and the *synaxis* are brought together, they are not conflated; they sit side by side—liturgical dualism.

Eschatologically Transparent Time

In view of liturgical dualism, Schmemann argues that early Christian eschatology is not world-renouncing. That is, it does not constitute a rejection of time and history, as Dix and others have postulated. The latter assumption often acts as the implicit basis of research conducted in the field of early Christian eschatology. When this misconception serves as the driving assumption, the liturgy of time is easily dismissed as a Hellenistic or late monastic development, and, once again, the Judaic origins are overlooked. Schmemann maintains that the Christian liturgy of time is compatible with early Christian eschatology. And this is the case precisely if Christian eschatology is properly appreciated as a continuation and fulfillment of Judaic eschatology and its account of time.

Schmemann calls the Hebraic account of time "eschatologically transparent time."[107] That is, the God of Abraham acts in time and gives it meaning by directing it toward the Lord's Day. Thus, time becomes history, salvation history.[108] In this sense of time, the Sabbath and all feasts

---

105. Schmemann, *Introduction to Liturgical Theology*, 59.
106. Schmemann, *Introduction to Liturgical Theology*, 55.
107. Schmemann, *Introduction to Liturgical Theology*, 71.
108. Schmemann, *Introduction to Liturgical Theology*, 88.

are reminders of the eschaton, the Lord's Day. Such time is not natural nor cyclical but is eschatological.

As the previous section showed, "the difference between Christianity and Judaism is not in their understanding or theology of time, but in their conception of the events by which this time is spiritually measured."[109] For Judaism, eschatology is still directed toward the Messiah and his kingdom; whereas, for Christianity, the Messiah has already come and the kingdom is at hand—the end of time has taken place. In light of this, Schmemann posits that Christianity recognizes the meaningfulness of time, and the church lives in this fullness. But if the Messiah has come, are not all subsequent temporal events without an end and therefore void of meaning? No, according to Schmemann, the end does not render subsequent historical events void but sheds light and meaning on these events.[110] To put it differently, post-Pascha events find their fulfillment in Pascha. Schmemann makes sense of this with liturgical dualism.

Through Christ's life, death, and resurrection, the future kingdom entered the world. By entering into the time of our world, Christ affirms the reality of "this time." Be that as it may, the Christ event is a "conquest of time not in the sense of rendering it empty and valueless, but rather in the sense of creating the possibility of being made partakers of or participants in the 'coming aeon,' in the fullness, joy and peace that is found in the Holy Spirit, while still living in 'this world.'"[111] This anagogical understanding of time fits within Schmemann's dualistic pattern: Christ affirms time, and Christ conquers time. In other words, the old eon ("this world") becomes the "time and space" where we encounter the new.[112] It is here that we encounter Christ, and so this world is necessarily important and meaningful. The Christian partakes of the old in light of the new.[113] At the same time, in that encounter with Christ, we are set free from the limits of the old.[114] In relation to this, the church, constituted in the Eucharist, is not of this world, for it belongs to the new eon, "which

---

109. Schmemann, *Introduction to Liturgical Theology*, 71.

110. Schmemann, *Introduction to Liturgical Theology*, 70.

111. Schmemann, *Introduction to Liturgical Theology*, 73.

112. According to Hans van Loon, Schmemann's conception of time is similar to Karl Barth's. See Loon, "Karl Barth."

113. The parallel to eschatological symbolism should be obvious.

114. Gregory of Nyssa's anagogical conception of time and space is similar. See Boersma, *Embodiment and Virtue*, 44–50.

in relation to this world is the Kingdom of the age to come."[115] Simultaneously, the church exists in this world and its eon because the kingdom, through Christ, entered this world and continues to in the church.[116] Schmemann argues that Christ established his church, setting it in time in order to redeem time ("this world") and give it meaning. The church's liturgy of time represents the church's existence in this world, while the eucharistic reality of the church reveals her foundation is the eschatological kingdom.

Another way of approaching this dualism is through the eucharistic pattern: Christ came into time, fulfilled and manifested history, and then ascended to the Father. It is an event of the past that must be understood as an end that is always present.[117] Schmemann is adamant that an eschatology that is not "eucharistically" informed renounces the world and, in so doing, belittles the historical incarnation. To put it differently, Christ's coming and Christ's leaving are equally important for understanding time. Christ entered into rather than abolished our time, and he left this world in order not to dominate or subsume it. This is why Schmemann repeatedly emphasizes that the church must *ascend* to the Lord's table and enter God's eternal time, the new eon, in order to return and impregnate the time of this world with meaning.

Schmemann argues that his dualistic account is contrary to a world-renouncing eschatology, for a eucharistic eschatology does not replace liturgical time. Eucharistic time is of a different eon than liturgical time, and the future (the new eon perceived in light of the old eon) cannot replace the present without destroying it. Hence, they must be kept apart yet related. In other words, eucharistic time cannot abolish liturgical time without rendering the time of this world unnecessary. As its end, eucharistic time must inform liturgical time.

To conclude and clarify, let us return to Dix's argument. Schmemann writes that, according to Dix, "there could be no liturgy rooted in time, having reference to the times and hours of human life, because the church herself regarded herself as a departure out of time, as the renunciation of that world which lives wholly in time and is subordinated to it and measured by it."[118] Schmemann posits that the problem with Dix is

115. Schmemann, *Introduction to Liturgical Theology*, 72.

116. Schmemann, *Eucharist*, 48.

117. See Schmemann, "Fast and Liturgy"; Schmemann, "Problems of Orthodoxy: Liturgical," 180; Schmemann, *Liturgy and Life*, 76.

118. Schmemann, *Introduction to Liturgical Theology*, 51.

that he does not recognize that early Christian eschatology is based on the Hebraic notion of eschatologically transparent time. According to the Hebraic account, time finds its meaning in the kingdom of YHWH and the coming of the Messiah. Schmemann argues that the church continues to see time in this fashion, except it recognizes that the Messiah has come. Therefore, Schmemann insists that to argue that eschatology is only future-oriented, and thus world-renouncing, is tantamount to denying that the Messiah has come. Nevertheless, Dix's orientation to the future is not completely misled. The Messiah came and then ascended (the eucharistic pattern) in order to allow time, aided by the church, to come to its fruition, its end. As part of Schmemann's dualism, the old and the new aeons overlap, and, through the church, the new penetrates into the old, giving it meaning by being its end. In point form, the argument beginning in the previous section and continued in this section is as follows:

1. The form of Christian worship is the same as Judaic worship.

2. The difference between Judaic and Christian worship is the content: Christians recognize that the Messiah has come.

3. The content gives new meaning to the forms, but the newness is understood as new only in view of the old. The old and the new remain together without conflation: liturgical dualism.

4. Judaic eschatologically transparent time is the form of time that the early Christian church embraced.

5. Eschatologically transparent time postulates that God acts in and through time and directs it toward the coming of the Messiah and the kingdom of YHWH.

6. Jesus is the Messiah. The kingdom has been inaugurated; the new eon has entered the old. According to eschatologically transparent time, Jesus makes sense of time and history.

7. The new eon, experienced in the Eucharist, does not subsume the old; eucharistic time and the liturgy of time follow the pattern of liturgical dualism.

8. Therefore, eschatology is not world-renouncing.

Time beyond Death: How Time Is Redeemed

Christianity began with a new experience of time, in which time ceases to be bound-up with death.[119]

We have looked at the broad sweep of time, in which God directs the world toward its *end*. However, there is another sense of time about which Schmemann writes that could be called existential time. While time as history involves the interplay between the cosmic, historic, and eschatological, existential time adds a fourth element: the individual person. To be clear, existential time includes the three aforementioned dimensions, but the focus shifts to the perennial problem of death. As such, this section acts as a segue for the next chapter.

Schmemann argues that we are historical beings. It is not possible to conceive of what it means to be human without taking temporality into account. Our experience of time is twofold. First, "man experiences time as cyclical; day follows night, spring follows winter, in an eternal rotation, an eternal cycle of beginning and ending enclosed within time."[120] This cycle symbolizes the completeness of time, in which beginning and end are connected. Schmemann sees this cosmic aspect of time as positive because of its completeness. It brings joy that is substantiated in our seasonal festivities. Second, time is experienced as the unstoppable movement toward death: we are beings toward death—Heidegger's recognition of the defining nature of death.[121] All life moves toward death, for "wherever time exists, death is always present."[122] Schmemann concludes that we live in the tension between the joy of life's completeness and the meaninglessness of death. However, it is the realization of death that overshadows our conception of life, the sobering realization that, every day, I progressively move closer toward my death. The completeness of cyclical time does not soothe the open sore of death. "Whether I die tomorrow or in thirty years, all I am trying to do, all that I am trying to be, is void of meaning because I will disappear. So, the time of human existence is meaningless unless there is something somewhere that can

---

119. Schmemann, *Church Year*, 26.

120. Schmemann, *Church Year*, 24.

121. "The end is imminent for Da-sein. Death is not something not yet objectively present, nor the last outstanding element reduced to a minimum, but rather an imminence" (Heidegger, *Being and Time*, 232–33). Schmemann writes, "Everything is resolved only when the question of death is resolved" (Schmemann, *Journals*, 48).

122. Schmemann, *Church Year*, 24.

overcome this meaninglessness."[123] In summary, time carries us toward death; time's end is death. Death, nonbeing (nothingness),[124] has the final word and renders life meaningless.

The broad narrative of our hopeless predicament acts as prolegomena for Schmemann and sets out the framework from within which he will work. Interestingly, Schmemann follows the same pattern of liturgical dualism: (1) the form remains (in this case, the existential framework concerning death), but the content changes; (2) an end or a telos is necessary to provide meaning; and (3) the end does not override the present but sits in fruitful tension with it.

Schmemann concurs with the existential experience of time. Therefore, his answer to our temporal predicament is based on how Christ entered into time and, consequently, into death. In short, time is transformed because Christ replaces the end of time—death—with himself—life. In order to better understand death and how it is overcome, Schmemann turns to the liturgy of Lazarus Saturday.[125] Typically, Saturday services within the Orthodox tradition are services that commemorate the dead. Lazarus Saturday is unique in that, paradoxically, it is a Sunday celebration (the day of resurrection) celebrated on a Saturday. Saturday, a day that remembers the dead, is turned into a celebration of the power of life over death. Schmemann contends that the resurrection of Lazarus provides the interpretive key to the paschal mystery, which is God's response to death.

Schmemann insists that Lazarus personifies the whole of humankind, and his home (Bethany) is a symbol of the whole world as our home. Through Lazarus Jesus experiences the meaningless power of death and destruction and he weeps. He weeps for his friend and thus weeps for humanity and the world, which are captive to death. Schmemann rhetorically asks why Jesus weeps all the while knowing that he will resurrect Lazarus. He weeps because here he encounters death, the sorrow of this world, the triumph of evil that destroys all he, as the *Logos*, created and loves. With Lazarus, Christ comes face to face with the power that destroys his creation, preparing the way for his own forthcoming battle

---

123. Schmemann, *Liturgy and Life*, 75.

124. Schmemann describes death as "above all, a lack of life, a destruction of life that has cut itself from its only source" (Schmemann, "Liturgical Explanation," 16).

125. I chose to place Lazarus Saturday into the middle of the argument because of Schmemann's assertion that Lazarus Saturday is the key to understanding Christ's death and resurrection.

with death. In Christ's tears we are shown the power that resurrects, i.e., love. Love is life, and Lazarus Saturday reveals that our enemy is death.

Christ's death is the ultimate sacrifice, the supreme act of love, and perfect obedience, and this destroys death. His sacrifice is a gift for his Father and for us. It is for his Father because it fulfills God's desire to save men from death. It is for us because Christ chose to die for us, instead of us. He was free from sin thus free from death, but he accepted death for our sake by virtue of his love for us, "and because Christ's death is a movement of love toward God, an act of obedience and trust, of faith and perfection—it is an act of life which destroys death. It is the death of death itself."[126] Schmemann is not simply using flowery prose. He literally means that Christ's obedience and love destroys death. This makes sense in light of Schmemann's account of the fall.

Death arose as a result of human choice. Adam and Eve chose an end that was not God. In this disobedient symbolic act man alienated himself from God and "having no life in himself and by himself, he dies."[127] To put it more philosophically than Schmemann does, there only is one end, i.e., God. To choose other than God is to choose nothing, nonbeing, anti-God, anti-creation, anti-life, death. By redirecting its route to another end than God humankind irrevocably moved toward the chasm of nonbeing. Through his incarnation the Son of God took humankind into himself and freely, in perfect love and obedience, gave it back to God. As a result, Christ steered humankind back to its proper life-giving end. By saving humankind through freedom, obedience and love, salvation was given to humankind in a form that fit with its nature. Schmemann maintains that "any other salvation would have been in opposition to the nature of man, and therefore, not a real salvation."[128] What he means is that it was humankind's free and disobedient act that separated us from God, marring the communion of love. Christ undid the fall through the proper use of the same three key elements that make us human: freedom, obedience, and love. In other words, by being not only the true image of God but also the true image of man Christ redeemed us.

The spiritual antonym of love and obedience is separation. Death, the result of disobedience, separates us from both divine and human relationships—death is separation. Christ enters into our humanity so that

---

126. Schmemann, "Liturgical Explanation," 16.
127. Schmemann, "Liturgical Explanation," 12.
128. Schmemann, "Liturgical Explanation," 16.

we can be reconciled with God and humans, made one—at-one-ment. In Jesus Christ, the God-Man, death runs into a problem. Here Schmemann comes at the problem of death from a different angle than laid out above. He argues that while man has no life in himself and thus can be separated from life, death cannot rob Christ of his life and of his goodness, for he *is* good and he *is* life. Paradoxically, death enveloped life (himself), but could not overcome it.[129] Therefore, death itself is no longer separation. It has become a passage onto life "and because His dying is love, compassion and co-suffering, in His death the very nature of death is changed. From punishment it becomes the radiant act of love and forgiveness, the end of alienation and solitude. Condemnation is transformed into forgiveness."[130]

What does Christ's entering into and overthrowing of death imply for Schmemann's conception of existential time? Existential time has been transformed. Death is no longer the end of time; time has a new end, a proper *telos*—Christ. As a result, meaningless time came to its end. "The Pascha of Jesus signified its end to 'this world' and it has been at its end since then. This end can last for hundreds of centuries, this does not alter the nature of time in which we live as the 'last time.' The form of this world is passing away...' (I Corinthians 7:31)."[131] Time is now intertwined with joy rather than death, for death has been transformed into a passage that leads to joy and life himself.

Christ overcame death, but we must still pass through it; the new has yet to subsume the old. Nonetheless, Christ sheds light into the old and changes our perception. A serious change has occurred:

> We are no longer people in meaningless time that leads to a meaningless end. We are given not only a new meaning in life, but even death itself has acquired a new significance. In the troparion [short hymn] of Pascha we say, "trampling down death by death." We do not say that He trampled down death by the Resurrection, but by death.[132]

Like all humankind, Christians must die, and it is only through death that we reach new life. Death precedes resurrection. We still live in the midnight of the old eon and must go through the world to reach the new eon. The form (death) remains, but the content changes from separation

---

129. Schmemann, "Liturgical Explanation," 16.
130. Schmemann, "Liturgical Explanation," 12.
131. Schmemann, "Liturgical Explanation," 5.
132. Schmemann, "Liturgical Explanation," 21.

to Christ. Schmemann writes that our death and resurrection wait to be appropriated by us; "it is already His Resurrection, but not yet ours. We will have to die, to accept the dying, the separation, the destruction. Our reality in this world, in this 'aeon,' is the reality of the Great Saturday."[133]

Christ's death and resurrection is the end of time, its *telos*. However, he is more than a distant end. The end is an event in the midst of human time (via the church), and, therefore, Pascha is a celebration of both the past (the historical event of Christ's passion) and the future (the consummation of the kingdom): "Pascha is always the end and always the beginning. We are always living *after* Pascha, and we are always going *towards* Pascha."[134] As the true *telos* who came into the world, all time centers on Jesus. Like a whirlpool, he gathers the past and future to himself, toward the new eon. We live in the middle of Christ's two comings (the old eon), what was and what will be. In this Saturday of our existence, he is present in the church. Thus, the new time inaugurated by Christ involves the past, present, and future.[135] Schmemann claims that, in a very practical way, these three tenses are essential to the Christian life and to time in its totality:

1. Christ has come: we discover the meaning of our lives.
2. Christ is present (in the church): this makes meaning possible.
3. Christ is coming: the present time is given meaning (leading to the fulfillment of the kingdom).[136]

In summary, Schmemann follows Heidegger's conclusion and agrees that the human person is a being in time and thereby is a being toward death. Schmemann concludes that, if death is final and is the *telos* of time, then time is meaningless. However, Christ overcame this meaninglessness by entering into death and trampling down death with death. Poetically concluding his point, Schmemann quotes from "The Lamentations of Matins of Holy and Great Saturday": "How, O Life, canst Thou die? Or abide in a grave. For Thou dost destroy the kingdom of death, O Lord, and Thou raisest up the dead of Hades' realm. . . . In a grave they laid Thee, O my Life and my Christ. Yet behold now, by Thy death, death is

---

133. Schmemann, "Liturgical Explanation," 19.
134. Schmemann, *Liturgy and Life*, 76.
135. We shall return to this in the next chapter.
136. Schmemann, *Liturgy and Life*, 87.

stricken down, and Thou pourest forth life's streams for all the world."[137] The "resurrection is the appearance in this world, completely dominated by time and therefore by death, of life that shall have no end."[138] As a result, the meaninglessness of time as death has been redeemed and transformed into a means to life. As a kingdom event within time, Pascha reaches into the past and the future of the old eon and impregnates it with life and meaning, and thus, in an anagogical fashion, the present is given meaning. As we shall see in chapters 3, 4, and 5, Ratzinger's conception of eschatology and temporality challenges Schmemann's anagogical approach and implicitly highlights the problems with liturgical dualism.

Conclusion

> The Church is to be seen as the presence and communication of the kingdom that is to come. The unique—I repeat, unique—function of worship in the life of the Church and in theology is to convey a sense of this eschatological reality.[139]

Eschatology is the lens through which Schmemann looks at theology. In fact, Schmemann offers us bifocals, and, looking through these, we see two different images of the same thing. First, looking from a distance, we see the kingdom. Theology, in this view, is always ordered and orientated to the kingdom.[140] Second, looking up close, we see Christ. He is the kingdom; he is the one who orients us; he is perfect thanksgiving, and, in him, we are filled with gratitude that transforms our life and vision.[141]

In Christ, we see proleptically and are given a vision of the sacramentality of the world—eschatological symbolism. As symbols, the things of this world are latent sacraments that find their fulfillment in Christ, the sacrament par excellence. Christ makes the things of this world epiphanic, and we wait for when they will be unhindered means of communion with God. Schmemann asserts that this is the Christian vision, and this is what makes sense of life.

137. Schmemann, "Liturgical Explanation," 17.
138. Schmemann, *Liturgy and Life*, 76.
139. Schmemann, *Liturgy and Tradition*, 95–96.
140. Schmemann, *Eucharist*, 34.
141. "He [Christ] is the end, the *Eschaton*, and our Eucharist is thus not in the past, the present, or the future. It is the *Eschaton*, in the glorified Christ" (Schmemann, *Liturgy and Tradition*, 112).

Akin to eschatological symbolism, liturgical dualism makes sense of temporality. It offers a way of holding together the old and the new. The Hebraic account of "eschatologically transparent time" understood temporality as salvation history. Early Christians held to this view but filled it with new meaning: the Messiah has come and has inaugurated the kingdom. In so doing, they recognized that time is made meaningful by the true *telos* of the paschal event. In other words, salvation history has been fulfilled and completed in Christ. Existentially, Christ's entering into death changed the very nature of time. What was once a steady progression toward death now culminates in Christ. Time, which once made life meaningless, now is anagogically significant. In Christ, we must rephrase Heidegger's "being toward death" to "being toward Christ." What undergirds all forms of temporality, for Schmemann, is the focus on ends: Christ is the *end* of time and history.

2

Schmemann and Personhood: Eucharistic Beings

> The *Eucharist*—thanksgiving, adoration, worship—is truly the ultimate and the total expression of his whole being. Man was created for *Eucharist*—for the pure love of God, for the sake of God, for the recognition of God as the content of his very life, as the Goal of all his goals, the Answer to all his questions, the Purpose of all his desires, the Object of all his knowledge, the Fulfillment of all his power and his thirst for love. Eucharist is the Divine element, the Image of God in us.
>
> —ALEXANDER SCHMEMANN

THE PREVIOUS CHAPTER ESTABLISHED the centrality of eschatology in Schmemann's theological vision and explored the ways in which it shapes temporality. According to Schmemann, eschatology guarantees the import of our temporal existence. This argument is based on an antinomic pattern set by his eschatological symbolism and liturgical dualism. In this pattern, the old remains separate from the new but in relation: the new is the *telos* of the old.

Since Schmemann aims to speak to the world for the life of the world, it is not surprising that he provides an account of what it means to be a human person. Nevertheless, Schmemann is not a systematician, and his theological anthropology is scattered throughout his various publications. It is my contention that the many snippets, passages, and paragraphs that concern personhood in Schmemann's work find their hermeneutical center in thanksgiving. As we have already seen, thanksgiving plays a vital role for Schmemann's construal of eschatology: thanksgiving is the eschatological experience of the kingdom. The high point of this experience occurs at the eucharistic meal—"do this in remembrance of me"—and it is under the aegis of thanksgiving and remembrance that Schmemann's notion of eschatology and personhood come together.

There are two related questions that underlie this chapter. How does eschatology shape personhood? What does it mean to be a person in time? Schmemann does not explicitly answer either question, and thus I pieced together various strands of his thought in order to explain and expand what Schmemann has hinted at. Since the two questions naturally conflate—Christian time always involves eschatology—I have, more often than not, abstained from forcefully separating them, allowing them to speak as one.

The Present Reality of Remembrance

All remembrance is ultimately remembrance of Christ, all thanksgiving is finally thanksgiving for Christ. . . . There is nothing else to remember, nothing else to be thankful for, because in Him everything finds its being, its life, its end.[1]

Liturgical remembrance is the linchpin that holds together eschatology (temporality), thanksgiving (Eucharist), and ontology (personal being). There are four aspects to this. First, remembrance is celebrated within the church, and it is through ecclesial remembrance that Christ makes himself present. He is present not simply within our memory but in reality, and we experience this as an event, an encounter. Second, his presence as event occurs through thanksgiving: Christ is made present in the Eucharist (thanksgiving). Third, in Christ, remembrance is a new experience of time in which past, present, and future come together.[2] This means that

---

1. Schmemann, *For Life of World*, 40.
2. Yves Congar's sacramental sense of time is similar to Schmemann's conception. Schmemann engages with Congar's work, so it is likely that Schmemann's account of time as holding together in Christ is inspired by the French Dominican friar. Hans Boersma offers a helpful overview of Congar's thought. See Boersma, *Heavenly Participation*, 122–27; Boersma, *Nouvelle Théologie*, 223–28.

remembrance is not concerned merely with historical reflection. Finally, as a kingdom event, remembrance becomes ontological (is real and personal) because the kingdom, along with the Eucharist, is Christ.

According to Schmemann, commemoration of the Last Supper is an ecclesial encounter/event, an event of the present. It is not a historical event that is imprisoned in the past, which we must mimetically re-enact in order to recall Christian history. Remembrance is ontological (it has reality/being), and Schmemann explicates this in two ways: (1) thanksgiving as Eucharist (or vice versa) and (2) God's memory and his remembering. We will return to the second aspect in the section titled "Memory of God."

The Eucharist is thanksgiving, and therefore thanksgiving is given a personal ontology. Christ embodies gratitude, gratitude to and for the Father.[3] In the eucharistic liturgy (the liturgy of gratitude), one participates in Christ and in his thanksgiving. At the table, the participant offers herself and the world in *gratitude* to God (restored priesthood).[4] To make my point that thanksgiving is given a person ontology, in the previous sentence, *gratitude* can be replaced with *Christ*: "At the table, the participant offers herself and the world in *Christ* to God." In Christ, the eternal, historical, and present come together (the ultimate symbol):

> And when, approaching for communion, we pray, "Of Thy Mystical Supper, O Son of God, accept me *today* as a communicant," this identification of what is accomplished *today* with what was accomplished *then* is *real*, and precisely in the full meaning of the word, for *today* we are gathered in the same kingdom, at the same table, where *then*, on that festal night, Christ was present among those whom "he loved to the end."[5]

For Schmemann, liturgical remembering is personal remembrance of the kingdom event, the Last Supper. It is remembrance of our participation in the Lord's Day as God's adopted sons and daughters.[6] Schmemann emphasizes the term *end* in the last line of the quoted prayer, "he loved to the *end*." The Last Supper is the end; it

---

3. See the section in this chapter titled "The Obedience of Christ." See Schmemann, *Liturgy and Life*, 52–59.
4. Schmemann, *Church, World, Mission*, 223.
5. Schmemann, *Eucharist*, 200.
6. Schmemann, *Church Year*, 122; see Schmemann, *Church, World, Mission*, 34.

is *Love itself*. And thus the last supper is the τέλοσ, the completion, the fulfilment of the *end*, for it is the manifestation of that kingdom of love, for the sake of which the world was created and in which it has its τέλοσ, its fulfilment.... And now, at this table, he manifests and grants this love as his kingdom, and his kingdom as "abiding" in love.[7]

"Hid with Christ" literally means we are in *Love itself*, in the kingdom. The Last Supper is the kingdom event into which we are lifted through the passage of the eucharistic liturgy. The Last Supper is not merely a past historical event but the kingdom event par excellence.[8]

Before concluding, we must clarify the distinction that exists between Pascha and the Last Supper. According to the previously cited quotation, the Last Supper is the "completion," "fulfilment," and "*telos*" of our existence. Yet, in the first chapter, we noted that Schmemann writes about Pascha as the *telos* ("Pascha is always the end and always the beginning").[9] Which one is the *telos*? Schmemann argues that everything that occurs after the Last Supper is a consequence of what the Last Supper initiated, the inauguration of the kingdom. The cross was the inevitable outcome, for the Last Supper was God's pronouncement against sin and evil. God's kingdom could not coexist with the kingdom of the "prince of the air" and all it entailed, "because it was in order to destroy the dominion of sin and death, to return his creation, stolen from him by the devil, to himself, to save the world, that God gave his only-begotten Son. Thus, Christ *condemned* himself to the cross with the last supper, with the manifestation in it of the kingdom of love."[10] The cross and resurrection mark the victory of God's kingdom, which was established at the Last Supper. In other words, Christ came to break bread, and Pascha is the culmination and the unifying event that follows, in which Christ delivers the kingdom to God so "that God may be all in all" (1 Cor 15:28). Pascha completes the Last Supper, and because they go hand-in-hand, Schmemann writes of both being the *telos*.

The adumbrated version of the relationship between thanksgiving and remembrance is as follows:

7. Schmemann, *Eucharist*, 200–201.
8. "The last supper, the Church and the eucharist are 'linked' not through an earthly cause-and-effect connection . . . , but through their common and single referral to the kingdom of God" (Schmemann, *Eucharist*, 202).
9. Schmemann, *Liturgy and Life*, 76.
10. Schmemann, *Eucharist*, 206.

1. To abide in Christ is to participate in the kingdom.
2. The Last Supper is abiding in Christ; therefore, the inauguration and the manifestation of the kingdom is an event *in* human history experienced in the Last Supper.
3. The kingdom is the new eon.
4. This world is the old eon.
5. As the one who is both eternal and historical, Christ unites the old and the new aeons.
6. In baptism, we are "hid with Christ in God" (Col 3:3), and through the Eucharist (Christ's thanksgiving), we participate in his life and his relationship with time and eternity.
7. Therefore, through the Eucharist/thanksgiving, we remember the Last Supper, for we truly participate in the new eon.

Schmemann insists that thanksgiving is not the response aroused by remembrance, but, rather, thanksgiving is what precedes and enables remembrance. Through Christ's thanksgiving, we are brought into the kingdom, and we reenter and truly participate in the Last Supper (the kingdom meal). In other words, thanksgiving is participation in Christ, which makes remembrance a personal act of remembering, in the same way that I personally remember writing this very sentence!

Remembrance, Reentrance, and Meaning

In order to clarify what appears to be a discrepancy in Schmemann's account of remembrance, one proviso must follow what was written in the previous section. In *Great Lent: Journey to Pascha*, Schmemann distinguishes between factual historical events and meaningful events. The former cannot literally be brought into the "today" of the liturgical experience, while the latter can: "Oh, to be sure, the Virgin does not give birth today, no one 'factually' stands before Pilate, and as facts these events belong to the past. But *today* we can remember these facts and the Church is primarily the gift and the power of that remembrance which transforms facts of the past into eternally meaningful events."[11] Does the distinction between a *factual* and *meaningful* event imply, contrary to *The Eucharist*, that remembrance of the Last Supper is simply about understanding the

---

11. Schmemann, *Great Lent*, 82.

particular historical event's meaning? What does Schmemann imply by "meaningful events"? Is remembrance ahistorical? Three points can be made that provide answers to the aforementioned questions.

First, Schmemann distinguishes the Last Supper from all other events; it is *sui generis*. The Last Supper is the beginning of the Easter event, the kingdom event that gives meaning to all other events,[12] and, as the new eon, the kingdom transcends the present without abandoning it. Easter is not a historical event per se but is an event of the new eon that touches down in history. In other words, the Last Supper is the focal point, in which all time finds its fulfillment, its meaning.

Second, Schmemann distinguishes between "natural memory" and "memory in Christ." He notes that "natural memory is first of all a 'presence of the absent,' so that the more he [a deceased loved one] whom we remember is present, the more acute is the pain of his absence. But in Christ, memory has become again the power to fill the time broken by sin and death, by hatred and forgetfulness."[13] In the eucharistic remembrance, "do this in remembrance of me," "we remember Him and He is here—not as a nostalgic image of the past, not as a sad 'never more,' but with such intensity of presence."[14] "Memory in Christ" makes sense of the uniqueness of Easter and its relation to the Last Supper and the new eon. But how does it affect other liturgical events (e.g., Lazarus Saturday)? This question leads to the next point.

Third, meaning for Schmemann is participatory—"memory *in* Christ," not memory *about* Christ. Meaning is not merely an abstraction. In liturgical participation, we reenter the reality of the event; we do not reenact it.[15] In his journal, Schmemann writes, "It is *not* Holy Week that is *coming back*; we are *returning to it*, touching it, communing with it.

---

12. Schmemann, *Liturgy and Life*, 76.

13. Schmemann, *Great Lent*, 82. See Schmemann, *Eucharist*, 124–25.

14. Schmemann, *Great Lent*, 82.

15. In *Introduction to Liturgy*, Schmemann distinguishes between the pagan reenactment of the mystery cults of the fourth and fifth centuries and the Christian approach of reentrance. He notes that "in Baptism Christ does not die and rise again, which would be its essence if it were a mystery, but the believer actualizes his faith in Christ, and in the Church, as Salvation and New Life." He makes the same point regarding the Eucharist: "People gain access to this Kingdom through His death and resurrection, but once again the Eucharist does not reproduce or symbolize these events, instead it manifests their efficacy and the Church's participation in the Body of Christ established by these events" (Schmemann, *Introduction to Liturgical Theology*, 109). This follows the logic that Louis Bouyer sets out. See Bouyer, *Life and Liturgy*, 86–98.

There—all is already eternity."[16] We return, touch, and commune with the event in the present. Thus, remembrance is not simply a meaningful reflection but a meaningful *event* of today. It is a present event because the efficacy of the historical event is manifested in the present. It is manifested in liturgical celebration, in tangible ecclesiastical experience, not simply in the participants' cerebral cortex. Through participation in Christ, we remain present yet at the same time return to the event. As the center of all meaning, Christ makes present those events that find their conclusion in him. In other words, liturgical celebration is present engagement with eternal reality, and we could acutely call these events eschatological events. Eschatological events function in the same way as eschatological symbols. They are incomplete kingdom events that find their meaning and fulfillment in the kingdom event par excellence, Christ's Pasch. Through the liturgy of the church, eschatological events (e.g., Lazarus Saturday) are made manifest to the participants. This is confirmed by the church's celebration, in which "an historical fact becomes an *event* for us, for me, a power in my life, a memory, a joy."[17] As a real personal encounter, I can truly celebrate. Schmemann quips, "One does not celebrate ideas!"[18] His repeated use and italicization of the word *event* and the phrase *meaningful event* is set in contrast with *ideas*. The conjoining of meaning with event, arguably what he intends with the term *event*, ensures that form and essence are not separated.[19] If separated, we are left with idea (essence) and piety (form), neither of which, according to Schmemann, are particularly Christian: we do not worship ideas, and there is no *we* in piety.[20]

In conclusion, for Schmemann, history is a meaningful progression of time only in light of Christ and his kingdom. The Last Supper is the manifestation and inauguration of the kingdom, the unique event that fills time. If Christ gives meaning to time and he is ontologically present, both of which Easter reveals, then, through his presence in the Divine Liturgy (the gathering, *epiklesis*, and the ascent), all liturgical celebrations take on meaning, become event, become tangible. The meaning, for example, of

16. Schmemann, *Journals*, 219.
17. Schmemann, *Great Lent*, 83.
18. Schmemann, *Great Lent*, 81.
19. Schmemann, *Of Water and Spirit*, 55–56.

20. Schmemann refers to two problematic approaches to the liturgy: the rational approach and the sentimental approach. The first centers on ideas and the second on personal piety (Schmemann, *Great Lent*, 80–81).

Lazarus Saturday—confirmation of the universal resurrection—is found in Christ. Lazarus Saturday, because of its relation to Pascha, becomes a real tangible meaningful event: an experience of joy, fullness, and love manifested in the present. The event is not the repetition or reenactment of Lazarus's resurrection but is the experience of meaning as reality (in contrast with abstracted meaning). Therefore, liturgical celebration is not mere recollection but is an experience of meaning made manifest. Construed in this manner, historical events remain events of the past yet, at the same time, are events of today. They are manifestations and, for that reason, meaningful events, via participation (reentrance), and carry the same meaning as the original events. Meaning is always personal (relational), and, because of this, meaning requires participation, not mere recollection. If it were recollection, absence rather than presence would be the dominant experience of remembrance. For example, we would be more aware of the distance that separates us from the past event than of its perduring meaning.

Remembrance in both its ultimate sense (the Last Supper) and in its "lesser" sense (eschatological events) is more than mere recollection of an event's meaning. We have looked at the personal, celebratory, and participatory nature of meaning (meaningful events), but what still needs clarification is the question concerning remembrance as ahistorical. This brings us back to Schmemann's notion of "memory in Christ," which provides an alternative to "natural memory" for conceiving of history. Natural memory leaves the past, so to speak, in the past: time is locked. Memory in Christ, on the other hand, frees us from the limits of the present without making remembrance ahistorical; on the contrary, it transforms the present into the "place" where the new eon, the kingdom, in all its manifestations, can be encountered (an event here and now—historical). Since we live in the old eon, we experience the new within the framework of world history. In both the historical and the meaningful event, Christ is central. Without Christ, the historical event is no longer a meaningful progression of time, and the meaningful event is simply remembrance as absence.

Conclusion

"Antinomical tension"[21] pervades Schmemann's eschatology and therefore temporality. Remembrance of the Last Supper is our experience of this tension, an experience of a kingdom event that happened in time in the person of Christ. Consequently, it transcends the past without abolishing it. We enter into this (supra)historical event in thanksgiving by becoming Eucharist. As the *telos* of time, Christ gives meaning to temporality; all time is measured in Christ and his Pasch. The paschal event—the eucharistic event—turns all acts of meaningful remembrance into current participatory experiences of meaning. In other words, through liturgical remembrance, Christians enter into the reality of meaning itself, i.e., Christ.

Memory of God

> There is no need for remembrance, since there is no gulf between the one who remembers and what is remembered, i.e., life itself.[22]

According to the *Oxford English Dictionary*, memory is "the faculty by which the mind stores and remembers information." To remember is the action that accords with the faculty of memory, and remembrance is "the action of remembering something." However, in the second point of the previous section, Schmemann clearly conflates memory and remembrance: "Natural memory is first of all a 'presence of the absent,'" and "memory has become again the power to fill."[23] Specifically with the latter example, it seems apparent that the word *remembrance* is more fitting than *memory*. Is this simply a misuse of language, something lost in translation—English was his third language—or did Schmemann purposefully employ these terms? English does not appear to hinder his ability to express himself,[24]

---

21. This is a phrase Schmemann used and others such as David Fagerberg have highlighted. See Schmemann, *Church, World, Mission*, 59; Fagerberg, "Cost of Understanding Schmemann." I wonder if the phrase is an attempt to put a positive spin on dualism.

22. Schmemann, *Journals*, 66.

23. Schmemann, *Great Lent*, 82.

24. Of Schmemann's major works, only his first two books, *The Historical Road of Eastern Orthodoxy* and *Introduction to Liturgical Theology*, employed a translator. *The Eucharist* was first written in Russian, but Schmemann supervised the translating of the first two chapters into English before his death.

SCHMEMANN AND PERSONHOOD: EUCHARISTIC BEINGS   43

so I think it is fair to dismiss the first option.[25] Thus, it is appropriate to ask why Schmemann uses these terms in this particular way. The answer is found in Schmemann's conception of the memory of God.[26]

Schmemann's conception of memory enriches the explication of remembrance in the previous section and accentuates the saving act of remembrance in overcoming our oblivion. In expounding the commemorating words of the Divine Liturgy, "May the Lord God remember all of you," Schmemann highlights the import of remembrance: "'Remember, O Lord . . . ' without any exaggeration one can say that the commemoration, i.e., the referral of everything to the *memory* of God, the prayer that God would 'remember,' constitutes the heartbeat of all of the Church's worship, her entire life."[27] As a result of the church's surrender to the scientific method, this understanding, with its seeming lack of theological objectivity, has been ignored. The scientific method reduces memory and remembrance to a referral on another's behalf (e.g., we recall those who have gone on before us) or to a sort of intellectualizing, in which remembrance is the intellectual exercise of focusing on the meaning of a past event. Schmemann aims to overturn the scientific understanding of memory and retrieve the depth of theological memory. Structurally, his notion of the memory of God is laid out as follows:

1. Introductory remarks about the centrality of the memory of God
2. What the church has lost by ignoring memory
3. The meaning of "natural memory"
4. Memory of God understood in the Old Testament
5. Our forgetting
6. Christ, as the incarnation of the memory of God, restores our memory of God

The first three points have briefly been covered, and so the following expands upon the last three points.

The memory of God in the Old Testament (point 4), asserts Schmemann,

---

25. "Father Schmemann's language and effort is artistic in that sense that it doesn't hit us with irrefutable axioms, but like the parables of Christ, it is an invitation to share in what he sees with his inner eye" (Vinogradov, "Father Alexander Schmemann").

26. Only in *The Eucharist* does Schmemann provide a sustained study on memory.

27. Schmemann, *Eucharist*, 123.

> refers to the attentiveness of God to his creation, the power of divine providential love, through which God "holds" the world and *gives it life*, so that life itself can be termed abiding in the memory of God, and death the falling out of this memory. In other words, memory, like everything else in God, is *real*, it *is* that life that he grants, that God "*remembers*"; it is the eternal overcoming of the "nothing" out of which God called us into "his wonderful light."[28]

The ontological implications of the block quote are obvious, and they reflect Schmemann's emphasis upon personal embodiment.[29] Furthermore, memory is a relational category. Memory is not simply internal within the mind of God, in some Cartesian manner, but is connected with love.[30] In regard to the human person, existence is necessarily contingent. Immortality is not part of human nature. Our existence rests in God's memory. Yet, the way that Schmemann writes of God's memory still seems odd. Is it not possible for him to speak of contingency and exclude memory? The key to making sense of this is context, i.e., the Eucharist. We shall return to the eucharistic context when we look at point 6 of the argument.

As revealed in the Old Testament, God's memory and his remembrance is the gift of life. The other side of God's remembrance is our reception of this gift, which Schmemann describes as "man's remembrance of God," which is "the constant *acquisition* of and increase in life."[31] Our greatest sin is that we have forgotten God, and, in forgetting God, we have cut ourselves off from life (point 5). This is the original sin recounted in Genesis, in which Adam and Eve chose to eat the fruit for its own end rather than as a means of communion with God. This was the beginning of Adam's and Eve's obliviousness, and it literally led to our demise. Like memory, *obliviousness*—the word Schmemann carefully chose because of its relation to oblivion—is ontological. Obliviousness is precisely the poisoning of life and the beginning of death. Schmemann develops the ontological implications:

---

28. Schmemann, *Eucharist*, 125.

29. "For just as there can be no love outside the 'lover,' i.e. a person that loves, there can be no hatred outside the 'hater,' i.e. a person that hates. And if the ultimate mystery of 'goodness' lies in the person, the ultimate mystery of evil must also be a personal one" (Schmemann, *Of Water and Spirit*, 22).

30. See Schmemann, *For Life of World*, 36.

31. Schmemann, *Eucharist*, 126.

> The absence of one whom I forget for me is *real*, he is actually *not* in my life, not a part of my life—he is dead for me, and I for him. If it is God, the giver of life and life itself whom I have forgotten, if he has ceased to be *my* memory and *my* life, my life itself becomes dying, and then memory, which is the knowledge and power of life, becomes knowledge of death and the constant tasting of mortality.[32]

Yet, natural memory—a poor reflection of God's memory (*imago Dei*)—in its remembering reaches out for life beyond death and hopes to bring back the past, only to fail and be reminded of absence rather than presence. Natural memory reveals the tragic irony of our attempt to resurrect the past (an unrecognized thirst for the kingdom), only to realize that it is impossible.

As the "incarnation of the memory of God"[33] and the restorer of our memory, Jesus Christ overcomes our obliviousness/oblivion (point 6). Christ's remembrance triumphs over time and heals our memory. He is the realization of our natural desire, and he accomplishes what we could not:

> He is the incarnation in man and for man, in the world and for the world, of God's remembrance, of the divine and lifecreating love directed toward the world. And he is the perfect manifestation and fulfilment in man of his remembrance of God, as the content, the power and the life of life itself.
>
> The incarnation of the memory of God: if man has forgotten God, God has not forgotten man, he has not "turned himself away" from him. He has transformed the fallen and mortal time of "this world" into the history of salvation.[34]

There is what we could term *vicarious memory*: Christ remembers for us and manifests the memory of God.[35] As a result, our memory is healed and is the organ of life, akin to God's memory. Time is turned into the history of salvation, and our obliviousness/oblivion is overcome.

Christ remembers for us and is also the object of our remembrance (e.g., the foretelling of the Old Testament and the Eucharist). Schmemann posits that this is the meaning of the Old Testament, "and it is impossible to separate Christ from it, to know him otherwise than through the

---

32. Schmemann, *Eucharist*, 126.
33. Schmemann, *Eucharist*, 127.
34. Schmemann, *Eucharist*, 127.
35. See Schmemann, *Journals*, 66.

Old Testament, because it is nothing other than the gradually disclosed *recognition* of Christ, the 'creation' of his 'memory' before his coming in time."[36] Schmemann points to three examples of "Old Testament remembrance": (1) Simeon's recognition of Jesus as the Christ (Luke 2:22–35), (2) John the Baptist's preparing and recognizing the way, and (3) Peter's confession, "You are the Christ, the Son of the living God" (Matt 16:16). Schmemann describes what occurred in these examples as our memory of the Savior and of salvation; it is "that *recognition*, in which God's remembrance of man is *fulfilled* as man's remembrance of God."[37] Christ restores our memory, so that we may know God and participate in his redemption and victory over death.

This final point leads back to the previous section and the relationship between the Eucharist/thanksgiving and the Last Supper (remembrance). The heart of the Christian life is the Eucharist; it constitutes the very life of the church, for in eucharistic remembrance, we encounter, not simply recall, Christ. Hence, the encounter that takes place in the eucharistic "do this in remembrance of me" is the experience/revelation that makes sense of all things—Schmemann's Christocentrism.[38] Therefore, if the memory of God in the Old Testament "refers to the attentiveness of God to his creation, the power of divine providential love, through which God 'holds' the world and gives it life,"[39] we, a posteriori, with the memory of Christ, recognize God's attentiveness, love, and life as Christ. Schmemann uses the language of memory because the faith of the church, expressed in the divine liturgy, knows no other language that suffices to express the fullness of faith than that expressed in the eucharistic practice of the Last Supper.

How does Schmemann's conception of the memory of God make sense of the conflation of memory and remembrance? First, God's thoughts have reality, and, therefore, "memory, like everything else in God, is real"[40] and is life. In God, act and being are inseparable; God's actions never contradict his being or his character.[41] Remembrance (act)

36. Schmemann, *Eucharist*, 128.
37. Schmemann, *Eucharist*, 128.
38. See Schmemann, *Journals*, 324.
39. Schmemann, *Eucharist*, 125.
40. Schmemann, *Eucharist*, 125.

41. The concern of this point does not necessitate expounding upon the energies essence distinction. A distinction, interestingly, that Schmemann all but ignores. In *The Eucharist*, Schmemann writes about being partakers of being and offhandedly he

and memory (being) are inseparable. Second, in remembrance, we enter into the memory of God. That is, memory as God's love, attentiveness, and life is manifested in time at the Last Supper. We can speak of God's memory in the aforementioned way only because we have participated in God's memory through remembrance. What this means is that, through eucharistic remembrance, our memory is restored as life-giving. Restoration is the result of participation in Christ's memory. Therefore, through participation (*en Christo*), our memory (being) conflates with remembrance (Christ's act).

In conclusion, memory and remembrance no longer foretell our oblivion. In remembrance, we enter into the life-sustaining memory of God; we are rooted deeply in the garden of God's being. Through the memory of Christ, the past is no longer absence, nor is the future a black hole. The fleeting present is no longer a moment surrounded by death. Rather, the present is Christ's remembrance—God remembering us and us remembering God—in which we reside in the "middle" of God's life-giving memory, "where" past and future are both experienced in light of the kingdom—hid with Christ in God. Grounded in God's memory, our memory becomes life-sustaining, and our remembrance becomes an act for the life of the world. To put it differently, our memory and our remembrance manifest reality, Christ. Therefore, we can extrapolate that the complete human person is one who remembers for those who have forgotten.

Homo Adorans and the High Priest

Schmemann's most sustained exposition on the notion of person is found in *The Eucharist* in the chapter titled "The Sacrament of Thanksgiving." The second most explicit writing on persons is in an article insipidly titled "Problems of Orthodoxy in America: The Spiritual Problem." Although the notion of person is not as explicitly explicated in his most popular book, *For the Life of the World*, as it is in the aforementioned works,

---

notes that Orthodox theology calls this "the divine *energies*" (Schmemann, *Eucharist*, 185). He briefly touches on Palamas in his historical writings (Schmemann, *Historical Road*, 234–37). In an article on St. Mark of Ephesus, Schmemann writes, "Can we not find in this controversy about the essence and 'energies' of God, a controversy that seems purely theological and so excessively abstract . . . ?" (Schmemann, "St. Mark of Ephesus," 18). Bear in mind that Schmemann has only disparaging things to say about abstraction.

personhood is part and parcel of its sacramental vision (our priestly ontology). All three texts are related.[42] In both *The Eucharist* and *For the Life of the World*, Schmemann asserts that thanksgiving is the act of offering everything back to God (the sacramental vision); this is our priestly role, our act of worship, and an essential human act. We are all called to be priests: "'*Homo sapiens*,' '*homo faber*' [man the creator] . . . yes, but, first of all, '*homo adorans*.' The first, the basic definition of man is that he is *the priest*."[43] In "The Spiritual Problem," along with the other two sibling articles, "The Canonical Problem" and "The Liturgical Problem,"[44] secularism is revealed as the key underlying problem that Orthodoxy faces in America. But what does secularism have to do with our priestly ontology and the essential human act of worship? Schmemann defines secularism as "above all a *negation of worship*. . . . It is the negation of man as a worshiping being, as *homo adorans*: the one for whom worship is the essential act which both 'posits' his humanity and fulfills it."[45] With this in mind, we shall unpack the following elements: (1) the secularistic reduction of the person and the Christian response of *martyria* and asceticism, (2) the role of the body for a worshipping being (a further sacramental reflection), (3) the essential personal act of naming, (4) the high priest and personhood, and (5) the vocation of *homo adorans* to "manifest" the church.

Martyria and Asceticism in Response to the Secularistic Reduction

In a similar fashion to Martin Heidegger's insightful notion of *Dasein*—a particular being in contradistinction from abstract humanity (generalities)—Schmemann desires to counter the secularist reduction of the human person to impersonal nature.[46] He asserts that there are two dangerous secular reductions, and both result in relativism: the historical reduction and the sociological reduction.[47] The historical reduc-

---

42. There are no major shifts in thought in Schmemann's work; he acknowledges this fact. See Schmemann, *Journals*, 71.

43. Schmemann, *For Life of World*, 15.

44. Schmemann, "Problems of Orthodoxy: Canonical"; Schmemann, "Liturgical Problem."

45. Schmemann, "Worship in Secular Age," 4.

46. Heidegger, *Being and Time*, 6.

47. Schmemann, "Problems of Orthodoxy: Spiritual," 177.

tion, arguably influenced by Heidegger's historicism, is the notion that truth is historically conditioned; past truths are not necessarily present truths.[48] The sociological reduction reduces the human person to a sociologically determined being; nationality, economic standing, technology, and so forth completely condition our ideas and behaviors. In both cases, truth as reality is dismissed. In the first case, there is nothing that transcends history. In the second case, truth can never be sought, for a person cannot know anything outside of her sociological predetermination. Schmemann pithily writes, "A relative truth attained by statistics: such is the formula of secularism."[49] Truth by consensus captures the anthropological aspect. In other words, these relativistic reductions emphasize people over person or human nature over the human person and thereby oppose the Christian emphasis upon the person. Schmemann is clear: Christianity "is not reducible to history and sociology."[50] At the same time, Schmemann counters the other extreme and makes clear that Christianity is not limited to individual salvation, for it is "cosmical and catholic."[51] Christianity is concerned with the salvation of the world; yet,

> the salvation of the world is announced and, in a sense, *entrusted to each person*, is made a personal vocation and responsibility and ultimately depends on each person. In the Christian teaching man is always a *person* and thus not only a "microcosm" reflecting the whole world, but also a unique bearer of its destiny and a potential "king of creation."[52]

Schmemann includes the collective ("not only a 'microcosm' reflecting the whole world"), and thus can consistently maintain that all fell with the first Adam and all is redeemed with the second Adam. However, the emphasis is upon personal participation. It is through persons (not individuals)[53] that the gospel is preached, and it is persons who believe, are baptized, and join the church. There is no impersonal encounter with the person of Christ:

48. Schmemann does not cite Heidegger in this regard, but he wrote at a time when Heidegger was certainly part of the theological conversation. For a clear description of Heidegger's historicism see Cayley, *Grant in Conversation*, 124. For more on Heidegger's historicism, see White, "On Historicism."
49. Schmemann, "Problems of Orthodoxy: Spiritual," 177.
50. Schmemann, "Problems of Orthodoxy: Spiritual," 177.
51. Schmemann, "Problems of Orthodoxy: Spiritual," 177.
52. Schmemann, "Problems of Orthodoxy: Spiritual," 178.
53. See section "The Body of Christ."

> In a very real sense no general "man"—be he American or any other—no "society," no "culture" has at any time truly *accepted* Christianity. . . . But at all times and in all "cultures" there were *persons* who did accept it and have lived by it. . . . They have always and everywhere left a deep impact on the "society" and the "culture" to which they belonged and have truly changed it from inside.[54]

Christianity is socially concerned, but it generally has a pessimistic view of the social, of this world, while maintaining an optimistic view of the possibilities of persons.

The optimistic view is based on *martyria* and asceticism. *Martyria* is the narrow way essential to the gospel, and the narrow way is always in conflict with the ways of this world. Baptism is the first Christian *martyria*, in which one dies to this world in Christ.[55] Baptism liberates us from the world and sets us beyond culture and society, so that we can see the world in Christ and live accordingly. Schmemann asserts that if, on one hand, Christianity is liberation from the world, then, on the other hand, Christianity is opposition to this world—asceticism. It is a fight "which is primarily, if not exclusively, a *personal* fight, i.e., an internal one—with the 'old man' in myself, with my own 'reduction' of myself to 'this world.'"[56] Without *martyria* and asceticism, we are reduced and enslaved to nature, "the triumph of 'nature' over the 'person,' a triumph which results in a fatal deterioration or *fall* of both nature and person, for the very calling of the person is to possess and thus to fulfill the nature."[57] Schmemann also argues that "human nature does not exist outside of persons."[58] But what is the nature that each person is called to possess and fulfill? We are called to fulfill the kingly office. Yet, to be consistent with Schmemann's other work, we must emphasize the royal priesthood (conflation of king and priest) and include the prophetic office. We will return to this later in the section titled "The Priesthood of Christ and Personhood."

In "The Spiritual Problem," Schmemann performs a bit of a juggling act in rejecting the secularistic reductions. Like Heidegger, he rejects the abstractions and generalizations in which the human person is reduced

54. Schmemann, "Problems of Orthodoxy: Spiritual," 179.
55. See Schmemann, *Of Water and Spirit*, 9.
56. Schmemann, "Problems of Orthodoxy: Spiritual," 179.
57. Schmemann, "Problems of Orthodoxy: Spiritual," 178.
58. Schmemann, *Of Water and Spirit*, 139.

to impersonal nature. At the same time, he avoids Heidegger's historicism by suggesting that there is human nature. Simply put, Schmemann sets forth a view that preserves the notion of person—the particular and unique—while maintaining that there is a true human nature or, in more Schmemannian terms, a true human vocation.[59] The coherency of this holding together of history and ontology is based upon Schmemann's definition of person—developed throughout the chapter—as one in relation with God. Our nature/vocation does not depersonalize, for it is found in a Person, Christ. Christ endows us with personhood and enables us as persons to fulfill the "personal" threefold office.[60]

The Resurrection of the Body

In *For the Life of the World*, Schmemann explicates the meaning of life.[61] He rhetorically asks, "What *life* is both motivation, and the beginning and the goal of Christian *mission*?"[62] Schmemann suggests that there are two general approaches given in response: spiritualist and activist. Both approaches problematically place the spiritual and material in fundamental opposition. The same pattern of opposition can be seen in various conceptions of the human person, specifically, the body-soul dichotomy. The human person is often understood in terms of a strict dualism, from which stems the idea of the immortality of the soul,[63] or in a strict physicalist sense, in which there is nothing beyond the physical body (e.g., Nancey Murphy).[64] Schmemann does not connect the spiritualist or activist approaches with the body and soul problem, but it mirrors his method. The likes of Murphy are not on his radar; however, Murphy's non-reductive physicalism[65] fittingly represents one extreme,

---

59. Priesthood is the continual vocation that is the essence of our existence, our very nature. *Vocation* implies movement, relationship, and divine dynamism, whereas *nature* implies motionlessness and solitary completeness.

60. See the section "Vocation: The Threefold Office of Christ."

61. A large part of this section was previously published in Kaethler, "Eucharistic Anthropology."

62. Schmemann, *For Life of World*, 12.

63. Schmemann, "Christian Concept of Death."

64. "My central thesis is, first, that we are our bodies—there is no additional metaphysical element such as a mind or soul or spirit" (Murphy, *Bodies and Souls*, ix).

65. The "non-reductive" clause, according to Murphy, means that the attributes traditionally attributed to the soul (reason, free will, morality, and spirituality) are all

matching, in some ways, the activist approach. Like Murphy, the pressing concern for Schmemann is the immortality of the soul. Nonetheless, it is easily deduced from Schmemann's rejection of the opposition of spirit and matter that physicalism is incongruent with his anthropological vision. Furthermore, he allows for a limited conception of the soul. This section attempts to answer the following questions. What role does the body play in regard to being a person? How does the body participate in our identity as *homo adorans*? What is the soul, and what part does it play in our personal identity?

Schmemann's account of the body is most explicit in his writings on death, and, usually, it is set in contrast with the immortality of the soul.[66] Behind these reflections is the paschal hope that Christ is risen. The affirmation "I believe in the resurrection of the body" of the Apostles' Creed is the corollary notion that follows. Schmemann fears that Christians have inadvertently moved away from the paschal hope and returned to the Platonic idea that, in death, the immortal soul leaves the imperfect, changing world and enters the perfect, unchanging afterlife.[67] He asserts, "Christ never spoke about the immortality of souls—he spoke about the resurrection of the dead! . . . Surely, if the question is strictly about the immortality of souls, then we need not concern ourselves with death as such, and what need have we of all these words about victory over death, about its destruction, and about resurrection?"[68] For Schmemann, resurrection of the body and immortality of the soul are incongruent. Belief in the immortality of the soul sanctions the notion of death as liberation.[69] Death is not liberation; resurrection overcomes death and aims to obliterate it. Death is opposed to life, and Christ is life; therefore, death is opposed to Christ. In addition, death is not created by God. Since it is not created by God, it is unnatural.[70] Schmemann goes so far as to say that

---

capacities of the body (Murphy, *Bodies and Souls*, 72).

66. Schmemann, "Concept of Death"; Schmemann, *O Death*; ch. 6 in Schmemann, *For Life of World*; ch. 2, subheading 7, in Schmemann, *Of Water and Spirit*, 60–66.

67. Rico Monge insightfully points out that Schmemann follows many of Nietzsche's (and Feuerbach's) criticisms of Christianity. Schmemann's rejection of Platonism is one example. Monge's description of Schmemann's engagement with Nietzsche and Feuerbach as "transformative affirmation (as opposed to, say, outright rejection or polemicization)" is particularly acute (Monge, "Alexander Schmemann," 28).

68. Schmemann, *O Death*, 26–27.

69. Schmemann, "Mystery of Easter," 18.

70. See Schmemann, *For Life of World*, 99–100; Schmemann, "Concept of Death"; Schmemann, *O Death*, 29–36.

"death is the denial of God, and . . . if it is the highest and immutable law about all creation, then there is no God."[71]

The world is given to us as our means of communion with God, and here is the crux of the argument: "The horror of death is, therefore, not in its being the 'end' and not in physical destruction. By being separation from the world and life, it is *separation from God*. The dead cannot glorify God."[72] Without a body, there is no interaction with this world;[73] therefore, there is no communion with God. The body is for communion: "without exception, everything in the body, in the human organism, is created for this relationship, for this communion, for this coming out of oneself. . . . The body is that which sees, hears, feels, and thereby leads me out of the isolation of my I."[74] The body is also the soul's freedom, "for the body is the soul as love, the soul as communion, the soul as life, the soul as movement."[75] And this is why, writes Schmemann, when the soul loses the body in death, "it loses life; it dies, even if this dying of the soul is not complete annihilation, but a dormition, or sleep."[76]

Schmemann writes much about the body but little about the soul. Nonetheless, we can deduce something about the soul from his comments on the transitory nature of the body and from his conception of death as sleep. Schmemann avers that the cells that form our bodies are replaced every seven years, and thus, "physiologically, every seven years we have a new body."[77] Accordingly, if all a person is is her body, then her identity is short-lived. This is why Schmemann describes our bodies as our "individual incarnation in the world."[78] What we glean from this is that it is the soul that maintains one's static identity. It is the soul that "sleeps" in biological death, waiting for the resurrection of the body. Without a body, the soul remains imprisoned in sleep. This separation is not liberation, "for Death is the severance of the soul from the body and it is this

71. Schmemann, *O Death*, 32.

72. Schmemann, *For Life of World*, 100.

73. "Each of our bodies is nothing other than our individual incarnation in the world, as the form of my dependence on the world, on the one hand, and of my life and of my activity in the world, on the other" (Schmemann, *O Death*, 42).

74. Schmemann, *O Death*, 42. He says almost the exact same thing in a journal entry in 1977 (Schmemann, *Journals*, 157).

75. Schmemann, *O Death*, 42–43.

76. Schmemann, *O Death*, 43.

77. Schmemann, *O Death*, 41.

78. Schmemann, *O Death*, 42.

severance which is evil, because God has united them that they live, and in this union implement the life of man."[79] Schmemann repeats this idea but with greater detail in his later article "The Christian Concept of Death": "It is precisely this union of spirit, soul and body that is called man in the Bible and in the Gospel. Man, as created by God, is an animate body and an incarnate spirit."[80] Without a body, the soul does not live, for it does not commune. In that sense, death is not destruction, "for creation may not destroy that which God has called from nothingness into being. But man is plunged into death, into the darkness of lifelessness and debility."[81] The life of the human person is in relationship, and, without the body, this is impossible. This is why there must be a resurrection of the body. In short, body equals relationship. But what sort of body is to be had in the eschaton? And what does the resurrected body reveal about our current bodies?

It is only in *O Death, Where Is Thy Sting?* that Schmemann reflects on the resurrected body:

> When Christianity speaks about the resurrection of the body, it does not speak about the vivification of bones and muscles, for bones and muscles and the whole material world, its whole fabric, is nothing more than certain basic elements, in the end—atoms. And in them there is nothing specifically personal, nothing eternally mine.
>
> Christianity speaks about the restoration of life as communion, it speaks about the spiritual body that over the course of our whole life we have developed through love, through our pursuits, through our relationships, through our coming out of ourselves. It speaks not about the eternity of matter, but about its final spiritualization; about the world that finally becomes truly a body—the life and love of mankind; about the world that has become fully communion with Life.[82]

There are six points concerning the new body that can be deduced from this quotation. First, the resurrected body will be entirely personal and unique to the degree that atoms are too limited to express the personal reality that will be eternally one's own. Second—and this is key—life will be restored as communion, and our new bodies will take us beyond the current communal limitations of the present body. Third, our new bodies

79. Schmemann, "Mystery of Easter," 18.
80. Schmemann, "Concept of Death."
81. Schmemann, "Concept of Death."
82. Schmemann, *O Death*, 43–44.

are called "spiritual bodies." I think what Schmemann seeks to express with "spiritual bodies" is that there will be no disjunction between the body and soul—a perfect mirroring, perfect oneness. One caveat, the new body is not the amalgamation of body and soul (old *and* new) but the complete spiritualization of matter (the old *becomes* new). This fits with Schmemann's emphasis upon God making the world anew.[83] Fourth, our spiritual bodies are formed in this present life. In other words, what we do in this life forms us for the hereafter; there is continuity. Fifth, although deeply unique, the spiritual body is somehow permeable to the other, open in such a way that there is no need to come out of the self. Sixth, as always intended, the spiritual body communes with God through the world; with the final destruction of death, the world reaches its climax of spiritualization and fully becomes a means of communion. Through the final resurrection, the world is recreated and restored to its original intent, and "God will transfigure it into 'a new heaven and a new earth,' into man's spiritual body, into the temple of God's presence and God's glory in creation."[84]

What do the six points reveal about our current bodies? First, respectively, our current bodies are limited in expressing personhood. Although the physicality of the body distinguishes one person from another, both literally in that I cannot leave my own skin and in the sense of our defining characteristics (brown curly hair, average height, long nose, etc.), physicality is limited—do we not all have a doppelgänger? Second, similar to the previous point, even though our bodies enable communion, they are limited: I am fixed within my own skin. Third, Schmemann may reject traditional body-soul dualisms, but there is disjunction in his conception of the person. In our current state of existence, there is not complete "spiritualization" of the body. Further evidence for this disjunction is revealed in the way that Schmemann describes sleep: "for in sleep it is precisely the body that sleeps and is inactive."[85] Fourth, this life is the beginning of life eternal and we are growing into our spiritual bodies. Time and space is where God forms us in relationship.[86] Everything we

83. Schmemann, *Liturgy and Tradition*, 97.

84. Schmemann, "Concept of Death."

85. Schmemann, *O Death*, 43.

86. Kallistos Ware acutely expresses this: "Time is part of the 'distancing' or 'contraction' on God's side which makes it possible for us humans freely to love. It is, as it were, the interspace which enables us to move towards God unconstrained and by our voluntary choice" (Ware, *Inner Kingdom*, 188).

do in this world matters, is part of our future. Or, as C. S. Lewis, explaining the virtue of courage, perspicuously put it, "Now it is quite true that there will probably be no occasion for just or courageous acts in the next world, but there will be every occasion for being the sort of people that we can become only as the result of doing such acts here."[87] Fifth, faith and communion involve an exodus of the self that begins on this side of the eschaton.[88] Hence, the importance of baptism as "the restoration of *true life*, the life that man has lost in sin."[89] The human person dies to the world and the self (self-sufficiency) in Christ (who reveals in his relationship with the Father absolute dependence), and, through this death, she rises in Christ. Therefore, in this life, in this body, we can enter into Christ and exit the self, yet this is a bodily act: baptism. It is also an act that we repeat. Liturgy, like the sacraments, is a passage. In every eucharistic service, we ascend to the kingdom of God, which enables us to follow Christ up Mount Tabor.[90] Although in this life and with this body we are hid with Christ in God (Col 3:3), we have yet to reach the fulfillment of personhood. Sin and the brokenness of this world weigh us down. Sixth, we are incarnated creatures, priests in and for the world, not separate. The world is God's gift to us, given to be transformed into life and to be offered back as our gift to God.[91] Therefore, "we should concentrate upon this world lovingly because it is full of God, because by way of the Eucharist we find Him everywhere."[92] Simply put, our bodies enable us to participate in God's created order, through which we commune with God in thanksgiving.

In conclusion, Schmemann argues that the immortality of the soul is not a Christian doctrine, because it imbibes the pre-Christian idea of death as liberation from the body. In contrast, our bodies, both in this age and the age to come, are for communion, for relationship. The soul separated from the body is a tragedy, for it has lost its means of communing. Thus, our bodies are central to being a person. In regard to constructive notions of the soul, Schmemann writes little, and we are simply left with the idea that the soul is one's static identity. With so little attention paid

---

87. Lewis, *Mere Christianity*, 81.

88. Schmemann, *Eucharist*, 144.

89. Schmemann, *Of Water and Spirit*, 20, 151. See Schmemann, "Mystery of Easter," 21–22.

90. Schmemann, *Liturgy and Life*, 82–83.

91. Schmemann, *Church, World, Mission*, 223.

92. Schmemann, *Church, World, Mission*, 226–27.

to the soul, it is not surprising that we run into some inconsistencies in Schmemann's thinking. We shall return to these at the end of the chapter.

Naming

Now, in the Bible a name is infinitely more than a means to distinguish one thing from another. It reveals the very essence of a thing, or rather its essence as God's gift. To name a thing is to manifest the meaning and value God gave it, to know it as coming from God and to know its place and function within the cosmos created by God.[93]

In the Orthodox Church, there is a series of prayers and rites concerning the naming of a child that takes place eight days after a child's birth. Schmemann laments that the rites are seldom performed because of the seemingly antiquated worldview they purport. In contrast, he avers that these naming prayers and rites are theologically important and are clear expressions of personhood, which are akin to the biblical story of Adam naming the beasts and the birds (Gen 2:19–20).[94] In what follows, I have highlighted two main features of naming. I have called the first feature the receptive aspect and the second feature the active aspect. The receptive aspect individuates and affirms the particularity of each person. The active aspect reveals our calling.

The Receptive Aspect

Schmemann describes the naming prayers as liturgical in form, a movement indicating that the child is on the way to the church. The prayers are similar to the prayer said for the reception of catechumens, in that the church "*takes possession* of the child in the name of Christ and engraves him with the Sign of the Cross, the sign of Christ's victory and lordship, and begins to prepare him for Baptism."[95] Schmemann suggests that the only unique element in the prayer is the actual naming of the child. Oddly, Schmemann overlooks the fact that this unique element fits well within the pattern laid out for catechumens. Beyond the obvious sharing in movement toward baptism, naming, like baptism, gives new identity.

---

93. Schmemann, *For Life of World*, 15.
94. See Schmemann, *Of Water and Spirit*, 131–33.
95. Schmemann, *Of Water and Spirit*, 139.

58   The Eschatological Person

Two important points need to be unfolded. First, connecting with the idea of new identity, Schmemann describes naming as the sacrament of person. Second, there is an important correlation between the eighth day as the day of naming and the eighth day as the Lord's Day.

The Sacrament of Person

Schmemann asserts that the rite of naming is "the acknowledgement by the Church of the *uniqueness* of this particular child, of the divine gift of 'personality' [given] to him."[96] It is clear that naming marks each newborn as unique, especially at a stage in which it is difficult to distinguish one baby from another. But what does it mean to acknowledge "the divine gift of 'personality'"? The basis for Schmemann's line of reasoning requires a certain amount of theological creativity, a reading between the lines. In the prayer of naming, the infant's name is referred to God's holy name: "And grant, O Lord, *that Thy Holy Name may remain unrejected by him.*"[97] Here, the church reveals that the infant's name is holy, because it is sanctified by God's name, and that the infant is recognized as a child of God and is called into relationship with God.[98] Schmemann uses Martin Buber's linguistic framework and argues, "My name is the 'I' which God creates by addressing it as 'Thou' and which therefore He Himself reveals as Person, as Holy Name, as the *Thou* of an eternal love and communion."[99] Schmemann's use of the word *communion* carries sacramental connotations, but, more explicitly, the sacrament of person is based on the connection of the Son and his name. He writes, "If for the Church, for all her Saints, for her entire experience, Christ Himself is present in His Name *Jesus*, if this Holy Name for us is presence, communion, joy, power, it is because the name is the sacrament of the person, the epiphany, the gift of its very essence."[100] Through the church's naming, Christ gives the gift of "that 'personality' created by God which is to be

---

96. Schmemann, *Of Water and Spirit*, 139.

97. Schmemann, *Of Water and Spirit*, 139.

98. Schmemann contrasts this with the impersonal dissolution of nirvana held by Eastern religions and modern spirituality. Likewise, Ratzinger contrasts Christianity with other religions by emphasizing the extraordinary personal element of Christianity (Ratzinger, *Truth and Tolerance*, 45).

99. Schmemann, *Of Water and Spirit*, 139.

100. Schmemann, *Of Water and Spirit*, 139. This sounds like onomatodoxy (the name of God *is* God). For more on this see Bulgakov, *Icons and Name*.

restored in Baptism and saved for God's Kingdom."[101] In Christ, we are brought into relationship (the recognition of one's name in the I-Thou recognition) with the Trinity. Through the divine relationship, we are brought into relationship with the world. Therefore, to speak of naming as the sacrament of person is to speak of it in the fullest sacramental sense: as both an epiphany (making clear the gifting of personality and its relational element) and as a bringing together (the human person with God, not as an abstract entity—human—but as an I with a Thou). For Schmemann, a person is one who is recognized by God. A person is constituted by relationship.

Schmemann argues that since a person is one who is in relationship with God, only a Christian is a full person:

> Confirmation is thus the personal Pentecost of man, his entrance into the new life in the Holy Spirit, which is the true life of the Church. It is his ordination as truly and fully man, for to be fully man is precisely to belong to the Kingdom of God.... The whole man is now made the temple of God, and his whole life is from now on a *liturgy*.... To be truly man means to be fully *oneself*. The confirmation is the confirmation of man in his own, unique "personality." It is, to use again the same image, his ordination to be *himself*, to become what God wants him to be, what He has loved in me from all eternity. It is the gift of vocation.... Confirmation is the opening of man to the wholeness of divine creation, to the true *catholicity of life*.[102]

The quotation is full of relational terminology: man belongs to the kingdom of God (Christ is the kingdom), man is the temple of God, man is the one loved by God, and man is opened to the wholeness of creation. Relationality is the foundation of personhood, and God desires that every human should be in relationship with him and, through him, with all creation, "the true catholicity of life." To use Schmemann's categories, in the cosmic sense, the human person was made and destined to be in communion with her Creator. However, humankind in Adam turned from this perfect communion. And again, much later in salvation history, the world "rejected and killed Christ—its Creator, Savior and Lord—'this world' sentenced itself to death, as it does not have 'life in itself' and rejected him of whom it was said, 'In him was life and this life was the light

---

101. Schmemann, *Of Water and Spirit*, 140.
102. Schmemann, *For Life of World*, 75–76.

of men' (Jn 1:4)."[103] This world's rejection leads to the eschatological sense: we must first die to the world before we can see God in the world. That is why Schmemann writes that our personality is "restored in baptism." We can approach this differently through the dichotomies of continuity and discontinuity. In "Worship in a Secular Age," Schmemann highlights that Christ is the fulfillment and transfiguration of all past worship. Christ brings all natural forms of worship to an end. Nonetheless, within this principle of continuity sits discontinuity: Christian worship is also a new beginning. It is not a new beginning "because of any ontological impossibility for the world to be the sacrament of Christ. No, it is because the world rejected Christ by killing Him, and by doing so rejected its own destiny and fulfillment."[104] What makes this text applicable is its statement about the world's ontological possibility. By applying the logic of this to personhood and the question of fullness, we can see that there is an underlying continuity, in which the human person, even the unbaptized, images God as a relational being (ontologically). The discontinuity is our brokenness, and, out of this brokenness, arises our need to appropriate what God has given us in Jesus Christ, a new beginning. To state it differently, every human being is fertilized *in vivo* with divine personality and waits to be birthed into the body of Christ through the waters of baptism. In the same manner that an eschatological symbol is a latent sacrament, so, too, is the human person. She has been named, and God has called her, recognizing and imparting the I of her existence; she reflects the divine image, for she is an inchoate person. Yet, she will not participate in this personal fullness until she, too, recognizes the divine Thou. With the transformation that occurs in baptismal rebirth, she becomes a sacrament, becomes a eucharistic being. In short, in Christ, we become what we were always intended to be. The fullness of personality is a potential reality gifted to all; it just needs to be appropriated.

The Eighth Day

Liturgically speaking, the eighth day refers to the Lord's Day. Sunday for Christian worship is the first day of the week in "old time," which is overshadowed by the eighth day, the time of the kingdom. How does the eighth day as a *statu die* (a set day in the old eon) relate to the eighth day

---

103. Schmemann, *Eucharist*, 34.
104. Schmemann, "Worship in Secular Age," 7.

of a newborn child? A child could be born on any day of the week. Does this multivalence of numbering not belittle the significance of time and Schmemann's insistence that the Lord's Day is a *statu die*? Schmemann does not raise this question. However, an applicable response can be deduced from what has been explicated in chapter 1. Pascha sits at the center of time, and, like a whirlpool, all time is pulled into its center. In a similar fashion, Schmemann writes that

> the naming of the child takes place on the eighth day after his birth. We already know that the eighth day is the symbol of the Kingdom of God, of the heavenly reality *beyond* "this world" and of which we are made partakers in Baptism and Chrismation. Therefore it is toward these sacraments that the service of naming is aimed. It is not the old but the new and eternal life that constitutes its horizon; it is beyond "this world" that the Church looks as she greets a child created for eternity.[105]

In other words, the naming on the eighth day essentially aims toward the kingdom. The eighth day of the child's life is woven into the fabric of the kingdom. As the Eucharist is the sacrament that fulfills all other sacraments, the established eighth day is the day that fulfills all other days. The eighth day of naming is drawn into the new eon and becomes the experience of the eighth day (the new eon), and the child's identity is thereby grounded in the kingdom.

The Active Aspect

Like all creatures, the human person is a hungry being who depends on food. In this sense, humankind is indistinguishable from the rest of creation. Even though our deepest hunger is for God, it is through the world that we commune with him.[106] Humankind's real uniqueness "in the universe is that he alone is to *bless* God for the food and the life he receives from Him. He alone is to respond to God's blessing with his blessing."[107] Our unique ability to bless is connected with naming. In naming the animals in the garden of Eden, Adam participated in manifesting the meaning and value God gave his creation—an act of blessing God. The logic mirrors what was written concerning the rite of naming

---

105. Schmemann, *Of Water and Spirit*, 140.
106. Schmemann, *For Life of World*, 14.
107. Schmemann, *For Life of World*, 14–15.

a child (the beginning of the I-Thou relationship), but the emphasis is placed upon the one who names, which highlights Adam's partnership in "manifesting" communion with God.[108] In the act of naming, one blesses God by revealing the essence of the named, i.e., a gift from God. Naming as blessing reveals humankind's relational imaging of God; we participate in revealing the essence of creation, and, in so doing, we are givers of gifts. Schmemann postulates, "As the world was created by the word of God *by blessing*—in the deepest, ontological significance of this expression—so is it saved and restored by thanksgiving and blessing, granted to us in the temple of Christ. . . . Through them [thanksgiving and blessing] we restore it [the world] into what it was created for and granted to us by God."[109] In short, humankind's participation in revealing and giving gifts restores the world to its intended purpose as a means of communion.

There are four other important notions to be extracted from naming that are revealed in the following quotation:

> Man is to *name* things. . . . To name a thing, in other words, is to bless God for it and in it. And in the Bible to bless God is not a "religious" or a "cultic" act, but the very *way of life*. God blessed the world, blessed man, blessed the seventh day (that is, time), and this means that He filled all that exists with His love and goodness, made all this "very good." So the only *natural* (and not "supernatural") reaction of man, to whom God gave this blessed and sanctified world, is to bless God in return, to thank Him, to *see* the world as God sees it and—in this act of gratitude and adoration—to know, name and possess the world.[110]

First, to name or bless is a way of life that marks us as human. Second, God blessed time; therefore, through thanksgiving and blessing, humankind has a responsibility to restore time. We are to reveal that time is no longer enslaved to death, but, rather, time is renewed in Christ—the new *telos* of time. We are to offer time back to God in order that it may be a "chalice of eternity."[111] Third, blessing and thanksgiving is our *natural* response. Humankind was always meant to bless and give thanks; thanksgiving is not a supernatural addition. In Christ, humankind is restored to its true self. Fourth, going beyond the immediate text, yet still consistent with

---

108. Another interesting way to think through this is in regard to the naming of the dead in the liturgy of death. See Schmemann, "Appendix II," 344.

109. Schmemann, *Eucharist*, 177.

110. Schmemann, *For Life of World*, 15.

111. Schmemann, *Journals*, 78.

Schmemann, we can deduce that through blessing and thanking God humankind fulfills the threefold office of Christ: prophet (to see properly), priest (to thank and name), and king (to possess).

The Priesthood of Christ and Personhood

He [Christ] remains the priest and intercessor for the world before the Father, and thus the Church, his body, a participant in his flesh and blood, takes part in his priesthood and intercedes by his intercession. She offers not a new sacrifice, for all the fulness of salvation has been given to the world . . . , but, being his body, *she is herself priesthood, offering and sacrifice*.[112]

We are *homo adorans*, which means that we are to accept the life-giving gifts of this world and, in gratitude, offer the gift of life back to God. This is our priestly ontology, which goes hand in hand with Schmemann's sacramental vision:

> Man was created as a priest: the world was created as the matter of a sacrament. But sin came, breaking this unity: this was no mere issue of broken rules alone, but rather the loss of a vision, the abandonment of a sacrament. Fallen man saw the world as one thing, secular and profane, and religion as something entirely separate, private, remote and "spiritual." The sacramental sense of the world was lost. Man forgot the priesthood which was the purpose and meaning of his life. He came to see himself as a dying organism in a cold, alien universe.[113]

Sin and brokenness, the abandonment of sacrament, and the bifurcation of secular and sacred, are the result of ingratitude, the result of our broken priestly ontology. Ingratitude is the source of "man's falling away from the 'hymning, blessing, praising, giving thanks and worshipping' through which he lives."[114] Circularly, it is through the practice of thanksgiving that we apprehend the centrality of gratitude, for, in thanksgiving, the church unveils and exposes the source of sin as ingratitude. For Schmemann, "*Eucharist*—thanksgiving, adoration, worship—is truly the ultimate and total expression of his [man's] whole being. Man was created for *Eucharist*. . . . Eucharist is the Divine element, the Image of God

---

112. Schmemann, *Eucharist*, 92.
113. Schmemann, *Church, World, Mission*, 223.
114. Schmemann, *Eucharist*, 187.

in us."¹¹⁵ Yet, we fell from the eucharistic life. Fortunately, as the perfect Eucharist, Christ redeems and restores us to the eucharistic life.

In what follows, we shall explore Schmemann's understanding of Jesus Christ as the perfect human, the high priest, and the Eucharist. There are three questions we shall examine. First, how does Christ's perfect obedience to the Father shape our understanding of person? Second, what does Christ reveal about our human vocation, the *munus triplex* (the threefold office)? Third, how are obedience and the *munus triplex* related to eschatology?

The Obedience of Christ

There are three moves that Schmemann makes concerning Christ, human persons, and obedience. First, Schmemann brings together thanksgiving and obedience as symbiotic. As the climax of the liturgy, the Eucharist orders and collects everything within itself. In other words, Christ gathers all things into himself and offers them to the Father:

> He offered Himself to His Father, a total, complete and pure Eucharist, the only one worthy of God. Therefore, there is no other Eucharist but Christ's and there is no other Eucharist but Christ. And, once more, we are *given it*, we are *united to it*, it has become our Eucharist, because we are His body, we are of "His bones and of His flesh."¹¹⁶

Christ's thanksgiving is obedience. According to Schmemann, obedience implies a sense of hierarchy but not subordination, "for obedience is based on a personal relationship whereas subordination is, in its very essence, an impersonal one."¹¹⁷ The Son is obedient to the Father because he knows him and is in perfect relationship with him. Subordination, on the other hand, implies imperfect knowledge and imperfect relationship. With subordination, there is an imbalance of power and the need for submission. According to Schmemann, Christ's obedience flows out of his love and thanksgiving for the Father.¹¹⁸

---

115. Schmemann, *Liturgy and Life*, 53.
116. Schmemann, *Liturgy and Life*, 54.
117. Schmemann, *Church, World, Mission*, 174.
118. See the same notion in Schmemann's depiction of Mary's yes. Schmemann, *For Life of World*, 84.

Second, in the same manner that Christ *is* Eucharist, Schmemann maintains that Christ *is* obedience.[119] There is no separation between Christ's being and Christ's life.[120] In perfect obedience, Christ is perfectly free. Why? Because Christ *is* obedience, and to be anything other would be false and imprisoning. What is important for the concerns of this chapter is the connection between ontological obedience (obedience as central to being) and personhood. Obedience is internal (ontological), whereas subordination is external. In other words, like thanksgiving, obedience is the essence of the human person. Schmemann argues that we are fully human—fully ourselves—when, like the virgin Mary, our response to God "becomes the movement of total self-giving and obedience to Him."[121] Such obedience is not external (subordination), because it is obedience not simply to God but to the Father; we are within a familial relationship. Schmemann argues that the Holy Spirit abolishes externality and manifests interiority, restoring and transforming the object into the subject, the "it" into the "thou."[122] God "becomes" Father, and we become children. We are brought into the absolute Other and recognized as an I. In Christ—perfect Eucharist and perfect Obedience—we are lifted up, and his obedience and thanksgiving become ours, as we become his.[123]

Third, obedience destroys death, for obedience is life. In Christ's free acceptance of his death, we see "fulfilled the measure of His obedience, and therefore, here is the destruction of the moral root of death, of death as the ransom for sin."[124] Again, obedience literally is life,[125] for obedience is the relational act of divine sonship, filial obedience. Disobedience, on the other hand, results in death, not in a juridical sense but in an ontological sense.[126] The human person has no life in herself; hence, the result of moving away from him who is life is death; after all, death is separation.

What does Christ's ontological obedience reveal about personhood? Beyond what has already been examined with naming—identity and life in relation with the Father—we are left with a vague sense of hierarchy

---

119. Schmemann, *Church, World, Mission*, 190.

120. Schmemann, *Eucharist*, 116–17. It is noteworthy that, in this section, Schmemann argues against *ex opere operato*.

121. Schmemann, *For Life of World*, 85.

122. Schmemann, *Church, World, Mission*, 187.

123. See Schmemann, *Eucharist*, 170.

124. Schmemann, "Liturgical Explanation."

125. Schmemann, "This Is Blessed Sabbath."

126. Schmemann, "Appendix II," 319.

and an underdeveloped notion of equality. To correct this ambiguity, we shall look at two quotations and bring together what appears to be disparity by turning to Schmemann's journals. In the first quotation, Schmemann is clear about the relationality (*sobornost*) of hierarchy, and, with the second, Schmemann gives the reader an obfuscated reflection on equality:

> Hierarchy, thus, is not a relationship of "power" and "submission," but of a perfect obedience of all to all in Christ, obedience being the recognition and the knowledge of the personal gifts and charisms of each by all. Whatever is truly conciliary is truly personal and, therefore, truly hierarchical.[127]
>
> The power and miracle of thanksgiving, as freedom and liberation, lies in the fact that it *makes the unequal equal*: God and man, creature and Creator, servant and Master. And it is not the "equality" inspired in man by the devil, whose secret impulse is in envy, in hatred for everything that is *above*, holy and lofty, in a plebeian repudiation of thanksgiving and worship, and therefore in a striving to make everything equal at the *lowest* point. Rather, it makes equal in that it *knows* man's dependence on God, objectively indisputable and ontologically absolute, *to be freedom*. . . . And if the itch for equality is, out of ignorance, the itch of the slave, then thanksgiving and worship come out of knowledge and vision, out of meeting with the holy and exalted one, out of entry into the freedom of being sons of God.[128]

What is the relationship between equality and hierarchy? Before this can be answered, equality must be defined. To do this, we must understand what Schmemann calls the "pathos for equality," which is based on the "principle of comparison."[129] The principle of comparison, which in name defines itself, is "the genealogy of the devil" and "an abstract invention."[130] It is the source of envy, pride, protest, anger, rebellion, and division (Schmemann gives this specific ordering, for one follows from the other). The ideas "all people are equal," "all people are free," and "love is always positive" grow out of the soil of comparison.[131] Comparison always reveals inequality, and, out of this, grow protest and the desire for equality.

127. Schmemann, *Church, World, Mission*, 175.
128. Schmemann, *Eucharist*, 180–81.
129. Schmemann, *Journals*, 107. For a more in-depth look at Schmemann's argument, see Kaethler, "Mary, Unity, and Pathos."
130. Schmemann, *Journals*, 107.
131. Schmemann, *Journals*, 106–7.

Schmemann argues that there are four main problems with equality. First, it is an abstraction. If we reflect on everyday life, we quickly see that reality reveals difference rather than equality. Thus, equality is an ideological reduction that reduces obvious difference to unreal sameness. Any abstraction for Schmemann leads to ideology and falsehood. Second, equality destroys persons, and "the person—man or woman—who hungers for equality is already emptied and impersonal because a personality is made of what distinguishes it from others and not submitted to the absurd law of equality."[132] Third, Christianity is about love, and love, he argues, has no room for comparison; love opposes comparison. It was Love that created this world, not principles, and thus equality cannot properly exist in this world. Fourth, equality rejects unity. It is because of difference and through love that we have unity, whereas "equality presupposes many equals, never turning into unity because the essence of equality consists of its careful safeguarding. In unity, distinctions do not disappear but become unity, life, creativity."[133]

Equality, defined as the rejection of difference, destroys personhood. The closest Christian equivalent to equality is unity. Unity is based in love and preserves difference, making it life-giving and creative. For example, in their differences and through mutual love, a husband and wife become one flesh (unity) and "create" life—a family. In fact, Schmemann sees the family as "the last bastion to expose the evil of equality."[134]

Equality as the child of comparison is purely a negative abstraction—equality inspired by the devil. The positive definition of equality given in the block quotation is linked with thanksgiving, knowledge, dependence, freedom, and divine sonship. With these in mind, it becomes apparent that, for Schmemann, equality as such has to do with opportunity rather than ontological status (e.g., I am as great as God): we are all called to be children of God. This connects with the image of family (the institution that elevates difference yet, through love, is unified). That means that the created human creature is invited to participate in the divine family life of God. As God's adopted family, in Christ and like Christ, we become Eucharist (thanksgiving). Through obedience and thanksgiving, we know God as Father, and, in praise, we recognize our

---

132. Schmemann, *Journals*, 107.
133. Schmemann, *Journals*, 107.
134. Schmemann, *Journals*, 108.

absolute dependence. That, maintains Schmemann, is equality, as well as true personhood.

By bringing together both block quotes, we see that hierarchy, equality (in the positive sense), and personhood go together. With personhood, there is distinction and difference, a real I-Thou distinction. God distinguishes a human person from all other persons, recognizing one's name, one's I, even in the midst of his own immense Thou. We enter into that relationship through familial obedience, thanksgiving, and knowledge of the Father. It is internal (ontological), and it makes one fully a person. Although the greatness and absolute otherness of God transcend one's meager existence, I, too, am truly person, and I, too, am a son via Christ's sonship. This is how Schmemann can speak of us being raised up to equality with God, without erasing hierarchy and falling into the genealogy of the devil.[135]

Vocation: The Threefold Office of Christ

Up to this point in the chapter, much has been written about our priestly calling, and therefore, this section, in large part, focuses on the other two offices of the threefold office of Christ, the kingly and prophetic. Oddly, outside of *Of Water and the Spirit*, these two offices are largely ignored, especially the prophetic office. This raises some interesting questions that must be addressed. Does Schmemann fully hold to the threefold office or to a single office? Is the prophetic and kingly office of little import? What does this imply about Schmemann's theological anthropology?

Schmemann's most extensive writing on vocation and the only place where he writes about *munus triplex* is in a chapter titled "The Sacrament of the Holy Spirit" in *Of Water and the Spirit*. This is appropriate, for it is the Holy Spirit who enables us to participate in Christ, and it is Christ who fulfills our vocation as priest, king, and prophet.[136] The key is participation. Through participation "in Christ, who is the King, the Priest and the Prophet, we are made *kings*, *priests* and *prophets* and, in the words of St. John Chrysostom, 'abundantly possess not one one but all three of these dignities.'"[137] The threefold office is our office; it is the office the old

---

135. For a more in-depth look at this argument, see Kaethler, "Mary, Unity, and Pathos."

136. Schmemann, *Of Water and Spirit*, 80.

137. Schmemann, *Of Water and Spirit*, 81.

Adam distorted and the new Adam redeemed. Schmemann thinks that contemporary Christianity has forgotten that the threefold office applies to us and not just Christ. This myopia resulted, argues Schmemann, in the impoverishment of the church and of those who constitute her.

King (Prophet) and Priest

There are two important points concerning the kingly office. First, God originally intended us to be kings of creation. Second, our calling now is to be crucified kings. Returning to the first point, man was given power and authority to lead creation to its fulfillment. This royal dignity still marks us, even after the fall. The royal vision, writes Schmemann, inspired the Orthodox Church's "anthropological maximalism."[138] Sadly, in our brokenness, we have used our kingly power and authority for self-benefit, to possess the world. We turned our gaze away from the source of our royal identity, and, consequently, we are consumed with this world and have become its slaves. In so doing, we have mutilated ourselves and the world. Nevertheless, our vocation, power, and creativity are themselves good, as is our need for beauty, knowledge, and worship.[139] They just need to be restored by Christ.

The cross is our way to enthronement with Christ. He is the crucified King, and, through our baptism, we, too, become crucified kings. Hence, crucified kingship is eschatological. It is only through the cross that we overcome this world and are freed from our enslavement. Schmemann turns to the liturgy of the week to clarify. In the liturgy of the church, Friday is the day of this world, in which this world's wickedness is revealed in the rejection and condemnation of Christ—the day of the cross. Saturday is the Sabbath and is the final day of the natural week, in which Christ appeared to be overcome by death. Sunday is the first day of the week and also the eighth day, in which the kingdom that is not of this world is revealed in the world. With these three days, we see the Christian antinomy between this world and its time. The cross is the way through this world to the kingdom, and it is with "kingdom eyes" that the world can be seen anew. The new royal power that Christ gives to us is "the power to transcend and overcome the finality of this world, its natural limitations, its closed horizons, the power to make the world

---

138. Schmemann, *Eucharist*, 185–89.
139. Schmemann, *Of Water and Spirit*, 85.

divine again, and not God 'worldly.' It is the power constantly to 'reject' this world as an end in itself."[140] Accordingly, Schmemann argues that we are now free to enjoy this world and to have dominion over it, for we see it as it is: a sign of God's kingdom.

The trajectory of the crucified king leads to the priest, the royal priest. With the power to reject this world and see it for what it is, the king is able respond properly: with thanksgiving. Therefore, Schmemann concludes that natural kingship is fulfilled in priesthood. Moreover, natural priesthood turns full circle and makes us kings of creation.[141] Although Schmemann does not explicitly make a similar claim concerning the prophet, the reciprocal pattern of the priest and king certainly applies to the prophetic office.

Like the priestly and kingly office, the prophetic office is part of our vocation that Christ restores. Schmemann asserts that prophecy is not the supernatural gift of foretelling the future but is "the power given to man always to discern the will of God, to hear His voice and to be—in creation, in the world—the witness and the agent of Divine Wisdom."[142] He describes it in two ways. First, prophecy is Christian sobriety. Schmemann expresses it as "inner *wholeness* and *integrity*, that harmony between soul and body, reason and heart, which alone can *discern* and therefore *understand* and therefore *possess* reality in its totality, *as it is*, to lead man to the only true 'objectivity.'"[143] Second, prophecy is the vertical dimension, that which connects all gifts and vocations (in the specific sense, e.g., scientist, teacher, etc.) with the truth of Christ. Thanksgiving is central to both ways. Thanksgiving enables one to see and have knowledge not *about* the world but *of* the world. In Kantian language, thanksgiving allows one to get beyond external knowledge to the things in and of themselves and, therefore, to see with sobriety.[144] Furthermore, thanksgiving (Eucharist) is the vertical dimension. One ascends to the kingdom through partaking of the Eucharist in the Divine Liturgy.

As mentioned at the outset of this section, the kingly office only rarely appears in Schmemann's work, and the prophetic office shows up only in *Of Water and the Spirit*, while the priestly office dominates his

---

140. Schmemann, *Of Water and Spirit*, 92.
141. Schmemann, *Of Water and Spirit*, 95.
142. Schmemann, *Of Water and Spirit*, 100.
143. Schmemann, *Of Water and Spirit*, 102.
144. Schmemann, *Eucharist*, 177.

work. Schmemann repeatedly calls the reader back to her priestly ontology: "Through the biblical 'still, small voice' we as Christians must rediscover our faith and recover our true vocation. At the same time, let us remember that our true vocation has already been defined: 'You are a chosen race, a royal priesthood, a holy nation, God's own people.'"[145] Why are the kingly and prophetic dimensions largely ignored? Perhaps Schmemann's magnification of the priestly to the exclusion of the other dimensions simply comes down to overcompensation. Schmemann does assert that, with our obliviousness, the priestly dimension has been forgotten more than the kingly dimension.[146] There is an element of truth to this, but it does not explain Schmemann's limited focus on the prophetic. I think that the answer, once again, concerns thanksgiving.

The kingly and prophetic dimensions are gathered up, initiated, and fulfilled through thanksgiving (our priestly act). This implies that our royal dignity and our prophetic nature begin and end with the priestly dimension. Schmemann does not disregard the kingly and prophetic; rather, he focuses on their root, our priestly act of thanksgiving.

Finally, we must ask what Schmemann's emphasis on the priestly implies about his theological anthropology. The answer is simple: Thanksgiving should be our first and foremost act, as well as our final act. All power and knowledge grow out of and lead back to thanksgiving. Power born outside of gratitude destroys the world and mutilates the one who wields it. Knowledge conceived outside of gratitude is merely knowledge *about* the world and not *of* the world. Power that does not end in gratitude enslaves one to the world. Knowledge that does not end in thanksgiving is knowledge without a *telos* and therefore misdirected. From Schmemann's perspective, we can be ourselves and live freely only in and through thanksgiving.

Eschatology

Thanksgiving, obedience, and perfect dependence are part of the eschatological vision that fills time. Schmemann writes that the referral of everything to the other "is the eschatological character of life itself and all that is in it," and this "means that the image of this world in Christ

---

145. Schmemann, "Fr. Schmemann Addresses."
146. Schmemann, *Of Water and Spirit*, 94.

and through Christ becomes passing, dynamic, open, outreaching."[147] It is the climbing of Mount Tabor and the dying to this world so that we may truly live:

> "For to me, to live is Christ and to die is gain" (Philippians 1:21). Then how should one live? Gather life for eternity, which means to live life as being eternal. To sow perishable goods so that "after" they would rise up indestructible. But one can also choose to live "gathering death," to live by "the lust of the flesh and the lust of the eyes and the pride of life" (1 John 2:16) which is already a torture, already death. One can choose to submit to daily bustle, to empty one's soul, to serve idols—a dead end—death.[148]

Christ filled time with his Eucharist and obedience so that we can approach the new eon. According to Schmemann, Christ does not provide us with an escape from the world or from ourselves as creatures, for "Christ saves us by restoring our nature, which inescapably makes us *part* of creation and calls us to be its *kings*. He is the Saviour *of* the world, not *from* the world. And he saves it by making us again that which we are."[149] Christ's perfect life was lived in time to redeem time and this life. Accordingly, by living in Christ, in obedience and as Eucharist, we participate as royal prophetic priests in making this life the chalice of eternity. Therefore, that which makes one fully a person (thanksgiving and obedience) is also that which redeems time and space: our eschatological being (participating in the life of the kingdom) does not separate us from the cosmic; rather, the eschatological brings to fruition the cosmic. Again, we see the connection between personhood and vocation. As persons in Christ, we are grounded eschatologically, and we unite this world, which is passing, with the everlasting kingdom, lifting the old into the new.

The Body of Christ

> "To that which you are—say Amen," writes St. Augustine, "and thus seal it with your answer. For you hear 'the body of Christ' and answer 'Amen.' *Be* a member of the body of Christ, which is realized by your Amen.... Fulfil that which you are."[150]

---

147. Schmemann, *Journals*, 24.
148. Schmemann, *Journals*, 47.
149. Schmemann, *Of Water and Spirit*, 84.
150. Augustine, as quoted in Schmemann, *Eucharist*, 48 (italics in Schmemann's

SCHMEMANN AND PERSONHOOD: EUCHARISTIC BEINGS

In this section, we shall examine the following three interrelated ideas. First, worship is the function of the church. The end of worship is the church, not the reverse. Even though Schmemann does not connect this with personhood, it brings clarity to the relationship between *homo adorans* and the body of Christ. Second, the church's role is to restore our eucharistic being. Third, the church transforms individuals into persons.

Schmemann argues that worship is the "expression, the edification and the fulfillment of the Church."[151] That is not to say that worship is secondary, for it is part of the church's essence to participate in the kingdom through worship. Nevertheless, the church's members gather with the goal of constituting the church, and this occurs through the Eucharist.[152] The primary function of the Eucharist is not to meet an individual's religious needs but to manifest the church. Therefore, in accord with Schmemann's logic, since worship falls within the domain of the church and we are worshiping beings (*homo adorans*), we can conclude that to be a human person in the fullest extent inherently means being part of the church.

The church restores and transforms individuals into eucharistic beings:

> The Church has been established in this world to celebrate the Eucharist, to save man by restoring his Eucharistic being. The Eucharist is impossible without the Church, that is, without a community that knows its unique character and vocation—to be love, truth, faith, and mission—all of these fulfilled in the Eucharist; even simpler, *to be* the Body of Christ.[153]

Schmemann equates our eucharistic being with the body of Christ. In fact, for Schmemann, the body of Christ can be seen as: (1) Christ, (2) the divine elements (the bread and wine), (3) the church, and (4) our eucharistic being. Our concern is with the latter two, even though all four are intimately connected, and the first is primary. The human person's eucharistic being is restored only in and through the first three ways. Yet, the three ways are also ends. We gather (sacrament of assembly), and, through the liturgical passage, we eat from the heavenly table, where, in and through Christ, we are transformed into his body, the church. As the

---

original).

151. Schmemann, "Liturgical Theology," 25.
152. Schmemann, "Liturgical Theology," 26.
153. Schmemann, *Journals*, 25.

church, we form Christ's body, and, through *his* Eucharist, we become Eucharist. The very fact that we become Eucharist reveals that the church does not exist for individuals, but, rather, it transforms individuals into eucharistic beings. This leads to the third idea.

Schmemann asserts that modern theology has ceased to understand and incorporate the Christian notion of person and has become individualistic. Individualistic theology sees rites, sacraments, and the church herself as various means to an individual's sanctification. As a result, "it has lost the very categories by which to express the Church and her life as that new reality which precisely overcomes and transcends all 'individualism,' transforms *individuals* into *persons*, and in which men are persons only because and inasmuch as they are united to God and, in Him, to one another and to the whole of life."[154] To be a eucharistic being is to be in the church[155] and thus united to God and, in him, to the whole of life. Individual is the opposite of person. An individual is self-reliant, and gratitude is a foreigner in his world, whereas a person is dependent upon relationship, and gratitude is her beginning and end, which makes her part of the church.

In summary, the church is both the means and ends of our existence. As *homo adorans*, we constitute and continue the life of the church, and the church transforms us from individuals into persons. In the same way that a new born child receives her life from the mother and belongs to the mother, the church is our mother, who sustains our life and makes us persons.[156] Communion is necessary for personhood.

Identity without Relationship?

According to Schmemann, the human body is our means of communion with the world and God.[157] Biologically speaking, however, every seven years, the cells that comprise our bodies are replaced. Consequently, constancy of identity cannot depend upon one's biological body. To resolve this quandary of identity, Schmemann posits that "static identity" rests in the soul. Here he runs into some problems.

---

154. Schmemann, *Of Water and Spirit*, 143.
155. Schmemann, "Liturgical Theology," 25.
156. Schmemann, *Of Water and Spirit*, 144–46.
157. A large part of this section was previously published in Kaethler, "Eucharistic Anthropology."

The problem is that, according to Schmemann, the body enables communion, not the soul; and if personal identity exists only in relation to God, the I-Thou relationship, we must ask what enables communion after bodily death. Unless Schmemann is willing to assert that death ends one's identity, which he is not, it must be possible to have communion with God without the body. Ironically, Schmemann's inconsistency arises as a result of too strong a dualism (body-soul dualism)—the very thing he aims to avoid. His account of relationality excludes the soul; he argues that it is through the body, both earthly and heavenly, that we commune. In other words, he separates body and soul according to functionality. The body communicates, relates, and leads one out of the imprisonment of individuality; the soul simply retains one's identity, which, again, is problematic, since identity is based on relationship.

A different understanding of the soul, with what we could call a weaker dualism, would solve the problem. Ratzinger encapsulates this with his notion of the immortality of the soul, which we shall explore in chapter 4. With a weaker dualism, Schmemann could speak of the horror of death and, at the same time, retain his strong relational understanding of existence and personhood. Counterintuitively, Schmemann needs a more developed notion of the soul in order to have a weaker dualism. If the soul shares the functional characteristics of the body and the body is the expression of the soul, then the two could be seen as working together—unified.[158] Similar to Schmemann's dualistic account, here, the soul is also incomplete without the body; after all, the human person is an embodied creature. Death is a horror, for it separates the human person from the body, leaving him or her an incomplete human. However, what rests "beyond" the grave, the soul, must still commune with God in order to be sustained as person and maintain identity.

It is arguable that Schmemann's error arises as a result of misreading Plato, an error commonly found among theologians of his time.[159] In reaction to Plato, Schmemann eagerly sought to minimize the role of the soul, and, in so doing, he unintentionally created a dualism that is

---

158. I am thinking along the lines of St. Thomas's account in which, as Ratzinger puts it, "the soul is the 'form' of the body" (Ratzinger, *Eschatology*, 148). See Aquinas, *Summa Contra Gentiles* 2.56.

159. For a perfect example of this, see Cullmann, *Immortality of the Soul*, 15–27. Cullmann's work had a large influence on Schmemann, as evidenced in *Introduction to Liturgical Theology*. For a brief overview of the development of this type of anti-Platonic approach, see Ratzinger, *Eschatology*, 72–75.

incompatible with his relational ontology. The incoherency and contradiction within Schmemann's body-soul construal is problematic; it reflects his avoidance of the "last things" and is the result of his teleological tunnel vision. In juxtaposition with Ratzinger's perspective, over the next two chapters, I will closely explicate the problems caused by Schmemann's overemphasis on the notion of ends.

Conclusion

For thanksgiving is truly the first and the essential act of man, the act by which he fulfills himself as man. The one who gives thanks is no longer a slave; there is no fear, no anxiety, no envy in adoration. Rendering thanks to God, one becomes free again, free in relation to God, free in relation to the world.[160]

Schmemann's theology of the person centers on *the* Eucharist. Christ is the Eucharist—perfect thanksgiving—and he is the perfect human. Schmemann writes, "Eucharist (thanksgiving) is the state of perfect man. Eucharist is the life of paradise. Eucharist is the only full and real response of the human person to God's creation, redemption, and gift of heaven. But this perfect man who stands before God is Christ."[161] It is Christ, as the incarnation of the memory of God, who remembers—and re-members—and offers thanks for humankind, saving us from obliviousness, our oblivion. Furthermore, in Christ, we see that filial identity is based on obedience to the Father. Such obedience is ontological, in that it is familial rather than external subordination. This means that our obedience to the Father through the Son is an internal familial work of the Spirit who forms us into who we are meant to be—sons and daughters of God—in which my I is fulfilled, not subsumed and lost. In remembrance and obedience, Christ restores us to our priestly existence and transforms us into royal sons and daughters of God who live in communion in, with, and through him. Through communion, we are transformed into full persons.

What it means to be a person in time is contingent upon eschatology, upon Christ as the new end of time. In remembrance of the Last Supper, we transcend the old eon and enter into the new, for Christ has transformed time into a passage that leads to him, to the kingdom. To

---

160. Schmemann, *Of Water and Spirit*, 46.
161. Schmemann, *For Life of World*, 38.

enter into the new eon, we must not be enslaved to this world. Therefore, *martyria* and asceticism are essential aspects of the Christian life that free us so that we can recognize that the temporal realm of the old is a means to encounter Christ (the new eon). As Christians, we are to lift this world (the old eon) to God in gratitude so that it may be filled with eternity. The ancient Orthodox rite of naming on the eighth day encapsulates this act, in which a child is given identity by being sacramentally "taken out" of the old eon and placed in reference to the new. According to Schmemann's logic, we should strive to liberate time rather than liberate ourselves from time; however, as I argue in the next three chapters, Schmemann's approach logically succumbs to the latter position.

The special value that Schmemann places on ascending, *martyria*, and asceticism does not mean that he has a low view of the body but the opposite. It is our bodies that enable us to commune both with God and other creatures. Through *martyria* and asceticism, we are able to recognize the sacramentality of the world and thus anagogically ascend. However, in Schmemann's zeal to defend the importance of the body, he pays little heed to the soul, making his relational account of identity problematic.

We are persons in time, and we fulfill our priestly vocation in the temporality of movement and relationship.[162] This entails that the person is to be understood dynamically rather than statically. Schmemann uses language that involves movement: preparation, pilgrimage, following Christ, and climbing up Mount Tabor.[163] The language of movement reiterates Schmemann's teleological and anagogical approach. He writes, "God revealed and offers us eternal Life and not eternal rest. And God revealed this eternal Life in the midst of time—and of its rush—as its secret meaning and goal. And thus he made time, and work in it, into the sacrament of the world to come, the liturgy of fulfillment and ascension."[164] For Schmemann, personhood grows as we ascend Mount Tabor toward transfiguration. The path up Mount Tabor is the way of the cross, and our personhood begins in baptism, is carried forth in *martyria* and asceticism, and made complete in *the* Eucharist.

---

162. Schmemann, *Liturgy and Life*, 75.
163. Schmemann, *Liturgy and Life*, 75. See Schmemann, *Great Lent*, 69.
164. Schmemann, *For Life of World*, 65.

3

Ratzinger: Eschatology as Christology

> Christ is the temple of the final age; he is heaven, the new Jerusalem; he is the cultic space for God.
>
> —JOSEPH RATZINGER

ESCHATOLOGY PLAYS AN IMPORTANT role in Ratzinger's work, but Ratzinger perceives it and engages with it differently from Schmemann. While Schmemann's prioritizing of eschatology moves accordingly with the theological current of the twentieth century (e.g., Rudolf Bultmann, Karl Barth, and Oscar Cullmann), Ratzinger's account goes against the tide. Ratzinger seeks to balance the political dimensions of eschatology with the "last things" (*Lehre von den letzten Dingen*, i.e., purgatory, heaven, hell, immortality of the soul, resurrection of the body, and the last judgment) and sets both within his Christocentric framework; relational ontology provides the impetus. It is this Christocentrism and relational ontology that affect Ratzinger's construal of time and eternity and, in turn, shape his eschatology.

This chapter is divided into four parts that address four sets of questions. First, how does Ratzinger understand eschatology, and what does he mean by the term? Second, how does Ratzinger employ eschatology? Where does it arise in his work? What does the omission or the inclusion of eschatology in Ratzinger's work reveal about the way he conceives of eschatology? Third, how do ontology, salvation history, and eschatology relate? How does Ratzinger understand the relationship between creation and redemption? Fourth, what is time, and what is history? What is eternity, and what does it reveal about temporality? What does the human phenomenon of the present reveal about temporality and eternity?

Eschatology: Looking toward Christ

What does Ratzinger mean when he uses the term *eschatology*? The answer is slowly unravelled in the introduction to *Eschatology: Death and Eternal Life*, in the form of a brief historical overview. Ratzinger argues that, in order to understand what eschatology is, one must be aware of the attitudes and the ethos that shape the theological landscape. By standing back and surveying the historical vista, one is better situated to evaluate past and current construals of eschatology. When he wrote *Eschatology*, eschatological awareness had so pervaded biblical studies that it subsumed "the entire confession of faith under the single theme of hope."[1] The predominance of eschatology in twentieth-century theology, Ratzinger argues, has nothing to do with the refinement of scholarly methods but rather with a "change in consciousness" (*eines veränderten Bewusstseins*). He conjectures that the change of historical consciousness—the intensification of eschatology—is the result of "the emerging crisis of European civilisation."[2] The European crisis opened the modern consciousness to a mindset of decline and fall. First occasioned by WWI, this awareness abruptly ended the optimism of liberal theology and its hope for a purely cultural Christianity. What grew out of this was an existential understanding of the eschaton (e.g., Rudolf Bultmann). This seemed to offer a reasonable interpretation of Jesus's proclamation about the end that was not in conflict with the experience of the war. Concurrently, another more powerful movement entered theology: Marxism.

---

1. Ratzinger, *Eschatology*, 2.

2. Ratzinger, *Eschatology*, 3. Ratzinger's contextual observation is applicable to the current theological movement, largely based in the United States, called apocalyptic theology. The movement is represented by figures such as J. Louis Marten and Douglas Campbell. The movement owes much of its inspiration to Ernst Käsemann. With the various wars on terror, the ever-increasing self-realization of the vapidness of American consumer culture, and the culture's seeming enslavement to the corporation, it should be no surprise that the eschatological focus continues. In this regard, although written over forty years ago, *Eschatology* continues to be relevant, especially as a counter voice to apocalyptic theology.

While the existential turn was inward, the Marxist turn was outward and concrete, and "here we encounter something of the primordial potency of Old Testament messianism, now gone anti-theistic and demanding an unconditional commitment through its claim that here at last all reality has become scientifically knowable."[3] Ratzinger describes this movement as marked by realism. Marxism became, and in many ways continues to be, the tangible means of fulfilling the eschatological message.[4] He argues that, with Marxism, faith is divorced from religion, and the Marxist simply retains religion: "It is thus possible in our day to write an eschatology which would be nothing but a dialogue (whether in agreement or disagreement) with the theology of futurity, the theology of hope and the theology of liberation."[5] The "last things" are completely ignored, if not rejected. For Ratzinger, the danger with the Marxist turn is that eschatology is reduced to a worldly hope that is guided by praxis. In other words, he is worried that eschatology has become completely politicized. In an edited volume on political theology, Robert W. Jenson wrote "that the scriptures' eschatology and the classical eschatology of the Christian church are directly and almost exclusively a discourse about politics, so that no extrapolations are needed to move between eschatology and politics, in either direction."[6] To be fair, Jenson does not separate faith and religion like Marxism; in fact, similarly to Ratzinger, he argues that eschatology relativizes this world's politics.[7] What Jenson makes clear is that Ratzinger's description of the state of eschatology continues to be relevant. Like Jenson, Ratzinger understands the political reality of hope and praxis that Christian eschatology offers. Yet, Ratzinger maintains that eschatology is not solely political. Eschatology is concerned with the last things, and the last things have political implications but are not entirely political.

How do these relate? Or, from another angle, how does Ratzinger bring together the medieval *dies irae* (day of wrath) and the respective concerns of the last things with the early Christian invocation *maranatha*? Did the medieval interest in the last things constitute a departure from

---

3. Ratzinger, *Eschatology*, 3.

4. The Marxist geographer David Harvey is a good example of the influence that Marxism continues to have. Harvey is among the top twenty authors cited in the humanities ("Most Cited Authors").

5. Ratzinger, *Eschatology*, 4.

6. Jenson, "Eschatology," 408.

7. Ratzinger, "Morality of Exile," 266.

the inner logic of the early church and her emphasis on the kingdom? Do we not need to return to the original political emphasis?

Ratzinger unpacks the meaning of *maranatha* by looking at both the inner makeup of Christian prayer and at the Eucharist. He admits that there is historical development in the church's eschatology and that the medieval emphasis differs from the early church's emphasis. The early church's use of *maranatha* belongs within the context of the eucharistic celebration, and thus it is within liturgical practice that we can best see its meaning. The Eucharist is paradoxically both the Lord's presence and the supplication that he may come. This paradox is also seen in the liturgical posturing of the early Christians. Ratzinger points out that early Christians faced East toward the rising sun when they prayed, for the rising sun is the symbol of the risen Christ who reigns over all, and "at the same time the rising sun is also the sign of the returning Christ who makes his definitive epiphany out of hiddenness, thus establishing the Kingdom of God in this world."[8] The posture of prayer reflects both presence and absence, experience and longing. In both the Eucharist and prayer, we see "how intimately related faith in the resurrection and hope for the parousia really are. The two are one in the figure of the Lord who has already returned as the risen One, continues to return in the Eucharist, and so remains he who is to come, the hope of the world."[9] Furthermore, the cross was traced on the east wall in the places that early Christians gathered, and "this cross was understood as a sign of the returning Son of Man, and also a threat of eschatological punishment."[10] Here, Ratzinger quotes Zechariah and Apocalypse: "Every eye will see him, every one who pierced him, and all tribes of the earth shall wail on account of him."[11] In the liturgical practice, both *dies irae* and *maranatha* were held together. The early Christian eschatological hope was linked to spiritual expectation, and what holds this together is Christ. Christian hope is personalized, and "its focus is not space and time, the question of 'Where?' and 'When?,' but relationship with Christ's person and longing for him to come close."[12]

The medieval focus on *dies irae* reflects a deep existential concern. Hope for the transformation of the present is insufficient when faced

---

8. Ratzinger, *Eschatology*, 6.
9. Ratzinger, *Eschatology*, 7.
10. Ratzinger, *Eschatology*, 7.
11. Ratzinger, *Eschatology*, 7.
12. Ratzinger, *Eschatology*, 8.

with the ever-present reality of death and the accompanying of divine judgment. This concern is not peculiar to the medieval period; the traced cross on the east wall caused similar concern for the ancient church. Ratzinger concedes that the medieval church overemphasized judgment, but this should not overshadow the other aspects of eschatology that were of shared concern with the early Christians. He highlights three points of convergence. First, eschatological meaning is a waiting for the Lord, a looking to the Lord. This is the driving force of eschatology, rather than temporal expectations. Second, the past of Christian history (as salvation history) is very important. It enabled Christians to have hope in the future. They could trust in God's goodness because of his past actions. Third, personal death is of the utmost concern. Ratzinger argues that "the eschatological question becomes the question of my own dying."[13] Eschatology involves the existential hope of salvation and eternal life. Christology unites the three points. Ratzinger argues that one can be existentially hopeful (looking to the Lord), because God has shown himself to be trustworthy through his acts in history (salvation history), and both of these await completion with the final coming of Christ.

Ratzinger seeks to clarify the dependence of the last things on eschatology and to elucidate the contemporary theologian's urgent task to carry forth and deepen this relationship:

> It is by an inner logic that the doctrine of the "last things" grew up within the framework of eschatology. That doctrine remains indispensable for eschatology today. But the negative aspect of what happened [*der Verlagerung*] is the real danger of reducing Christianity to individualism and otherworldliness. Both of these rob the Christian faith of its vital power [*Lebenskraft*]. Here, in fact, lies the task of contemporary eschatology: to marry perspectives, so that person and community, present and future, are seen in their unity.[14]

According to Ratzinger, the last things are a natural and appropriate theological development that is indispensable for eschatology. In summary, eschatology is concerned with the resurrection of Jesus Christ, the kingdom of God, and the last things.[15] As we shall see throughout this chapter and the next, Ratzinger's theology is robustly Christocentric.

---

13. Ratzinger, *Eschatology*, 12.
14. Ratzinger, *Eschatology*, 12.
15. Ratzinger, *Joseph Ratzinger in Communio*, 1:12.

Therefore, eschatology in its perfect expression is always about looking toward Christ,[16] and, for this reason, we can conclude that Ratzinger's account of eschatology is irreducibly relational.[17]

Eschatology in Ratzinger's Work

In chapter 1, we saw that, for Schmemann, eschatology is the very tenor of theology. For Ratzinger, eschatology functions differently. Unlike Schmemann's work, the term *eschatology*, along with its correlate *the kingdom of God*, is not found on every page, let alone in every article that Ratzinger penned. Nonetheless, it is certainly important. *Eschatology* is often considered his most scholarly work. Emery de Gaál describes it as "by far the most revised and also most systematic of his writings."[18] It was the last book that Ratzinger wrote prior to taking on the extensive responsibilities in service to the church that demanded his attention and time up until his resignation in 2013. Gaál insightfully observes that "this book is no accident. There is no denying that the eschatological arena intrigued him so much that he dedicated twenty-five titles to this area alone."[19] This section examines the ways in which eschatology shaped Ratzinger's work, particularly his doctrine of creation. Furthermore, it will explicate what his use of eschatology reveals about his larger theological vision.

Creation

By connecting paradise and thanksgiving with both creation's primordial beginning and its end, Schmemann stitches together creation and eschatology. Ratzinger does something similar by employing the notion of *exitus et reditus* (exit and return), but, for Ratzinger, this notion is less centered on time and narrative than it is for Schmemann and more focused on relations (e.g., freedom and love). The other way in which Ratzinger brings together creation and eschatology is with creation and

---

16. Ratzinger is undeniably a Christocentric theologian. See Gaál, *Theology*, 276.

17. This is twofold: first, our movement of *reditus* is relational, as it involves being joined to Christ. Second, since eschatology is Christocentric, it points to the heart of all reality as relationally grounded in the second person of the Trinity, the *Logos*.

18. Gaál, *Theology*, 277.

19. Gaál, *Theology*, 277.

covenant; covenant is the end of creation (its goal). Like *exitus et reditus*, creation and covenant are deeply relational notions.

Exitus et Reditus

Ratzinger contrasts pagan and Christian notions of *exitus et reditus* in order to highlight the fundamental relational orientation of the Christian God. He explains that, according to the pagan philosopher Plotinus, "the exodus by which non-divine being makes its appearance is seen, not as a going out, but as a falling down, a precipitation from the heights of the divine, and by the laws of falling it hurtles into ever greater depths, farther and farther into remoteness from God. . . . Finitude is already a kind of sin, something negative."[20] Unlike pagan concepts of *exitus et reditus*, the Christian version sees both movements, not just *reditus*, as positive. *Exitus* is God's free act of creation, in which he brings about a contingent other as something good. It is God's will that the other "should exist as something good in relation to himself, from which a response of freedom and love can be given back to him."[21] Here, we see three important interrelated concepts: creation, relation, and freedom. Creation is something other than God. Relation highlights the contingent nature of creation. Even though creation is other than God, it has no existence and reality apart from God. Freedom: God's act of creation is totally free; God does not need to create. Creation is an act of love, and love is always free.[22] As a result "the principle of freedom is present in being itself, from its ground upwards."[23] This leads to the movement of return, *reditus*. We were freely made in relation to God and out of God's love, and thus, for us to be fully ourselves, we must respond in kind (freely). Our *reditus*, the free act of response and return, is our coming home to ourselves. Since freedom is present in being itself, our very being would be destroyed if we were forced to return. The fall was our free refusal to return, the refusal of dependence and the assertion of autonomy. In this, "the arch from *exitus* to *reditus* is broken. The return is no longer desired, and ascent by one's powers proves to be impossible."[24] Ratzinger avers that this is where the

---

20. Ratzinger, *Spirit of the Liturgy*, 30.
21. Ratzinger, *Spirit of the Liturgy*, 32.
22. Ratzinger, *Truth and Tolerance*, 105.
23. Ratzinger, *Spirit of the Liturgy*, 32.
24. Ratzinger, *Spirit of the Liturgy*, 33.

Redeemer enters. As the Good Shepherd, "he makes his way to us and takes the sheep onto his shoulders, that is, he assumes human nature, and as the God-Man he carries man the creature home to God. And so the *reditus* becomes possible. Man is given a homecoming."[25] Yet, God does not force our return and destroy our being, nor does he externally command our return. Instead, *he* becomes fully human, and, in *his* humanity, he freely chooses to return. There is a second act of freedom that follows: we must freely appropriate Christ's sacrificial act.

By entering into time, Christ's sacrifice takes the shape of the cross. Ratzinger defines sacrifice as "returning to love and therefore divination."[26] Thus, the cross is an act of love and has nothing to do with destruction. Ratzinger argues that the cross "is an act of new creation, the restoration of creation to its true identity."[27] The cross makes possible *reditus*, which is the movement that God desires for his creatures. *Exitus* as beginning and *reditus* as end (not in a static sense but as a constant movement into the triune life of God) are inseparable not simply because every story needs both a beginning and an end, but because they are relationally bound. By breaking this relational arch—the dialogue of love between God and humankind—we cease to be ourselves. It is only in *reditus* that human persons become Jesus Christ's brothers and sisters.[28] Our being is found only in the journey home. In a homily on the creation of humankind, Ratzinger christologically reflects that "human persons are not to be understood merely from the perspective of their past histories or from that isolated moment that we refer to as the present. They are oriented toward their future, and only it permits who they really are to appear completely."[29] For Ratzinger, it is the relational context of *exitus et reditus* that makes sense of how eschatology informs creation.[30]

---

25. Ratzinger, *Spirit of the Liturgy*, 34. This is remarkably similar to what Karl Barth poetically wrote: "It was God who went into the far country, and it is man who returns home" (Barth, *Church Dogmatics* 4/2, 19).

26. Ratzinger, *Spirit of the Liturgy*, 33.

27. Ratzinger, *Spirit of the Liturgy*, 34.

28. Ratzinger, *In the Beginning*, 48.

29. Ratzinger, *In the Beginning*, 49.

30. See Ratzinger, "Dignity of Human Person," 121. Here, Ratzinger criticizes the authors of §12 of *Gaudium et Spes* for basing their theological anthropology on creation and introducing Christology only at the end, "even though it [Christology] forces itself on the attention here as an indispensable component of a Christian anthropology" (Ratzinger, "Dignity of Human Person," 121).

Creation and Covenant

And for God, since he is entirely relationship, covenant would not be something external in history, apart from his being, but the manifestation of his self, the "radiance of his countenance."[31]

The relationship between creation and covenant fulfills a number of important roles for Ratzinger. First, it brings together ontology and history. In other words, it preserves the continuity of being. The incarnate Son does not rupture the wineskin of creation, but, rather, he fulfills and completes creation. At the same time, covenant occurs and develops within time. Second, it reveals the nature of our relationship with God. Third, it brings to the fore Christ's involvement as both the Alpha and the Omega.

The doctrine of creation is important for Ratzinger, particularly as a counterbalance to the historical approaches that neglect, or simply reject, the cosmic and ontological (metaphysical) implications of Christianity. Ratzinger offers a number of examples of theologians who do this, such as Martin Luther and his "model of the two Adams that the historical Adam is but wood and stone compared with the new existence opened by faith." For Luther, the two Adams sit in absolute discontinuity, and therefore, in principle, ontology no longer exists, for ontology involves "a continuity and identity of being that embraces the differences of history."[32] Ratzinger directly links this to Luther's account of creation. He argues that, for Luther, redemption is a break from creation, a freeing from creation, in which creation is seen as a burden. Commenting on Luther's statement that "man comes from God and from his own nothingness, which is why he who returns to his own nothingness returns to God," Ratzinger critically remarks that "grace is seen here in radical opposition to creation, which is marked through and through by sin; it implies an attempt to get behind creation."[33] In addition to Luther, Ratzinger highlights the disjunction between history and ontology in Barth and Bultmann.[34] He claims that, for the early Barth, faith is an act of God, and there is no true encounter between God and man. In other words, the human person remains ontologically unchanged by her encounter with

---

31. Ratzinger, *Many Religions, One Covenant*, 77.
32. Ratzinger, *Principles of Catholic Theology*, 161.
33. Ratzinger, *In the Beginning*, 88.
34. Ratzinger, *Principles of Catholic Theology*, 161.

God. Although Ratzinger does not provide a source, he may possibly be alluding to Barth's *Der Römerbrief.* For example, Barth writes,

> There is no such thing as a mature and assured possession of faith: regarded psychologically, it is always a leap into the darkness of the unknown, a flight into the empty air. . . . I heard yesterday I must hear again to-day; and if I am to hear it afresh tomorrow, it must by revealed by the Father of Jesus, who is in heaven, and by Him only.[35]

Ratzinger uses Bultmann as a representative of a theologian who emphasizes the momentary and sets it in contrast with that which perdures. According to Ratzinger, Bultmann sees faith as "the momentary 'now' of decision, a 'now' that exists only at the moment of acting."[36] This is not the place to fully examine the accuracy of Ratzinger's depictions of the aforementioned theologians. Regardless, what is clear is that Ratzinger does not want to place ontology and history in opposition (dialectic), nor does he want to conflate them. He concludes, "All of these, however, are but variations of the one effort to reject the categories of being and describe faith as salvation in purely historical terms, to solve the problem of history's mediation in the realm of ontology by canceling it and declaring history alone to be that which is and is essential."[37]

---

35. Barth, *Epistle to the Romans*, 98. Here is an expanded example: "That the promises of the faithfulness of God have been fulfilled in Jesus the Christ is not, and never will be, a self-evident truth, since in Him it appears in its final hiddenness and its most profound secrecy. The truth, in fact, can never be self-evident, because it is a matter neither of historical nor of psychological experience, and because it is neither a cosmic happening within the natural order, nor even the most supreme event of our imaginings. . . . It can neither be taught nor handed down by tradition. . . . Faith is the faithfulness of God, ever secreted in and beyond all human ideas and affirmations about Him, and beyond every positive religious achievement. . . . In Jesus, God becomes veritably a secret; He is made known as the Unknown, speaking in eternal silence; He protects himself from every intimate companionship and from all the impertinence of religion. . . . Faith in Jesus, like its theme, the righteousness of God, is the radical 'Nevertheless.' Faith in Jesus is to feel and comprehend the unheard of 'love-less' love of God, to do the ever scandalous and outrageous will of God, to call upon God in His incomprehensibility and hiddenness. . . . For all it [faith] is a leap into the void. And it is possible for all, only because it is equally impossible" (Barth, *Epistle to the Romans*, 98–99). Whether this is comprehensive of Barth's view of faith is negligible; it demonstrates that Ratzinger's description of early Barth is not unfounded.

36. Ratzinger, *Principles of Catholic Theology*, 161.

37. Ratzinger, *Principles of Catholic Theology*, 161. As we shall see, in the end, Bultmann abandoned salvation history and embraced a purely eschatological position. Nevertheless, Bultmann's eschatological focus is based upon historical terms, in that

In summary, Luther disconnects creation from redemption, and humankind ontologically becomes nothing. Early Barth does not necessarily reject ontology per se, but, according to Ratzinger, ontology appears to be of little importance for Barth. To put it in more Barthian terms, there is no room for habitual grace. This is made clear in Barth's later thought, in which he writes, "*Habitus* comes from *habere*, and therefore denotes possession. But grace is divine giving and human receiving. It can be 'had' only in the course of this history."[38] Clearly, we see the priority of history (event) over and against ontology. Finally, with Bultmann, the focus is on the immediate existential reality of the receiver of the word, and thus continuity (ontology) is not in his purview.

The philosophical equivalent, which is also a move away from ontology, is found in Karl Marx.[39] For Marx, systems and the future are more important than the individual person.[40] The Christian vision of the ontological goodness of creation is swept aside by Marx and turned into something that must be worked, formed, and remolded. Ratzinger writes, "The decisive option underlying all the thought of Karl Marx is ultimately a protest against the dependence that creation signifies: the hatred of life as we encounter it."[41] Thus, we can see that, for Ratzinger, creation plays an important role in either balancing or countering theological and philosophical positions that downplay the importance of ontology. What comes to the fore with Ratzinger's engagement with Marx is Ratzinger's concern that, without a well-developed doctrine of creation, we lose the inherent goodness and dignity of the human person—the continuity of being.

By linking creation and covenant, Ratzinger brings together the cosmic and ontological with the historical. It is also a linking of the end and the beginning, which mirrors *exitus et reditus*. He argues that creation

---

he is concerned with the immediate. Ratzinger also included Moltmann in the list just quoted, but he does not make clear why Moltmann is included, beyond mentioning Moltmann's theology of hope. It can be deduced that Moltmann makes the list because of his major influence in the development of liberation theology, which has a Marxist preclusion of ontology.

38. Barth, *Church Dogmatics* 4.2, 91.

39. The dominance of the historical question is also seen in Hegel, Comte, and, if we turn to the natural sciences, Darwin. See Ratzinger, *Introduction to Christianity*, 79–100.

40. Ratzinger describes Marx's notion of history as "partisan history." The party is always right. Any aberration from the communist party is always wrong. See Ratzinger, *Church, Ecumenism, and Politics*, 180–82.

41. Ratzinger, *In the Beginning*, 91.

moves toward the Sabbath, and "the Sabbath is the sign of the covenant between God and man; it sums up the inward essence of the covenant. If this is so . . . creation exists to be a place for the covenant that God wants to make with man. The goal of creation is the covenant, the love story of God and man."[42] In the same document, he explicitly states the relational significance: "If, then, everything is directed to the covenant, it is important to see that the covenant is a relationship."[43] This relationship is two-sided, and, from our side, it means worshipping God. What exactly is worship? Worship is the surrendering of the self to God, which consists of the union of humankind and creation with God. As previously noted, Ratzinger insists that sacrifice, which is our surrender, is not a move toward *nonbeing* but toward *new-being*. The state of new-being is the state of oneness with God, separation overcome. It is this understanding, Ratzinger avers, that makes sense of why "St. Augustine could say that the true 'sacrifice' is the *civitas Dei*, that is, love-transformed mankind, the divinization of creation and surrender of all things to God: God all in all (cf. I Cor 15:28) That is the purpose of the world. That is the essence of sacrifice and worship."[44] Thus, creation moves toward covenant, which is fulfilled when man truly becomes *homo adorans*, that is, when he is deified (*theosis*).[45] Covenant does not stand opposed to creation, and man's deification does not involve his destruction but his fulfillment—in other words, as the Good Shepherd Christ enters into the historical fray of creation and pushes the ontological process, initiated with creation, further along toward the goal: deification, or the spiritualization of matter. Ratzinger argues that the "'last day,' the 'end of the world,' the 'resurrection of the flesh,' would then be figures for the completion of this process [spiritual unification], a completion which, once again, can happen only from the outside, through the entry onto the scene of something qualitatively new and different, yet a completion which corresponds to the innermost 'drift' of cosmic being."[46] He maintains that spirit unifies matter and overcomes separation. To be clear, according to Ratzinger, the material world and the spiritual world do not exist in juxtaposition. He asserts that, by placing them in disjunction, we contradict creation, the meaning of history, and Scripture. The resurrection of the

42. Ratzinger, *Spirit of the Liturgy*, 26.
43. Ratzinger, *Spirit of the Liturgy*, 26.
44. Ratzinger, *Spirit of the Liturgy*, 28.
45. In this text, Ratzinger uses the term "divinization," a term he uses more often than *theosis*. See Ratzinger, *Joseph Ratzinger in Communio*, 1:192.
46. Ratzinger, *Eschatology*, 191–92.

flesh reflects what Ratzinger calls "the dynamism of the cosmos," which leads toward this goal.[47] What is clear in Ratzinger's work is that eschatology is the end toward which creation moves (*reditus*), rather than a radical breaking *into* and breaking *of* creation.[48] It is true that Jesus must enter as the Good Shepherd and rescue us by carrying humanity home; but this does not go against, to use John Howard Yoder's expression, "the grain of the universe."[49]

God and the Cosmos: History, Ontology, and Sacraments

In chapter 1, Schmemann's sacramental vision was explicated because it goes hand in hand with his eschatology—eschatological symbolism. Ratzinger, on the other hand, is far more interested in sacraments than he is in sacramentals.[50] The same themes that permeate Ratzinger's thoughts on creation are seen in his work on the Eucharist: relationship, freedom, ontology, and history.[51] The lack of concern with sacramentals is a reflection of Ratzinger's eschatology. The relationship between humankind and God is what fuels his eschatology and not the inverse, whereas eschatology is at the center of Schmemann's theology, shaping his view of the divine-human relationship. Nonetheless, I think it is arguable that Schmemann's relational pairing of eschatology and sacramentalism (eschatological symbolism) is similar to Ratzinger's pairing of ontology and history. These two pairs of relations are not identical, but they do similar work, so to speak. That is, they both secure the "already and not yet," in which creation is the means of communion with God and humankind. Ratzinger's assertion that the question concerning humankind and the relationship between history and ontology is "the fundamental crisis of our age"[52] is echoed by Schmemann's intent to answer the question he poses at the outset of *For the Life of the World*: "What *life* is both

---

47. Ratzinger, *Eschatology*, 194.
48. See Ratzinger, *Dogma and Preaching*, 143–61.
49. Yoder, "Armaments and Eschatology," 58.
50. See Ratzinger, "On Meaning of Sacrament," 32–35.
51. Scriptural interpretation is also an important part of his reflection on creation and sacrament.
52. Ratzinger, *Principles of Catholic Theology*, 160.

motivation, and the beginning and the goal of Christian *mission*?"[53] In what follows, two moves are made. First, Ratzinger's understanding of ontology and its relation to historical events is explicated. Second, we shall return to Ratzinger's thought on the Eucharist and see how it connects with the aforementioned point.

Ontology and History

In *Principles of Catholic Theology*, Ratzinger traces out a brief history of the relationship between ontology and history. As previously explained, ontology concerns the continuity of being, and this raises the following questions. Can we speak of being or only of becoming? Or, in more theological terms, what is the relationship between creation and redemption? These are not simply abstract questions. Ratzinger recognizes that there is something more important at stake than academic queries, i.e., the relationship between ontology and history affects the way we understand faith, identity (anthropology), and freedom. In what follows, I will expound Ratzinger's insightful, albeit convoluted, historical overview of the theological development from metaphysics to salvation history, and from salvation history to eschatology, as it is presented in *Principles of Catholic Theology*. This overview leads to Ratzinger's conclusion that, through a theology of the resurrection, metaphysics/ontology,[54] salvation history, and eschatology can be held together without diminishing the respective import of each.

History as Salvation

As a preliminary, Ratzinger looks at the general human experience of history *as* salvation. He argues that the story of history *as* salvation finds its roots with individuals coming together in solidarity with others to face the dangers of life. "Wherever men escape from their daily confrontation with the saving and threatening powers of the cosmos and apprehend themselves as a community that meets the pressing needs of existence that perdures through generations, there history as a form of salvation

---

53. Schmemann, *For Life of World*, 12.

54. Ratzinger takes up the older usage of ontology, which is used synonymously with metaphysics. For a historical overview of the relationship between ontology and metaphysics, see Schumacher, "Mapping the Theo-Political."

has its origin."⁵⁵ Race, nation, and culture provide forms of existence that preserve life, safety, and freedom; a form of salvation is offered.⁵⁶

Ratzinger maintains that this structure can also be found within Christian history during periods of peace. In this situation, the individual entrusts himself to the church's faith not because of his faith in the realities pointed to in the New Testament, but because he "finds in a world formed by and filled with faith a firm basis that gives his life meaning, salvation and shelter.... The concrete presence of Christian history gives form and freedom to his life and is, therefore, accepted as salvation."⁵⁷ Yet, a problem arises when the story of history no longer appears congruent with one's experience of life. When this happens, history fails to be salvific, and the two are torn apart. This foreshadows Ratzinger's portrayal of Martin Luther and clarifies Luther's reaction, which was not against salvation history per se but against history *as* salvation. When experience rends history as salvation, salvation can turn on history and revolt against it. Ratzinger offers several historical examples. The first example is Buddhism. Buddhism rejects both history and being, for being exists in history. As a result, nonbeing "becomes" God. Ratzinger describes Buddhism as not simply an attack on history but "as the complete antithesis to history, as turning toward 'nothingness.'"⁵⁸ Next, he turns to Platonism. As a result of Socrates's death at the hands of the *polis*, Plato loses his faith in the Greek story of history. Nevertheless, history is not done away with completely; rather, Plato posits that there is a vast gap between history and being. History will never overcome this gap; it has lost its salvific value. Nonetheless, history is not neutral, and there should be human effort to purify it and to bring it closer to the reality it reflects. Finally, Ratzinger turns to Marx. Marx radically rejects history, as it has been historically conceived, but not in order to turn to pure being or toward nonbeing. Salvation is still to be sought in history but in a new form of history, a history that must be made.

With the examples that Ratzinger offers, we are given three variant responses to the problem of history as salvation: (1) rejection of history, (2) recognition of the limits of history (it is not ultimate), and (3) redefinition of history. The three responses could easily be located

55. Ratzinger, *Principles of Catholic Theology*, 153.

56. William Cavanaugh brings this same notion of salvation narratives into the political arena. See Cavanaugh, *Theopolitical Imagination*.

57. Ratzinger, *Principles of Catholic Theology*, 154.

58. Ratzinger, *Principles of Catholic Theology*, 155.

chronologically in the history of thought. This is best seen in an interesting parallel we could make with what Ratzinger refers to as "basic human orientations" or what we could call paradigms of thought. Tracing the historical trajectory that led to the scientific orientation (our current orientation), he describes the movement as a shift from the metaphysical to the historical and from the historical to the technological (scientific or *techné*).[59] Each paradigm shift moves away from the hidden and invisible (metaphysics) to the visible (history), and from the reality of being (the givenness of what is) to the primacy of making (*techné*). Ratzinger's underlying concern is that each paradigm shift alters the way in which we understand what it means to be human.

The metaphysical orientation that characterizes the ancient world and the Middle Ages begins with God—thereby grounding thought in being (metaphysics)—and then moves toward humanity. Here "man can rethink the *logos*, the meaning of being, because his own *logos*, his own reason, is *logos* of the one *logos*, thought of the original thought, of the creative spirit that permeates and governs his being."[60] By beginning with God, the human person is imbued with significance: his logos is in relation to the *Logos*. Unlike the metaphysical paradigm, the historical paradigm limited thought to our own thinking and making.[61] Lastly, the technological paradigm avoids the ambiguities of interpretation that compromised the historical paradigm, and it grounds its knowledge on the pure empiricism of the repeatable. The latter two, in contradistinction to the metaphysical, begin and end with humanity. Thus, humanity fell from the heavens and became a fact and eventually an artifact. That is not to say that God was removed from the picture, just that the ordering was reversed. With the technological fact, humans became manipulable, something to be crafted into the "divine"; "he [technological man] does not need to regard it impossible to make himself into the God who now stands at the end as *faciendum*, as something makable, not at

---

59. Ratzinger, *Introduction to Christianity*, 57–77.

60. Ratzinger, *Introduction to Christianity*, 59.

61. Ratzinger argues that the historical paradigm began with Descartes (1596–1650) and reached its apogee in Kant. He also lists Giambattista Vico (1668–1744) as "the first to formulate a completely new idea of truth and knowledge and who, in a piece of bold anticipation, coined the typical formula of the modern spirit when it comes to dealing with the question of truth and reality. Against the Scholastic equation *verum est ens* (being is truth) he advances his own formula *verum quia factum*. That is to say, all that we can truly know is what we have made ourselves" (Ratzinger, *Introduction to Christianity*, 59).

the beginning, as *logos*, meaning."[62] In short, by beginning with ourselves instead of God, we became objects and lost our dignity.

There is one further aspect to add. Ratzinger correlates the paradigm shifts with a change of focus on temporality. Metaphysics focused on the eternal. The historical paradigm found its center in the past, and the technological in the future:[63]

Basic Orientations	History as Salvation	Temporality
(Pure) Metaphysics	Rejection	Eternal
Historical	Recognition	Past
Technological	Redefinition	Future

To be clear, Ratzinger does not explicitly articulate the parallel I have outlined, and this is not a seamless parallel. But by bringing together these two strands of Ratzinger's thought, we are able to see more accurately what is at stake. This also sheds light on why Ratzinger, as we shall see, focuses on the metaphysical and the historical rather than on the eschatological. That is, an orientation toward the future that does not sit within the boundaries of the metaphysical and historical too easily collapses into the technological paradigm (e.g., Marxism and certain versions of liberation theology).

Jesus: The End of All Partial Salvation Histories

Ratzinger argues that, according to St. Paul, Jesus breaks the old history, including the late Judaic concept of history, and initiates a new history (*Heilsgeschichte*), which is the end of history and the end of temporary salvation; world history cannot save. Ratzinger claims that the rising Christian historical consciousness is

> characterized simultaneously by both personalization (individualization) and universalization. The beginning and end of this new history is the Person of Jesus of Nazareth, who is

---

62. Ratzinger, *Introduction to Christianity*, 66.

63. The term *pure* is bracketed to emphasize that it is only metaphysics in its purest sense that would completely reject history. Surely any Christian metaphysician, past or present, would accept the value of history to some degree (e.g., the incarnation).

recognized as the last man (the second Adam), that is, as the long-awaited manifestation of what is truly human.... For this very reason, it is oriented toward the whole human race and presumes the abrogation of all partial histories, whose partial salvation is looked upon as essentially an absence of salvation.[64]

All other offers of salvation hold humankind back from reaching its end, "lulling him," as Ratzinger puts it, "from his very humanness."[65]

Ratzinger argues that Jesus's new history is concretized by the new community of believers. This is expressed either as ἐκκλησίαι (*ekklēsia*) or παροικία (*paroikia*). Both terms are not without problems. ἐκκλησίαι refers to the community as living alongside the ordinary everyday community, whereas the term παροικία emphasizes the temporality of the community, a society of sojourners. With both, there is a level of separation from the other coexisting historical communities (e.g., alongside, rather than within; sojourner, rather than permanent dweller), and it is this separation that is the early Christian concrete historical expression of the "already and not yet." The early church did not reject history altogether, but, to use St. Augustine's distinction, she clearly recognized the difference between the City of God and the City of Man[66] and, in practice, still lived "with—and from—the past."[67] Even though the early Christians recognized the import of the past, they understood that they were participating in a history that was just beginning. This new history, their new faith, reduced their past history and their contemporary history to the status of "nonhistory and nonsalvation."[68] Finally—and this is an important point that sets up Ratzinger's argument—although the new history reduced the past and contemporary history, "it did not abrogate this contemporary history; it merely lowered its status. On the other hand, the new history that came into being was just a secondary history (of sojourners!); it could preserve its salvational character only by hope, that is, in the relationship of what was experienced to what was not yet experienced."[69] Ratzinger highlights the Platonic parallel: one remains in the current history while at the same time transcending history in such

---

64. Ratzinger, *Principles of Catholic Theology*, 156.

65. Ratzinger, *Principles of Catholic Theology*, 156.

66. Ratzinger does not point out this correlation to St. Augustine, but it fits with the text and with his Augustinian leanings.

67. Ratzinger, *Principles of Catholic Theology*, 156.

68. Ratzinger, *Principles of Catholic Theology*, 156.

69. Ratzinger, *Principles of Catholic Theology*, 156.

a way that the transcending enters into history. He argues that Platonic thought therefore entered into Christian discourse early on and helped the early Christians work through their initial hope of an imminent end/eschaton. The Platonic concept of the transcendence of history provided the basis for the new understanding of Christian hope.

Salvation History Overturns Ontology

The question of validity in regard to the Platonic development in Christian thought has "plagued Western consciousness with burning trenchancy ever since Luther. Luther's appearance signalled the collapse of the prevailing Christian historical consciousness."[70] Immediately following this quotation, Ratzinger sets out the context in which Luther lived in and to which he reacted. Ratzinger jumps from a Platonically informed eschatology to the last days of medieval Christendom, and he argues that, in the sixteenth century, the Christian West lost its sense of existence as a sojourner. Instead, present history was seen as Christian history, heaven and earth fused. Put differently, the Platonic gap was overcome, and Christendom was seen as the embodiment of what once was hoped for (history *as* salvation). The vision of two overlapping realities was lost, and Christianity no longer offered an alternative history. Those caught in the oppressive forces of its history were at a point of crisis. Ratzinger argues that this is Luther's situation. Luther experienced this historical context as anti-Christian. As a result, he did not seek Christianity within this story of history but against it. It seems that there is a certain amount of sympathy in Ratzinger's telling of Luther's situation. The Christian West had closed the gap between the "two cities," which was a problem that needed to be addressed. Therefore the question is: did Luther react appropriately? Ratzinger's view is clear: Luther threw out the baby with the bathwater, so to speak.[71]

Luther's account of the relationship between faith and understanding was firmly formed by his historical crisis. He had an aversion toward what can best be summarized by the term *continuity*. He could not accept the story of history within which he dwelt and demanded a rupture. Ratzinger argues that Luther's handing over of the Christian order to the

---

70. Ratzinger, *Principles of Catholic Theology*, 157.

71. For a more sustained look at Luther and the major differences between Catholicism and Lutheranism see Ratzinger, *Church, Ecumenism, and Politics*, 100–120.

secular powers was intended "to expose the lack of historical actuality in the Church that was herself unable to form her own history or communicate salvation by her continuity."[72] Listed below are the marks of difference that Ratzinger sees between Christianity perceived prior to Luther and Christianity understood in light of Luther:

Western Christianity prior to Luther	Christianity influenced by Luther
Apostolic succession as continuity	The working of the Spirit here and now
Christianity represented by community and church	Christianity represented by personal orientation ("pro me")
Typology (promise and fulfillment)	An appeal to what was in the beginning
History interpreted in light of promise and fulfillment	History interpreted in light of the contradiction between law and gospel
Ontology as the philosophical expression of continuity	Salvation history understood as the antithesis of ontology
Emphasis on the incarnation	Emphasis on the cross

The fundamental difference is the distinction between continuity and discontinuity. The Reformers, siding with discontinuity, sought to escape what Ratzinger calls "organized historical forms."[73] Ratzinger maintains that the question concerning continuity and discontinuity continues into the twentieth century. It is the dividing line between Protestants and Catholics. Typically, Protestant theology is rooted in salvation history, while Catholic theology is grounded in ontology/metaphysics. But, as Ratzinger made clear, it is Buddhism that holds the anti-historical position. No Christian position is completely void of salvation history. The

---

72. Ratzinger, *Principles of Catholic Theology*, 157.
73. Ratzinger, *Principles of Catholic Theology*, 158. See Ratzinger, "Truth and Freedom," 20.

difference concerns how history is understood in relation to ontology. At this point, it is important to consider that the original German title of *Principles of Catholic Theology*—the main source for Ratzinger's engagement with ontology, history, and eschatology—is *Theologische Prinzipienlehre*. "Catholic" is not in the title. This testifies to Ratzinger's desire for ecumenicity.[74] Ratzinger is not attempting to further divide Catholics and Lutherans, but, rather, he is sketching out a history of thought in order to gain greater clarity.[75] He is not defending the church. In fact, Ratzinger is clear that, in Luther's context, the church had lost sight of her reality as sojourner, and she too closely united her current historical reality with the kingdom of God (history *as* salvation).

Salvation History in the Twentieth Century and Karl Rahner's Attempt at Reconciliation

In the twentieth century, the question of salvation history continued to be of the utmost significance. Ratzinger does not find this surprising. The two world wars, along with the transition to the new form of civilization (the secular city), once again caused a historical crisis, a questioning of the mediation of history. The questions in this period take on two forms: the traditional form, which continues to rehash the distinctions listed above, and the revolutionary form, which was born out of a theology of hope and manifested itself as political theology (e.g., J. B. Metz).

The overarching concerns in both forms center around "a question of being as such: Is there a continuity of 'humanness'? And, if there is, at what point does the mediation of history begin?" As noted earlier, this is specifically what Ratzinger refers to as "the fundamental crisis of our age."[76] The general Protestant response, as he sees it, continues to follow Luther's lead, intensifying the problem of alienation, prioritizing discontinuity over continuity, and rejecting ontology (e.g., early Barth,

---

74. This is pointed out in Twomey, *Pope Benedict XVI*, 57. For more on Ratzinger's ecumenical perspective, see Ratzinger, *Pilgrim Fellowship of Faith*, 258.

75. Tracey Rowland's writes, "When the 'Joint Declaration on the Doctrine of Justification' was signed in 1999 with leaders of the Lutheran community, Bishop George Andrews (the head of the Evangelical Lutheran Church of America) said, 'it was Ratzinger who untied the knots. Without him we might not have an agreement'" (Rowland, *Ratzinger's Faith*, 98).

76. Ratzinger, *Principles of Catholic Theology*, 160.

Bultmann, and Oscar Cullmann).[77] In disagreement with this position, Ratzinger argues that history must be seen as a type of mediation of being. Clearly, Ratzinger does not mean all history; as Gaál notes, for Ratzinger, "history is redeemed by Jesus Christ *in* history but not *through* history."[78] Ratzinger links continuity to Christ who, as the second Adam, is distinguishable from the first Adam but not completely separate; hence, the continuation of the title *Adam*. The church of antiquity always saw this as the unity of Adam's being, and

> in contrast to the Greek concept of being, then, creatureliness means having one's origin, not in a passive idea, but in a creative freedom; it includes, therefore, in a positive way, the temporality of being as the mode of its self-fulfillment, history as substantiality, not mere accidentality, but in such a way that time has its unity in the *Creator Spiritus* and because it is sequential, is still a continuity of being by way of succession.[79]

Nevertheless, Ratzinger realizes that this is not a simple solution, and that it raises another important question concerning the relationship between the particular and the general. Although little work has been done in this direction, it is in this area that he sees Catholic theology as especially capable of contributing. Karl Rahner is the Catholic theologian who has contributed the most to this conversation. Ratzinger adumbrates Rahner's position, and, in spite of Rahner's ingenuity, Ratzinger argues that his position is deeply problematic. Ultimately, Rahner fails to hold the particular (historical) and the universal (ontological) together. He collapses the distinction: the particular is the universal. For example, Rahner claims that the Christian person is simply the human person as she really is. All that she must do is look deep within herself to find her Christian person.

According to Ratzinger, the main problem with Rahner's work is that, by collapsing being into history, he destroys freedom and thereby succumbs to a philosophy of necessity—freedom is assimilated into predestination. Methodologically, like Hegel, Rahner's attempt fails because he tries to create an airtight system that explains the whole. Any such explanatory system pushes freedom out of the picture. Since there is, and

---

77. Ratzinger argues that Cullmann rejects metaphysics because of its relation to time (Ratzinger, *Eschatology*, 51).

78. Gaál, *Theology*, 149.

79. Ratzinger, *Principles of Catholic Theology*, 162.

should be, a spiritual tension between history and being, and because Christianity is grounded in freedom, there can be no all-embracing Christian synthesis. Ratzinger writes, "The key thought of a Christian philosophy and theology would, therefore, have to be freedom—that true freedom that includes also the nondeducible and hence excludes perfect conceptual cohesion."[80]

Ratzinger's response to Rahner, what Ratzinger calls a "philosophy of conversion," foreshadows Ratzinger's concluding remarks on the relationship between ontology, salvation history, and eschatology. Ratzinger argues that "Jesus Christ, as the Event of the new and unexpected, is, then, the central expression of this freedom ['the non deducible' freedom that is key to Christian theology and philosophy]."[81] This phrase in Ratzinger's quotation, "the Event of the new and unexpected," is key to what follows. The Christ event reveals that no one could have foreseen—for it was new and unexpected—the context in which God was going to guide every freedom to salvation. Rahner's insistence, that at the core of every person we find a Christian, is problematic because it does not account for the externality of the Christ event. Salvation came to us externally; we did not find it by turning inward to the self, and this "means that the liberation of man consists in his being freed from himself and, in relinquishing himself, truly finding himself. It means that by accepting the other, the particular, the apparently not-necessary and free, he finds what is whole and real."[82] Furthermore, Ratzinger argues that it means that the tension between history and ontology is within human nature. That is, we are ontologically wired in such a manner that the self is found externally in an encounter. The self "has its foundation in the mystery of God, which is freedom and which, therefore, calls each individual by a name that is known to no other. Thus, the whole is communicated to him in the particular."[83]

Eschatology and the Rejection of Salvation History

Ratzinger demonstrates that Rahner's failed yet laudable attempt to understand the relationship between history and ontology is not seen in

---

80. Ratzinger, *Principles of Catholic Theology*, 170.
81. Ratzinger, *Principles of Catholic Theology*, 170–71.
82. Ratzinger, *Principles of Catholic Theology*, 171.
83. Ratzinger, *Principles of Catholic Theology*, 171.

the general Protestant theologies of the twentieth century. Instead, within Protestantism, there was a widespread move of opposition, in which salvation history was held to as a counter to Catholic theology. Ratzinger admits that, in many ways, this opposition rings true. The dominant voice in Catholic theology prior to Vatican II, neo-scholasticism/neo-Thomism, was characterized by a rejection of history. Confirming this point, Fergus Kerr succinctly notes that "neoscholastic theology 'identified truth and life with immutability and rationality; it opposed being to history and ignored concreteness in human life and in the economy of salvation'. For neothomists, as for Enlightenment philosophers, appealing to experience, tradition and historical studies was the wrong way to get to truth."[84] Under the influence of the *ressourcement* theologians, Vatican II shifted its focus, even following the terminology used within German Protestant theology: *historia salutis* (salvation history).[85] Interestingly, as Catholics began to engage seriously with the questions of history, Protestants developed a new attitude toward it.[86] There was what Ratzinger calls a "direct reversal" away from salvation history to eschatology, and the key figure behind this reversal is Bultmann. Nonetheless, one cannot ignore Barth's influence. Barth opened the door with his passionate polemic that "a Christianity that is not wholly, entirely and absolutely eschatology has wholly, entirely and absolutely nothing to do with Christ."[87] But it was Bultmann who took this to its logical conclusion. Unlike Barth, his main concern was to make present the eschatological and this "question of re-actualisation, the problem of the 'presentness' of the Christian message, became the crucial springboard of his whole theological effort."[88] Bultmann's academic disciples followed the thread, which led to a complete dismissal of salvation history. Historical events were emptied of their import and neutralized as word-events, in which "theological meaningful 'history' is withdrawn from the objectively determined realism of

---

84. Kerr, *Twentieth-Century Catholic Theologians*, 2.

85. Ratzinger notes that the question concerning God's action in history has always been present within the Christian tradition (Catholicism). In patristic terms, it is expressed as the relationship of *dispositio* and *natura*. For a good overview of *ressourcement* theology, see Boersma, *Nouvelle Théologie*.

86. Ratzinger lists Gottlieb Söhngen and Jean Daniélou as the primary Catholics who began to engage in the conversation (Ratzinger, *Principles of Catholic Theology*, 172).

87. Karl Barth, *Epistle to the Romans*, as quoted in Ratzinger, *Principles of Catholic Theology*, 176.

88. Ratzinger, *Principles of Catholic Theology*, 176.

historical events and moved into the nonobjectifiable."[89] To put it differently, Bultmann and his followers placed word (the message) above history. No longer was the actuality of history important, for how can a past event affect our present?[90] In contrast, the meaning made present in word was recognized as existentially potent.

Bultmann's existential-eschatological approach also made its way into Catholic theology. It helped relieve the Catholic burden of reconciling metaphysics and salvation history, a struggle that Catholic theologians had difficulties resolving. Inevitably, the rejection of salvation history in Catholic thought and the new impetus of the eschatological led to political theology, a theology of liberation and revolution. Bultmann's existentialism "prepared the way for the new concept by its relativization of past history and, ipso facto, of its Christian content."[91] With Christian content pushed aside, the technological paradigm (what Ratzinger refers to as the know-make relation) and its orientation for redefining history and remaking humankind entered into (political) theology. The future replaced the past and ontological continuity.

Reading History in Continuity: Ratzinger's Approach

Ratzinger's historical overview leads to a tripartite methodological conclusion. First, theology must always be understood within its historical context. There is no pure neutral exegesis. By tracing the origins of exegetical interpretations, we can gain a greater sense of objectivity and understanding. The explanation of history as salvation, with which Ratzinger began his exploration into the question of ontology and history, is an interpretive tool that makes sense of theological developments as responses motivated by historical crises. That does not mean that such developments should necessarily be rejected, but it does imply that looking through a larger lens enables one to have a fuller and more critical understanding. Second, "we must neither over- nor underestimate the value of theological programs."[92] This is especially the case when the program seeks to be all-encompassing. Vincent Twomey, a former PhD

---

89. Ratzinger, *Principles of Catholic Theology*, 176.

90. Ratzinger looks at this question from a number of different angles in *Introduction to Christianity* (52–57, 193–215).

91. Ratzinger, *Principles of Catholic Theology*, 180.

92. Ratzinger, *Principles of Catholic Theology*, 181.

student of Ratzinger's, writes about Ratzinger's "courage to be imperfect."[93] This phrase not only explains much about Ratzinger as a person but also about his approach to theology.[94] In short, Ratzinger recognizes the limits of theology; human finitude is always part of the equation. Third, theology should have a hermeneutic of continuity. Theologians should seek to make sense of the faith and teachings of the church as a consistent development.[95] Ratzinger approaches exegesis, the councils, and theology in this way.[96] The hermeneutic of continuity enables Ratzinger to build bridges and connect what appear to be disparate loose ends. This is exactly what he does with ontology, salvation history, and eschatology. What underlies all three points is the importance of history. Theology is not accomplished in a historical vacuum.

Ratzinger: Ontology, Salvation History, and Eschatology United in the Resurrection

As seen in the historical overview, it is clearly demonstrable that, with the various approaches (ontology, salvation history, and eschatology), there is a canon within a canon, a core way of making sense of theology.[97] For example, according to Oscar Cullmann—a representative of salvation history—the core is a series of decisive events in our history brought about by God. We are to insert ourselves into these events through faith.

93. Twomey, *Pope Benedict XVI*, 16.

94. It is arguable that, as a theologian, Ratzinger has the "courage to be imperfect" because of his belief that the church, not theology, safeguards the faith. See Ratzinger, *Nature and Mission*, 62–63.

95. See the following two articles for a good example of a scholar who takes up a position of discontinuity in contrast with Ratzinger: Boeve, "Revelation, Scripture and Tradition"; and Boeve, "Europe in Crisis."

96. For a brief overview of Ratzinger's exegetical approach of continuity, see: Ratzinger, "Biblical Interpretation in Crisis"; Ratzinger, *Many Religions, One Covenant*, 36–41; Gaál, *Theology*, 99. In regard to continuity and councils, see: Ratzinger and Messori, *Ratzinger Report*, 27–38; Ratzinger, "Theological Locus"; Gaál, *Theology*, 104; Rowland, *Benedict XVI*, 46–47. Ayres et al. clearly argue that Ratzinger's mode of theology is "within an overall sense of the fundamental unity of the Christian tradition" (Ayres et al., "Benedict XVI," 430).

97. Ratzinger points out that with the eschatological turn and the rejection of salvation history, a division was created in the New Testament. The eschatological camp clung to St. Paul's writings, and the Gospels of John and Luke were read as misinterpretations of Jesus's message because of their framework of salvation history (Ratzinger, *Principles of Catholic Theology*, 177).

For Bultmann, the core concerns our eschatological existence. What is the core of the gospel, according to Ratzinger? He concludes that the Christian faith all gathers around one key sentence: "Jesus has risen." Ratzinger avers, "This sentence is thus, above all, the true *articulus stantis et cadentis ecclesiae* [by which the church stands or falls] by which the structure of faith and theology are chiefly to be determined."[98] Yet, he writes that when a Catholic is asked about the core of the gospel, the most frequent answer is "Jesus, the man, is God."[99] In this statement, we have the Chalcedonian ontological *is*, which presumes the incarnation event and is motivated by the existential concern about the meaning of Christ for contemporary reality. Ratzinger considers this to be important but argues that we cannot stop here, for this points back to the root of every confession that Jesus *is* the Christ. The *is* in the statement points back to an event: Christ's anointing. The event of anointing is Christ's resurrection.[100] The resurrection is absolutely central, but the statement "Jesus, the man, is God" demonstrates that the resurrection is not without ontological and existential implications. Continuity of belief (e.g., the interdependence of the creeds) preserves the continuity of existence (ontology).

It is obvious to Ratzinger "that all Christian theology, if it is to be true to its origin, must be first and foremost a theology of Resurrection."[101] He clearly distinguishes his account from Luther's theology of the cross and, arguably, not for Catholic polemical purposes but for theological reasons. Ratzinger argues that the cross makes no sense without the resurrection. In fact, on its own, the cross would simply reveal that death has won. The resurrection is the interpretive key. This is glaringly obvious, but the implicit point is that, while a theology of the cross can easily ignore the ontological claims, a theology of the resurrection cannot. Ratzinger makes four claims about what a theology of resurrection reveals, and these four claims tie together ontology, salvation history, and eschatology.

---

98. Ratzinger, *Principles of Catholic Theology*, 184.

99. Ratzinger, *Principles of Catholic Theology*, 182.

100. See Ratzinger, "Theological Locus," 486–87; Ratzinger, "Liturgy and Church Music." For a brief historical overview of the Catholic Church's development in regards to the priority of the resurrection see Ratzinger, "Catholicism After the Council," 15–17.

101. Ratzinger, *Principles of Catholic Theology*, 184.

I. Resurrection: Preeminence of History?

First, the resurrection reveals the preeminence of history over metaphysics, what Ratzinger calls the "*prae* of God's action."[102] That idea arose earlier in this chapter, but there are a few implications that were not discussed. The Christian emphasis upon a God who first acts clashes with the Greek emphasis of a God who exists purely in the realm of substance (ουσια, *ousia*). The primary biblical categories are relationship and action, and the two basic statements we can say about God are that he creates and that he reveals. As revealed in the resurrection, God is not simply timeless: he engages with creation within the realm of temporality. However, this prioritizing of history over ontology is not as simple as it first appears. In the final footnote in the section on ontology and history in *Principles of Catholic Theology*, Ratzinger writes,

> In the view of the fundamental meaning of this "is," I would stress more strongly today than I have in these pages the irreplaceability and preeminence of the ontological aspect and, therefore, of metaphysics as the basis of any history. Precisely as a confession of Jesus Christ, Christian faith—and in this it is completely loyal to the faith of Abraham—is faith in a living God. The fact that the first article of faith forms the basis of all Christian belief includes, theologically, the basic character of the ontological statements and the indispensability of the metaphysical, that is, of the Creator God who is before all becoming.[103]

The footnote then references a few of his other writings. This same concern is expressed in a footnote a few pages earlier: "Where it does not continue to be method but becomes a point of view, the exclusion of the ontological question, as happens in the phenomenological method, leads of necessity to a restriction to the φαινεσθαι [*phainesthai*, appearances] and hence to a construction that is close to Docetism."[104] Out of this concern, three points can be made: (1) without metaphysics, we cannot preserve truth (reality); (2) metaphysics safeguards the "'specifically human quality' of man,"[105] along with (3) the unity of subjective and objective knowing. Let's look at each of these three points in turn.

---

102. Ratzinger, *Principles of Catholic Theology*, 185.
103. Ratzinger, *Principles of Catholic Theology*, 190n172.
104. Ratzinger, *Principles of Catholic Theology*, 183n160.
105. Ratzinger, *God of Jesus Christ*, 46.

In regard to the first point, Ratzinger points the reader to the end of *Principles of Catholic Theology*, where he reflects on the question, what is theology?[106] The section is centered on two statements: God is the subject of theology, and theological speculation is linked to philosophical inquiry. Ratzinger realizes that the latter claim does not resonate with the current trends in theology. Nonetheless, he argues,

> I am convinced, in fact, that the crisis we are experiencing in the Church and in humanity is closely allied to the exclusion of God as a topic with which reason can properly be concerned—an exclusion that has led to the degeneration of theology first into historicism, then into sociologism and, at the same time, to the impoverishment of philosophy.[107]

Since theology is primarily concerned with God and not salvation history, it must think in philosophical terms. Here, Ratzinger appropriately brings St. Thomas into the conversation and juxtaposes Thomas's "theo-logy," in which the subject is God, with Peter Lombard's theology, in which the object is the doctrine of reality and signs. These two views, along with the controversy of their status, continue in the present under the division of theology and economy. Ratzinger asks, "Is economy to be called theology? Or are the two to be kept always separate?"[108] To answer the question, he qualifies the distinction by characterizing the two positions in medieval fashion as *scientia speculativa* (Thomistic/theology) and *scientia practica* (Franciscan/economy). The first concerns orthodoxy and the second orthopraxis. If the latter is pushed to the extreme—praxis as theology—then theology excludes the question of truth and simply becomes the exercise of forming new practices in light of old practices. In fact, praxis becomes truth; thus, truth becomes a product of human creation. The how replaces the what. Contra to this position, Ratzinger argues for the priority of orthodoxy.[109] He cites Romano Guardini and St. Irenaeus of Lyons as clearly articulating the proper approach. Both theologians prioritize *logos* over *ethos* and see Christ as leading humans to an encounter with God. While a Christocentric approach is often conceived as

---

106. *Principles of Catholic Theology* is a compilation of articles written in the 1960s and 1970s. Thus, different parts of the book have different emphases that reflect an earlier or later position in Ratzinger's thought.

107. Ratzinger, *Principles of Catholic Theology*, 316.

108. Ratzinger, *Principles of Catholic Theology*, 317.

109. See Ratzinger, *Nature and Mission*, 32–41; Ratzinger, *Truth and Tolerance*, 162–83.

the linchpin for both salvation history and eschatology, Ratzinger turns it around. Christ always points beyond himself to the Father ("the meaning of christocentrism consists in transcending oneself"). Christology therefore fails "when it remains locked in a historico-anthropological circle and does not become a real theo-logy, in which the metaphysical reality of God is what is discussed."[110] Thus, Ratzinger concludes that metaphysics does not betray salvation history, but, rather, salvation history always leads into metaphysics. From metaphysics (*scientia speculativa*), one can move to *scientia practica*. Following Bonaventure's lead, Ratzinger insists that the two must be in relation. A purely metaphysical or academic theology is highly problematic, for "just as we cannot learn to swim without water, so we cannot learn theology without the spiritual praxis in which it lives."[111] Ratzinger repeatedly expresses the same idea by emphasizing the inseparable relation of truth and love.[112] Christianity's basis as a religion of truth must be based equally on orthopraxy and orthodoxy. He argues that "at the most profound level its content will necessarily consist . . . in love and reason coming together as the two pillars of reality: the true reason is love, and love is the true reason. They are in their unity the true basis and the goal of all reality."[113]

In *The God of Jesus Christ*, Ratzinger also highlights the importance of metaphysics but from another angle. In chapter 1, he argues that "it is impossible to separate the question of whether God exists from the question of who or what God is."[114] To talk about the who, Ratzinger turns to Exodus 3, where God reveals himself to Moses as "I am who I am," and, here, Ratzinger highlights that God has a name. This mysterious name reveals that God's name is not one among many names but is set apart and incomparable. Ratzinger argues that it means "he is always presence: 'I am.' He is contemporary with every time and antecedent to every time. I can call on this God here and now: he belongs to the 'now' and responds to my 'now.'"[115] In contradistinction is the beast in Revelation, who has no name but is just numbers (666). According to Ratzinger, this means that the beast is pure function, who turns all others into utility, whereas God

---

110. Ratzinger, *Principles of Catholic Theology*, 319.
111. Ratzinger, *Principles of Catholic Theology*, 322.
112. Ratzinger, *Truth and Tolerance*, 230–31.
113. Ratzinger, *Truth and Tolerance*, 183.
114. Ratzinger, *God of Jesus Christ*, 19.
115. Ratzinger, *God of Jesus Christ*, 22.

has a name and is therefore personal; persons are never reduced to mere functions. The name of God reaches its apogee in Jesus whose Hebrew form includes the word *Yahweh* and adds a further element to it: God saves.[116] Now the "I am who I am" becomes "'I am the one who saves you.' His Being is salvation."[117] God comes to us as person and loves us as persons. His who explains his existence, his acts.

Turning to the second point, metaphysics safeguarding the particular human quality, in chapter 2 of *The God of Jesus Christ*, Ratzinger argues that "the first proposition of the Christian faith and the fundamental orientation of Christian conversion is: 'God is.'"[118] While the first chapter highlights God's identity, the second chapter highlights what the *is* of God reveals about the human context. God precedes all things human, and we are contingent beings. Thus, what is true and right is superior to all our interests and goals; we are only creatures. Yet, we are the products of his loving will; we are not the products of chance. Finally, chapter 3 emphasizes the inseparable relationship between history and ontology. Christian orthodoxy has always linked creation and redemption; the Creator God is also the Redeemer God.[119] This is vitally important for ethics, particularly with the current hatred of the body, in which the body is degraded to a mere thing and is excluded from ethics. By hating his body, Ratzinger avers, the human person despises himself, this life, and reality as a whole. Out of this hatred comes a cry for gnostic revolution, which tears the human person in two. Certainly, to ignore the metaphysics of creation is to ignore something central about what it is to be human. It is in this sense that Ratzinger argues that there is a "'specific human quality' of man, who cannot declare the trampling underfoot of creation to be his own liberation without deceiving himself on a very profound level."[120]

The unity of subjective and objective knowing is framed by the following question: what does it mean when a person believes in God, the Father Almighty, Creator of heaven and earth? In response to this question, Ratzinger highlights and answers the following questions that are repeatedly thrown at the Christian faith.[121] Is faith simply a placebo

---

116. Ratzinger, *God of Jesus Christ*, 24.
117. Ratzinger, *God of Jesus Christ*, 24.
118. Ratzinger, *God of Jesus Christ*, 27.
119. See Ratzinger, *Yes of Jesus Christ*, 88–89.
120. Ratzinger, *God of Jesus Christ*, 46.
121. Ratzinger, *Principles of Catholic Theology*, 67–75.

without any real content (Marx)? Was faith simply invented to ensure that the weak would submit to the strong (Nietzsche)? The heart of both questions concerns praxis. We could appropriately format two more questions. What bearing does the first line of the Apostles' Creed have on reality? Are there not other means besides Christianity of placating and controlling the people? All the questions assume that God can be replaced by something else, which may be more effective. Again, it is the prioritizing or replacing of orthodoxy with orthopraxy. In response, Ratzinger makes a very simple yet effective argument: "The Bible makes it abundantly clear that a world under God's sway is quite different from a world without God—that nothing, in fact, remains the same if God is taken away and that, by the same token, everything changes when one turns to God."[122] The content changes the form. Yet, Ratzinger does not stop here. He asserts that God has a name—God is a person—and is not simply an idea or philosophical assertion to be explicated. God, as person, is known in relationship. Ratzinger calls this way of knowing and believing "an active-passive process."[123] God first acts, and humans can either accept his love or reject it. Ratzinger is clear: "God is not a resting object but the ground of our being, who establishes his own credentials, who makes his presence known at the very center of our being and who can, precisely for this reason, be ignored because we are so easily inclined to live far from the center of ourselves."[124] The "active-passive" is the answer to the questions. Faith is a passive response to a God who actively reveals himself, whereas the aforementioned questions stem from an assumption of orthopraxis, in which the practitioner is first and foremost an active knower. The position of the active knower closes him down to receptivity, to the ground of his being, i.e., God. Therefore, from the outset, the active knower has failed to take into consideration the possibility of God's existence. If he has taken God's existence into consideration, the God he has considered is merely God as idea or principle and not God as person.

The validity, or lack of validity, of God's existence affects the foundations of the world. Hence, God is not merely to be understood in the subjective sense, what Ratzinger describes as Luther's "pro me." Neither is God to be understood solely as a salient principle that undergirds all other principles (e.g., Aristotle). The subject-object distinction does not

---

122. Ratzinger, *Principles of Catholic Theology*, 68.
123. Ratzinger, *Principles of Catholic Theology*, 69.
124. Ratzinger, *Principles of Catholic Theology*, 69.

do justice to a universe in which God is both Creator and Redeemer. The Christian God is known in both the personal sense (Thou) and the objective sense (the ground of all reality). He is the ground of my being and also the ground of all being. With penetrating clarity, Ratzinger writes that

> what is so striking here [God as both Thou and as the ground of all being] is, of course, the fact that this whole ground of being is, at the same time, a relationship; not less than I, who know, think, feel and love, but rather more than I, so that I can know only because I am known, love only because I am already loved.[125]

In short, there is no knowing without God. If God exists, the world should never be understood with the strict delineation of the subject-object divide.

In conclusion, all three of Ratzinger's concerns about the importance of metaphysics/ontology have bearing upon human identity (ontology) and human action (ethics). In regard to the relationship between history and metaphysics, we must ask if any greater clarity has been achieved. As we saw in *The Principles of Catholic Theology*, Ratzinger initially emphasizes the historical, in which metaphysics simply follows behind God's actions. Then, in the concluding footnote, he reverses this. Yet, turning to the sources that he references, we continue to see the pairing of ontology and history, creation and redemption. The only difference with these sources is that they start with a metaphysical/ontological reflection and are then followed by the language of history, event, or redemption. It is apparent that Ratzinger walks a thin line and tries his best not to land on either side because, if disconnected, both sides are full of theological difficulties.

I think the language of preeminence might be taken to say more than Ratzinger actually means. Ratzinger emphasizes the need for metaphysics for two main reasons. First, he desires to preserve the priority of God: God exists in and of himself, in a perfect triune relationship. God does not exist for me, but he dies for me. This instills a sense of our contingency, along with the recognition that life is a gift and not a right. Theology is first about God and then about humankind. Second, Ratzinger does not want salvation history nor eschatology to erode the continuity of God. God moves in the midst of history, but he never ceases to be the ground of our existence; God does not equal history. He engages with

---

125. Ratzinger, *Principles of Catholic Theology*, 74.

humans but never ceases to be God (e.g., Chalcedonian Christology). Salvation history is the story about God's love for us and only secondarily is it about our love for God. At the same time, the God in whom "we live and have our being" (Acts 17:28) is person. He takes the initiative and actively pursues us and dialogues with us. This dialogue enters into history and becomes event but is also more than history.[126] It is also an existential encounter in which God continually makes himself present. Clearly, Ratzinger seeks to balance all three aspects (ontology, salvation history, and eschatology), so why speak of preeminence? Perhaps the answer simply concerns context. Sometimes, balance can be achieved only by counterbalance.

II. Resurrection: An Eschatological Event

What does it mean to speak of the resurrection as an eschatological action of God? Ratzinger contends that the Gospel writers' understanding of the resurrection can be fully appreciated only in light of Israel's notion of the eschaton. Israel expected that, in the eschaton, the dead will be awakened, and this is the apocalyptic sense that the Gospels incorporate. For the Gospel writers, Christ's resurrection is no "ordinary" resurrection that a miracle worker could have brought about. The resurrection of Christ is an event that destroys death, an event that changes everything. Ratzinger claims that "the realm of history has been transcended, that he [Jesus] who arose from the dead did not return, as anyone else might have done, to a this-worldly history but stands above it, though by no means without relationship to it."[127] The resurrection is not a historical event in the same sense as the crucifixion. As the resurrected Christ, Jesus is not imprisoned within history; yet, it is the same Jesus who was born in a stable and lived as a first-century Jew. Unlike the late Judaic expectation, the resurrection did not come at the end of history but in the midst of history. In Christ, the eschatological and the historical touch, and this is why the resurrection is called an "eschatological *event*."

---

126. Michaela C. Hastetter argues that, for Ratzinger, Jesus Christ is the primary form of dynamic existence. The Trinitarian God in Christ, so to speak, comes out of himself and leads us into the inner Trinitarian dialogue. Her argument emphasizes the God who acts. See Hastetter, "Dynamik der Theologie," 97.

127. Ratzinger, *Principles of Catholic Theology*, 186.

III. Resurrection: Cosmic and Future

The resurrection has both cosmic and future implications; "the Christian faith is a faith of hope in the fullness of a promise that encompasses the whole cosmos."[128] From this point, Ratzinger extrapolates that Christianity undoes the individualizing of the human person, transforming her from the *I* to the *we* (*Sein-mit-anderen*). Christology is not simply concerned with freeing individuals qua individuals from their sin but with the entire human race. Christology traditionally has two facets that are expressed in the doctrine of original sin and in the biblical notion of Christ as the "last man." With the second, we see that Christ is necessary to bring the human race to its *telos*. The first provides the context. That is, "God conquers man's past—conquers sin—by calling him into the future—into Christ."[129] Therefore, Ratzinger concludes that salvation is objective. It draws man out of his subjectivity into his true existence, into reality.

IV. Resurrection: An Orientation toward Human Existence

The resurrection is directed toward the heart of human existence. It is the ultimate Passover that gathers all history and interprets all salvation histories, making evident that salvation history is an exodus history:

> In a very literal sense, it becomes a theology of existence, a theology of *ex-sistere*, of that exodus by which the human individual goes out from himself and through which alone he can find himself. In this movement of *ex-sistere*, faith and love are ultimately united—the deepest significance of each is that *Exi*, that call to transcend and sacrifice the *I* that is the basic law of the history of God's covenant with man and, ipso facto, the truly basic law of all human existence.... God's action is, precisely in the objectivity of its "in-itself-ness," not a hopeless objectivity, but the true formula of human existence, which has its "in-itself-ness" outside itself and can find its true center only in *ex-sistere*, in going-out-from itself.[130]

---

128. Ratzinger, *Principles of Catholic Theology*, 186.
129. Ratzinger, *Principles of Catholic Theology*, 188.
130. Ratzinger, *Principles of Catholic Theology*, 189–90.

The parallel to *exitus et reditus* is obvious. With this parallel in mind, we can assert that each person is called to this exodus, in which his *exi* is actually his return (*reditus*) to the ground of his being. *Exitus et reditus*, the basic reality of creation, and the God-directed movement of salvation history, is also the center of our human existence/nature revealed to us in the resurrection.

Conclusion

According to Ratzinger, the question concerning history and ontology cannot be answered by exegesis. It is a complex question that must recognize the impact history has on interpretation. Ratzinger seeks to make sense of the underlying currents by historically tracing the various ways in which the question has been answered. In so doing, he hopes to be less prejudiced by contemporary concerns and therefore less one-sided. He concludes that, if we accept only the historical (e.g., Luther), we run into ethical problems (i.e., rejection of the body). If we ignore history and accept only the ontological, Christianity is reduced to principles. Thus, we risk losing the personal element (God is person, not a principle) of Christianity, along with the eschatological "already and not yet" reality of this world. As a result of the latter, Christian faith becomes a theology of glory—the incarnation without the cross and resurrection. If history and ontology are conflated (e.g., Rahner), we lose freedom and genuine love and ignore the overarching Christian narrative of exodus. If we turn away from history and ontology in favor of an eschatological/existential focus, we lose the objectivity of God and his reality. This results in the acceptance of the subject-object distinction, and Christianity is reduced to the interior personal experience of the individual. In light of all this, Ratzinger argues that we must turn to the resurrection. What he finds in the resurrection enables him to hold ontology, history, and eschatology together, without conflation.

Ratzinger oscillates between which aspect, history or ontology, has preeminence. It is not clear what his final position is, but we know that ontology and history engage and affect one another (without conflation). Ratzinger focuses so intently on this complex relation that it appears as if eschatology is forgotten or at least relegated to a lesser position. However, this is not the case. Ratzinger places eschatology under the umbrella of ontology:

> Eschatology is not necessarily bound to any philosophy of history but only to ontology.... Its pivotal point is not a scenario for the rest of history but a concept of God that becomes concrete in Christology. The absorption [*Aufnahme*] of eschatology into Christology which occurred in principle with the decision to believe in Christ, means that it was also absorbed [*Hineinnahme*] into the concept of God and that the apocalyptic pattern of the theology of history retreated into the background. This new location of eschatology within the theological system is surely the central reason why its thrust could be combined with the tradition of Platonic thought.[131]

Jesus is the kingdom. Quoting Origen, Christ "is *hēautobasileia*, 'the Kingdom in person' [*das Reich in Person*]."[132] Eschatology concerns Christ's being, ontology. The "apocalyptic pattern of history" refers to a philosophy of history in which all time is conceived as part of a mappable and understandable historical evolution that emphasizes an imminent end. Ratzinger argues that eschatology should not be about history, in as much as it is about personal relations. For him, "God's Kingdom is an event [*Geschehen*], not a sphere."[133] This event is the total person of Jesus. The personal element does not, however, simply slide into a Bultmannian existentialism. The ontological emphasis on the person of Christ does not allow for it. But what does the "ontologizing" of eschatology actually do for Ratzinger's schema, besides avoid Bultmann's position? Without lessening the import of history, it places the eschaton into the hands of God, rather than into the hands of humankind, and the emphasis is placed on participation, rather than on liberation. Furthermore, it emphasizes the personal reality that undergirds all reality: the *Logos*. Even time itself, as we shall see, must be understood in personal terms.

The Eucharist

The same concerns listed above—ontology, history, eschatology, and relationality—are seen in Ratzinger's theology of the Eucharist. Here are two examples from *Die sacramentale Begründung christlicher Existenz*:

---

131. Ratzinger, *Joseph Ratzinger in Communio*, 1:20. See Ratzinger, *Eschatology*, 34–35.
132. Ratzinger, *Eschatology*, 34.
133. Ratzinger, *Eschatology*, 35.

If it were only about the solitary soul, as individual, being addressed by its God and receiving mercy (*or grace: *Gnade*), then indeed it would be impossible to see what, in this highly intimate, totally internal and spiritual process, the intervention of the Church and the material media of the sacraments could actually mean. If, however, there is no such thing as the autonomy of the human mind, if it is not a relationshipless mental atom (*Geistatom*), but rather, as a human being, lives only in an incarnated and historical way, with other human beings, then the question poses itself in a fundamentally different way.[134]

Thus, praying in church and in the vicinity of the Eucharistic sacrament means that we are situating our relationship to God in the mystery of the Church as the concrete locus where God meets us. And this is ultimately the meaning of going to church: situating my self in God's history with humankind, where alone I have my true human existence as a human being, and which therefore opens up for the true space for my encounter with God's eternal love.[135]

The rejection of the autonomous individual, the historical situatedness of human existence and "God's eternal love" address the ontological, historical, and relational concerns. In *The Spirit of the Liturgy*, Ratzinger includes the eschatological in his conception of the Eucharist: "The Blessed Sacrament contains a dynamism, which has the goal of transforming mankind and the world into the New Heaven and New Earth, into the unity of the risen Body."[136] A few pages later, he writes, "The New Jerusalem is anticipated in the humble species of bread."[137] Nevertheless, eschatology is the least mentioned concern in Ratzinger's writings on the Eucharist. In *God Is Near Us: The Eucharist, the Heart of Life*, Ratzinger concludes with an article titled "My Joy Is to Be in Thy Presence: On the Christian Belief in Eternal Life." Prior to this article, eschatology hardly makes an appearance in the book. With this in mind, there are two points I want to make. First, as already covered, ontology, history, eschatology, and relationality are important for Ratzinger's eucharistic theology. The fact that ontology and history are important notions for this area of Ratzinger's theology demonstrate the point I made at the outset of this chapter: the

---

134. Ratzinger, *Ratzinger Reader*, 76–77. The German terms in parentheses are the editors' notes.

135. Ratzinger, *Ratzinger Reader*, 78.

136. Ratzinger, *Spirit of the Liturgy*, 87.

137. Ratzinger, *Spirit of the Liturgy*, 90.

pairing of ontology and history performs a similar task for Ratzinger as eschatological symbolism does for Schmemann. Second, it should not be surprising that eschatology, particularly in reference to the kingdom, is not a dominant theme in Ratzinger's theology. Again, in Ratzinger's theology, eschatology falls under Christology. What lies ahead in the (not) distant future is less important than the relationship with the eternal that takes place in the present.

Time, History, and Eternity

God is not simply the bottomless abyss or infinite height that sustains all things but never itself enters the sphere of the finite. God is not simply infinite distance; he is also infinite nearness. One can confide in him and speak to him: he hears and sees and loves. Although he is not within time, he has time: even for me.[138]

We have looked briefly at what eschatology is, in what ways eschatology informs Ratzinger's theology of creation, and how Ratzinger holds together ontology, history, and eschatology. With the last construal, history was contrasted with ontology. This could be recounted in various ways: becoming was contrasted with being, discontinuity was contrasted with continuity, event was contrasted with permanence. What was not explicated is Ratzinger's understanding of temporality. According to Ratzinger, temporality finds meaning in relation to what is eternal. Here, we return to Ratzinger's relational Christology, for eternity and eternal life can be understood only in light of a God who actively loves.

Three Senses of Time

Ratzinger writes about cosmic time, biological time, and time as history.[139] Under the umbrella of cosmic time, we have solar time, in which the earth orbits around the sun and gives the rhythm of time: night and day and the seasons. Likewise, there is lunar time, the moon's rotation around the earth. Both rhythms are used to measure our existence. Alongside this is biological time, an organic rhythm of time, as seen in plants, trees, and humans. With biological time, each entity has its own individual time,

---

138. Ratzinger, *Dogma and Preaching*, 121.
139. See Ratzinger, "End of Time," 5–7; Ratzinger, *Spirit of the Liturgy*, 93–94.

the span from birth to death.[140] Like the other senses of time, cosmic time is also concerned with beginnings and endings (e.g., the big bang or questions concerning the sun's death). But, with all senses of time, we must ask, "How is an end to be conceived? Simply as extinction, defeat, ruin, death—paralleling the death of the individual or a culture's dying out?"[141] Or, like the life of an individual, is there some sort of underlying continuation (e.g., for ill or good, I am influenced by the lives of my ancestors). Is it proper to make time anthropocentric by paralleling time with the experience of human death? It is clear that humans are part of both biological time and cosmic time, but is this relatedness two-sided, or does the cosmos ultimately remain unaffected by the human person and our history? The answers to the questions depend upon how we understand time as movement.

Two Modes of Movement

"Please, Aslan," said Lucy, "what do you call soon?" "I call all times soon," said Aslan. . . . "Come," said the Magician. "All times may be soon to Aslan; but in my home all hungry times are one o'clock."[142]

With all three senses, time concerns movement. Ratzinger argues that there are two modes of movement: physical movement and heart or spirit movement.[143] Ratzinger also refers to the second mode as anthropological time, and he maintains that it can be understood only through Augustine's notion of *memoria*-time. We shall return to the second sense of movement in the next section. The first mode is taken from Aristotle's vision of time. According to Ratzinger, for Aristotle, time is nothing but movement (physical), whereas eternity is defined by non-movement (nonphysical). This approach has seeped into various theologies, and, in light of Aristotle's vision, it has been advocated "that temporality is connected to bodiliness, and that as a consequence the movement of human beings from life into death is at the same time a movement out of time and into non-time."[144] The move from temporal to nontemporal means

---

140. Ratzinger, *Spirit of the Liturgy*, 93.
141. Ratzinger, "End of Time," 6.
142. Lewis, *Voyage of Dawn Treader*, 139.
143. Ratzinger, "End of Time," 10.
144. Ratzinger, "End of Time," 8.

that, in death (physical time), one moves into the realm of non-time where history is already fulfilled. Ratzinger points out the absurdity of this conclusion: "The end of history has nothing to do with history itself."[145] For "in this way history as time could placidly keep on going, while on the other side, history is always already fulfilled."[146] Ratzinger argues that such dualism is unintelligible; time as physical movement is insufficient. There are two important points to highlight. First, Ratzinger desires a concept of time that preserves the importance of temporality. Second, his understanding of time is tied to the "last things."

Eternity and Anthropological Time

Time is not simply physical movement but incorporates movement of the heart or spirit—anthropological time.[147] Anthropological time can be understood only in relation to eternity and the eternal entering into time. Therefore, in order to understand anthropological time, we must understand eternity. There are three important aspects of eternity in Ratzinger's work. First, eternity is dominion over time. Second, eternal life is a quality of existence woven into the fabric of time. Third, eternity exists at the core of human experience. All three aspects hinge upon relationality and the import of history.

I. Eternity as Dominion over Time

Contrary to Aristotle, Ratzinger maintains that eternity is not equivalent with non-time. Aristotle's view does not square with the account of the eternity of the Christian God, the God who establishes a covenant and enters into human history. Ratzinger writes, "God's eternity is not mere time-lessness, the negation of time, but a power over time that is really present with time and in time."[148] The conclusive manifestation of this is the incarnation, in which the eternal God and temporal human unite.

---

145. Ratzinger, "End of Time," 10.

146. Ratzinger, "End of Time," 9. See Ratzinger, *Joseph Ratzinger in Communio*, 2:8.

147. Thomas Rausch acutely expresses this sense of time with his paraphrase of Johann Baptist Metz's "dangerous memory": "Jesus frees us from the grip of evolutionary or chronological time, interpreted as a history of triumph and conquest." Interestingly, Rausch points out the similarity between Ratzinger and Metz's sense of temporality (Rausch, *Eschatology, Liturgy, and Christology*, 126).

148. Ratzinger, *Spirit of the Liturgy*, 92. See Ratzinger, "End of Time," 11.

For "in Jesus we temporal beings can speak to the temporal one, our contemporary; but in him, who with us is time, we simultaneously make contact with the Eternal One, because with us Jesus is time, and with God he is eternity."[149] Ratzinger pastorally notes that "God is not the prisoner of his eternity: in Jesus he has time—for us, and Jesus is thus in actual fact 'the throne of grace' to which at any time we can 'with confidence draw near' (Heb 4:16)."[150]

In less pastoral terms, eternity is not to be understood as antithetical to time but as the "place" where past, present, and future meet.[151] It is where the human experience of time takes on its definitive form. We shall return to anthropological time; for now, it is enough to say that, in death, the human person does not enter into timelessness but into the fullness of time. Thus, those who have died and gone to be with Christ are not at the end of history. They, like us, wait for history to conclude. In other words, eternity does not subsume and destroy history. This cannot be overemphasized. For Ratzinger, history cannot be belittled, because it is in the temporality of human existence that one forges relationships. These relationships are laden with eternal value, which is clearly demonstrated in Jesus. The Son of God entered time in order to restore the broken relationship between God and humankind (*ipso facto*, human relations). The relationship he redeemed two thousand years ago—in history—continues on infinitely; love endures. Likewise, the love (or lack thereof) in our relationships continues forth in history until judgment day. To disparage history by placing its end outside of history is to diminish the greatness of love and to ignore the relational reality of existence itself. To state the obvious, God does not exist in eternity; he is eternal, and all who exist with him participate in his eternality;[152] he is love, and love is relational. Therefore, the God of love can never be the timeless god of Aristotle. The eternality of God who is relation holds time together.

---

149. Ratzinger, *Introduction to Christianity*, 317.
150. Ratzinger, *Introduction to Christianity*, 318.
151. Ratzinger, *Spirit of the Liturgy*, 60.
152. Ratzinger, *God Is Near Us*, 132.

II. Eternity as a Quality of Existence

According to Ratzinger, eternal life is not life with endless duration.[153] This would be the case only if one understood timelessness in relation to physical time. Ratzinger describes eternal life as "a new quality of existence, in which everything flows together into the 'now' of love, into that new quality of being that is freed from the fragmentation of existence in the accelerating flight of moments."[154] The "new quality of being" stems from participation in God. If we focus on the self, eternal life withdraws, but if we exit the self and turn our gaze to God, we share in his eternity.[155] With this in mind, Ratzinger can coherently write about the interpenetration of time and eternity. We can experience, albeit in a fragmentary way, eternal life in the midst of earthly life. Whenever or wherever we accept the will of God and live in the midst of truth, love, and justice, we encounter the eternal Holy City of the new Jerusalem.

Eternal life transforms us from within and liberates us from subjective isolation. In Christ, our will and our gaze joins the Father's. When our will joins God's, we are brought into his good will for all, and we find ourselves looking toward all others; eternity dissolves individualism. All who participate in God participate in his all in all, and "that is why the purely private existence of the isolated self no long exists, but 'all that is mine is yours.'"[156] This is why Ratzinger sees the presence of eternity in the flowering of justice, truth, and love. In a slightly cryptic manner, Ratzinger argues that, in eternity, "the mutual impermeability of I and thou can no longer exist, as this is closely associated with the fragmentation of time."[157] What he means is that without the quality of eternity, each person is locked within his own present—whether that be the recollection of the past or thoughts of the future—and thereby separated from the other.

Ratzinger contrasts this eschatological vision of eternal life with utopia, implicitly pointing out the failings of Marxism. The Christian vision of eternal life, argues Ratzinger, does not alienate us from this life.

---

153. Ratzinger wittily notes that if eternal life was life with endless duration, we would be faced with the challenge of overcoming eternal boredom! (Ratzinger, *God Is Near Us*, 137).

154. Ratzinger, *God Is Near Us*, 137.

155. Ratzinger, *God Is Near Us*, 132.

156. Ratzinger, *God Is Near Us*, 145.

157. Ratzinger, *God Is Near Us*, 143.

Eternal life is not a wish-fulfilling opiate. In fact, it is quite the opposite. It is the political utopias that estrange us from real life. Political utopian visions are oriented toward the future, the future that is always out of reach.[158] Ratzinger compares these political visions to the myth of Tantalus; whereas Christian eschatology is a hope that, because it is eternal, is a present reality:

> For the Kingdom of God is much closer than the Tantalus-fruit of utopia because it is not a chronological future, does not come chronologically later, but refers at all times to the wholly other, which for that very reason is able to embed itself within time, so as simply to take it up within itself and make of it pure presence. Eternal life, which takes its beginning in communion with God here and now, seizes this here and now and takes it up within the great expanse of true reality, which is no longer fragmented by the stream of time.[159]

In summary, eternal life is a life lived in participation with God. It is a life that dissolves the isolated self. It is experienced in the present wherever God's will is accepted, for that is where truth, love, and justice come to be.[160] Eternity is not simply an end toward which to strive but is the reality of the wholly Other who transforms this time into the time of love. Ratzinger writes, "His 'I am' is not only the present reality of God; it is also his constancy. In every transition he is present; yesterday, today, tomorrow. Eternity is not the past. It is this absolute reliability and constancy that always bears us up."[161] Thus, God's eternity in time defragments time, giving it constancy. Eternity is where the historical fragmentation of love, truth, and justice is made complete. To live in this mode of existence (eternal life) is to live in the porosity of reality where the *I* is also always a *we* (*Sein-mit-anderen*).

III. Eternity as Anthropological

The experience of eternity in the midst of time is what was referred to above as anthropological time. As a corporeal being, the human person

---

158. Here we can see the inspiration of Joseph Pieper. See Pieper, *Hope and History*, 89–90.

159. Ratzinger, *God Is Near Us*, 143.

160. Ratzinger, *God Is Near Us*, 143.

161. Ratzinger, *God of Jesus Christ*, 22.

lives within a measurable course of time, biological and cosmic time. Concurrently, the human person is spirit, and thus she participates in the movement of the spirit. This is why Ratzinger claims that human history is a specific form of time that incorporates the "organic and the spiritual-intellectual."[162] In *Eschatology*, he writes that "a human being lives in time not just physically but anthropologically."[163] This leads to two important aspects of Ratzinger's thought. First, eternity is best understood in light of memory: *memoria*-time. This way of understanding eternity gives form to the notion of time as the movement of the spirit. Second, in conjunction with the first point, time is anthropocentric.

Ratzinger avers that the distinction between physical time and time as humanly experienced is the fundamental insight on which Augustine hits with his writings on memory. To be clear, as physical creatures, we cannot separate ourselves from physical time, for even our intellectual decisions are connected with the body and can be dated. Nevertheless, physical time is insufficient. One's experience of the present is not completely based on the calendar

> but much more by his mental attention [*der Spannung des Geistes*], the section of reality which he grasps as present, as effectively Now. To this present belong his hopes and fears, that is, what is chronologically future, as well as his fidelity and gratitude, what is chronologically past. "The present" in this sense is a strictly human phenomenon, differing from one human being to another (in different human beings different "presents" intersect); physical time has only moments. Augustine tried to designate this specifically human phenomenon by the term "memory" [*Gedächtnis*].[164]

Determined by my decisions, memory unites the chronological past and future with my present. Ratzinger highlights that such time, *memoria*-time, does not share in the constancy nor in the irreversibility of physical time. Human acts are unique in that they cannot be repeated (physical time), yet, at the same time, they persist (*memoria*-time). For example, within physical time, I cannot literally repeat my wedding (what would I do with my children?); on the other hand, I can, in an act of recall, make certain elements of my wedding present. Within the constructs of pure

---

162. Ratzinger, *Spirit of the Liturgy*, 93.
163. Ratzinger, *Eschatology*, 184.
164. Ratzinger, *Joseph Ratzinger in Communio*, 2:7.

physical time, my wedding has come and gone and does not perdure. However, within *memoria*-time, what occurred at my wedding continues forth and is not simply a moot point concerning the past. Ratzinger argues, "Love in its very essence endures, truth, once discovered, abides; my human experiences are a real part of my living self. Present consciousness, which is able to summon what is past into the present of recollection, thus makes possible some notion of what 'eternity' is."[165] Since eternity is experienced anthropologically (*memoria*-time), it is not in opposition to temporality. Eternity is not the exact opposite of human time but its fulfillment.

There is one other element already alluded to that should be noted. That is, temporality is relational:

> Man is temporal as a traveller along the way of knowing and loving, decaying and maturing. His specific temporality also derives from his relationality—from the fact that he becomes himself only in being with others [*Sein-mit-anderen*] and being towards others. Entering upon love, or indeed refusing love, binds one to another person and so to the temporality of that person, his "before" and "after." The fabric of shared humanity is a fabric of shared temporality.[166]

The temporality of human relations has a before and an after, in that I am affected by another's existence. All persons are affected by relationships, and so, for example, there is a before I met my wife and an after. Ratzinger uses the term *temporality* not to highlight the ephemeral but, rather, the relational: "Time characterizes man in his humanity," for his temporality "derives from his relationality—from the fact that he becomes himself only in being with others and being towards others."[167]

Memoria-time is connected to the world and its corporeality, along with the temporality of relations. Nevertheless, Ratzinger makes clear that *memoria*-time "is not wholly tied to that world nor can it be dissolved into it."[168] When we step out of this world and this life (*bios*), *memoria*-time is separated from physical time and enters eternity. Since *memoria*-time comes with us, so to speak, it highlights the import of

---

165. Ratzinger, *Joseph Ratzinger in Communio*, 2:8. See Ratzinger, *Principles of Catholic Theology*, 22–25.

166. Ratzinger, *Eschatology*, 183–84.

167. Ratzinger, *Eschatology*, 183.

168. Ratzinger, *Eschatology*, 184.

the actions of this life and our need of purification. To put it differently, *memoria*-time enables us to recognize continuity between this life and life everlasting. Most importantly, and what was noted in the section on "Eternity as Dominion over Time," the temporality and relationality of *memoria*-time preserves the significance of ongoing history, even when my history is concluded, i.e., death. To come at this from another angle, if eternity is like *memoria*-time, then it is best understood as the perfect present and not the negation of time; and thus salvation history continues until Christ's return, when history shall conclude. Even in death, I will not lose my relation with history. Relationality belongs to my very essence as a person in *memoria*-time.

There is an "indestructible relation . . . between human life and history."[169] This is shown to us on the deepest level with Christ's incarnation where "in the man Jesus God has bound himself permanently to human history."[170] Poetically, Ratzinger writes, "The God whom we come to know in Christ's cross . . . for him, history is so real that it leads him down to Sheol, so real that heaven can be really and truly heaven only when it forms the canopy of a new earth."[171] There are two ways in which one is connected to history after death: by guilt or by love. The ripple effects of my life that continue to cause pain and suffering also continue to affect me; the guilt is part of me and binds me to time. Unlike guilt, love is not bound to time. Like guilt, love is in relation to time—but only because it is open to time and relationships. Ratzinger argues that "the nature of love is always to be 'for' someone. Love cannot, then, close itself against others or be without them so long as time, and with it suffering, is real."[172] Ultimately, it is love that overcomes guilt and frees us from the bondage of time, for it is God (who is love and is the ultimate *for*)[173] who, through the Son, brings the kingdom into our midst.

Memoria-time not only reveals something about eternity but also about the human person. We live life in the midst of physical time and *memoria*-time, and this is unique to us. We know that time shapes us, but do we shape time? How does time relate to eternity? Ratzinger avers that "cosmic time, which is determined by the sun, becomes a representation

---

169. Ratzinger, *Eschatology*, 187.
170. Ratzinger, *Eschatology*, 187.
171. Ratzinger, *Eschatology*, 189.
172. Ratzinger, *Eschatology*, 188.
173. Ratzinger, *Truth and Tolerance*, 258.

of human time and of historical time, which moves toward the union of God and world, of history and the universe, of matter and spirit—in a word, toward the New City whose light is God himself. Thus time becomes eternity, and eternity is imparted in time."[174] It is important to note the direction of logic. Historical time does not move into cosmic time but the inverse. In fact, Ratzinger clearly states that "the historical does not serve the cosmic; no, the cosmic serves the historical. Only in history is the cosmos given its centre and goal. To believe in the Incarnation means to be bound to Christianity's origins, their particularity, and, in human terms, their contingency."[175] Since eternity entered the world through the incarnation, and presently through us in our participation in Christ, the cosmos is anthropocentric (*"Der Mensch steht über der Zeit, ja, die Zeit existiert nur in ihm und durch ihn."*).[176] For it is through our history, salvation history—the story of God's love for us—that the cosmos is given meaning and is brought into union with God. In line with this, we can say that eschatology makes our human experience of time history, for without the end and the *telos*, time is just a successive series of endless movement.

History

THE REDEEMER OF MAN, Jesus Christ, is the centre of the universe and of history.[177]

The eschatological dimension of history as previously expounded does not complete Ratzinger's understanding of history. We have seen how eschatology folds into Christology, and this hints at the answer. Ratzinger argues that the *Logos* is at the center and end of history, an idea he takes

---

174. Ratzinger, *Spirit of the Liturgy*, 94.

175. Ratzinger, *Spirit of the Liturgy*, 104. Clearly, history in this context is *Heilsgeschichte*.

176. In English, it reads, "Man stands over time, yes, time exists only in him and through him" (Ratzinger, *Offenbarungsverständnis und Geschichtstheologie Bonaventuras*, 736). Ratzinger sets Augustine's anthropological time in stark contrast to Aristotle's notion of time, in which humans are subordinate to cosmic time. This is seen in the context of the previous German citation: "Man darf also mit Recht von einem durchaus anthropologischen Zeitbegriff sprechen, der sich in denkbar scharfem Gegensatz zu dem des Aristoteles befindet: Der Mensch steht über der Zeit, ja, die Zeit existiert nur in ihm und durch ihn" (Ratzinger, *Offenbarungsverständnis und Geschichtstheologie Bonaventuras*, 736).

177. John Paul II, *Redemptor Hominis*.

from Bonaventure's theology of history. Bonaventure applies the concept of Christ as mediator to time and states that "the 'fullness of time' is simultaneously the 'center of time.'"[178] The pattern of *exitus et reditus* is the basic pattern of history (Bonaventure uses the terms *egressus* and *regressus*). Like the church fathers, Bonaventure, and Ratzinger in his wake, sees the pattern of history as a mirror of God's relationship with the human person; the human person is a microcosm of the cosmos.

Ratzinger holds to a relational account of history. Since the *Logos* is both the center and the end, "the fulfillment of history," as Christopher Collins puts it, "comes not when the 'end of the line' is reached, but when *love* comes to fruition and prevails in the hearts and lives of the people to whom this love has been offered from the person of Christ."[179] Collins, interestingly and for good reason, hesitates to use the language of *end*. "Christ as *Center*, not *End*, of History" is the subtitle for the section just quoted. Yet, Ratzinger, explaining Pope John Paul II's use of "the fullness of times," asserts

> that Christ brings the decisive milestone into world history itself and that, in the uncertainties of history, which are becoming ever more dramatic, he remains not only the departure but also the destination. Oriented to him, we are on our way to an end. An end that is not simply destruction but is consummation, which brings history to an inner totality.[180]

Here Ratzinger clearly describes the end as consummation, and this validates Collins's point and his use of the term *fulfillment*. At the same time, the quotation reveals that there is a place for speaking of Christ as the end of history. What Collins helpfully clarifies is that history has not ended with the Christ event. Collins explains that "the 'end,' or better the fulfillment, of history happens when the extension of the Word made flesh in history becomes 'all in all' (1 Cor 15:28)—when love is all that remains (1 Cor 13:13)."[181] In Ratzinger's words,

> we can say, as a matter of fact, that the actual meaning of history is being announced to us here. In the breakthrough from the world to God, everything that went before and everything that followed afterward is given its proper significance as the great

---

178. Ratzinger, *Theology of History*, 110.
179. Collins, *Word Made Love*, 31.
180. Ratzinger and Seewald, *Salt of the Earth*, 277–78 (italics added).
181. Collins, *Word Made Love*, 31.

movement of the cosmos is drawn into the process of deification, into a return to the state from which it originated.[182]

Ratzinger's vision of history is both circular and linear and matches the way he describes Bonaventure's view in terms of a spiral. Bonaventure recognizes the unique and unrepeatable character of history (linear) alongside the notion of *egressus* and *regressus* (circular).[183] The spiral incorporates both. The most important point to be taken from this image is that Ratzinger does not divide history into a before and after (exactly what happens if time is understood in a strict linear fashion). He argues,

> God has not divided history into a light and a dark one. He has not divided people into those who are redeemed and those he has forgotten. There is only one, indivisible history, and it is characterized as a whole by the weakness and wretchedness of man, and as a whole it stands beneath the merciful love of God, who constantly surrounds and supports this history.[184]

Ratzinger maintains that this undivided view of history was held by Christians in the first millennium of Christianity. The view in which history is divided into a before and after Christ is a thirteenth-century development prompted by Joachim of Fiore.[185] In this remarkably insightful little book, *What It Means to Be a Christian: Three Sermons*, Ratzinger persuasively argues that "Advent is our present, our reality."[186] The liturgical celebration of Advent is therefore not a reminder of the past but of our present. The meaning of the term itself, as Ratzinger explains, makes this clear: "It [Advent] is a translation of the Greek word *parousia*, which means 'presence' or, more accurately, 'arrival,' that is, the beginning of a presence... the presence begun."[187]

Finally, Ratzinger writes that exodus is "the fundamental rule of salvation history," which once again highlights history as relational. God loved and chose Israel not simply for Israel's sake but for the sake of the world. Israel was called to step outside of its own interests in order to bless

---

182. Ratzinger, *What It Means*, 53.
183. Ratzinger, *Theology of History*, 147.
184. Ratzinger, *What It Means*, 35.
185. See note in Ratzinger, *What It Means*, 35–36.
186. Ratzinger, *What It Means*, 18. This is counter to Jean Daniélou who holds a position closer to Schmemann's (Daniélou, "Conception of History").
187. Ratzinger, *Dogma and Preaching*, 321.

the surrounding nations. God calls the church and each of her members to do likewise. Ratzinger avers that

> everything is intended to express this one basic movement of freeing oneself from existing merely for one's own sake. Christ the Lord expressed it most profoundly in the rule about the grain of wheat, which shows, at the same time, that this fundamental law sets its mark, not only on the whole of history, but, even before that, on the whole of God's creation.[188]

As the *Logos* stands at the center of history, the church, the body of Christ, is called to do the same. We are called to share in the *ekstatic* love of Christ, so that we can share in his love for the world and participate in the underlying movement of history.

In conclusion, relationality is the key to understanding Ratzinger's conception of history. Linear constructions of time place God too far from the central workings of history, and, as a result, history becomes impersonal. Even if we introduce a Platonic image of God into the linear construct, in which God hovers over history and history is the moving image of eternity, we are still confronted with an image of creation that is not inbuilt with *reditus*. Without this relationship between God and the world, deistic tendencies slip into view.[189] This is the direction to which Schmemann's conception of time dangerously leads. We shall look at this in greater detail in the next section and in the following chapter. The other danger of a linear conception of time is that it easily allows for a Marxist reading of history, in which history is our making—Ratzinger's apprehension about liberation theology.

Since the *Logos* is at the center of history, we can say that salvation history is the real history of this world. In other words, salvation history is not just one form of history amid other alternatives. With this in mind, we can say that Jesus is the end of history (see section "Jesus: The End of All Partial Salvation Histories"); Christ reveals that all other forms of (sal-vation) history are "nonhistory and nonsalvation."[190] Nevertheless, these ersatz forms of history continue to exist. The church as the body of Christ is to repeatedly draw the world out from the inward gazing forms of such

---

188. Ratzinger, *What It Means*, 57–58.

189. In a discussion with Johann Baptist Metz, Ratzinger said that "there is some-thing of the *deist* hidden deep down in all of us: We no longer envision God as a subject who is really active in history" (Metz and Ratzinger, "God, Sin, and Suffering," 50 [italics added]).

190. Ratzinger, *Principles of Catholic Theology*, 156.

history into the love of Christ, true salvation history. But, as Vatican II made clear, the church herself is on the way (eschatologically oriented toward the day in which God will be all in all). She does not reach back from a static position into the midst of "nonhistory." Instead, as the living and dynamic church, she journeys upon the *Logos's* established paths, and, as a shepherd, she gathers sheep along the way, as she looks toward the coming of the Lord. Here the language of *end* in relation with *center* is helpful. With this dynamic view of the church in mind, "the Church is not a rounded-off and finished reality, defined once and for all and thus something beyond time and space. Rather, in its real essence the Church remains a Church on the way and represents in itself the history of God's dealing with mankind."[191]

The Historical or Ahistorical Church? Ratzinger contra Schmemann

Ratzinger's conception of the dynamic church goes against Schmemann's vision of the church. According to Schmemann, salvation history is complete:

> The philosophy of history seeks to discover the significance of the historical process, its teleology,—and in this sense, the only real pattern of a philosophy of history is the sacred history of the Old Testament, the history of Salvation, "Heilsgeschichte," wholly moving towards its own fulfillment, to the Incarnation of the Son of God. And this history was fulfilled. "But when the fullness of the time was come, God sent forth His Son" (Gal IV.–4).[192]

For Schmemann, history ended with Christ; whereas, for Ratzinger, all other histories have ended or reached their conclusion, but salvation history continues, as it awaits for the day when all that is left is love.[193] History, in Schmemann's conception, is divided into the old and the new aeons, with Christ sitting between the two aeons. These overlap in the life of the church; the church is in the world but of the kingdom.[194] In con-

191. Ratzinger, *Theological Highlights*, 75.
192. Schmemann, "'Unity,' 'Division,' 'Reunion,'" 248.
193. Schmemann writes, "From the point of view of Heilsgeschichte the Church has no history, it is already in statu patriae, and is always the actualization of it fullness of salvation accomplished by Christ ἅπαξ—once for all" (Schmemann, "'Unity,' 'Division,' 'Reunion,'" 248).
194. See Schmemann, "Ecclesiological Notes."

trast, according to Ratzinger, there is no before and after; we still live in Advent. History is still the arena for the dialogical movement of *reditus*, in which God lovingly draws us home. It is the indivisible movement with which God has actively engaged since creation (*exitus*) and in which he continues to engage through the church.[195]

The deficiency inherent to Schmemann's position is twofold and concerns the pervasiveness of evil and the conflation of the church with the kingdom. By dividing history into two halves, one is reasonably forced to make one of two arguments concerning the problem of evil. First, the world has drastically improved since Christ's coming. David Bentley Hart makes an argument akin to this (excluding the word *drastically*), and does so in a nuanced and convincing manner. However, even Hart admits that we still live in a broken world: humans have always killed each other and will continue to do so.[196] The Christian revolution is far more subtle than it is revolutionary. Second, according to Schmemann's position, the new eon is beyond this world and remains detached from this world that continues to run amuck. He argues that, since the world rejected Christ, the world cannot be the place of Christ's kingdom.[197] Thus, the old remains broken, and it is only in the new that Christ is really present. Nevertheless, Schmemann and Ratzinger agree that the kingdom breaks into our world in various ways (e.g., church, sacraments, Christians, etc.), but it is not equivalent with our world, and, as a result, neither theologian succumbs to an over-realized eschatology. Yet, with Schmemann's position, which highlights the radical nature of Christ's breaking into history, we are left with the lingering question that leads back to the first argument: if God radically came into time and divided history into before and after

---

195. Ratzinger writes, "It is an eschatology of the present that John [in the Gospel of John] has developed. It does not abandon the expectation of a definitive coming that will change the world, but it shows that the interim time is not empty: it is marked by the *adventus medius*, the middle coming, of which Bernard speaks. This anticipatory presence is an essential element in Christian eschatology, in Christian life. . . . The 'middle coming' takes place in a great variety of ways. The Lord comes through his word; he comes in the sacraments, especially in the most Holy Eucharist; he comes into my life through words or events. Yet he also comes in ways that change the world. The ministry of the two great figures Francis and Dominic in the twelfth and thirteenth centuries was one way in which *Christ entered anew into history*, communicating his word and his love with fresh vigor" (Ratzinger, *Jesus of Nazareth*, 291 [italics added]).

196. Hart, *Atheist Delusions*. On the positive side, Hart maintains that Christianity revolutionized morality (e.g., compassion for others who are outside of one's family, social standing, or nationality).

197. See Schmemann, *Liturgy and Tradition*, 78.

Christ, would not history bear evidence of his healing wounds in an obvious way? Schmemann argues that this is not the case; this world remains unaltered. It is only the baptized, those who are dead to this world, who are transformed. They are transformed by dying to this world and being lifted up into the kingdom through the church and her sacraments. Thus, there is a strong sense that the Christian person truly is an alien resident, one who constantly transcends this world. In this fashion, this world is altered only in that it becomes a little brighter from all Christ's shining saints who reflect the glow of the banquet table from which they partake. This light reveals the way, the way to the new eon. In this sense, the second argument falls back into the first argument (the world has improved). In fact, if Schmemann's approach did not fold into the first argument, it would destroy one of his main emphases: Christianity is for the life of the world. But what fails about the first argument? Simply put, the subtle changes of the Christian revolution seem to be outweighed by the atrocities of world history. That is not to say that the subtle changes are not noticeable, but, as Ratzinger notes,

> if we are honest, we will no longer be able to paint things black and white, dividing up both history and maps in zones of salvation and iniquity. History as a whole, and mankind as a whole, will appear to us rather as a mass of gray, in which time and again there appear flickers of that goodness which can never quite be extinguished, in which, time and again, men set out toward something better, but in which also, time and again, collapses occur into all the horrors of evil.[198]

Since Ratzinger's account of history is not divided into a before and after Christ, it is more adept at facing the realities of evil than Schmemann's account. For Ratzinger, it is clear that we still live in Advent, expectantly waiting for Christ's return, when history will truly end. Therefore, it is not surprising that, on the one hand, we can see historical transformation since the birth of Jesus and the founding of his church,[199] for God has always supported and surrounded history; we can point to his great works in the same manner as the Jews (e.g., the exodus of the Israelites). On the other hand, evil persists, often overshadowing that God has walked

---

198. Ratzinger, *What It Means*, 17–18.

199. For a brief list of these consequences of the "Christian Revolution," see Ratzinger, *Dogma and Preaching*, 224–26.

among us (e.g., the Israelites soon went back into exile, and false teachers arose alongside the establishment of the church).

The second problem, the conflation of church and kingdom, follows the same logic as the first. Schmemann's understanding of the church as the coming together of heaven and earth emphasizes the static reality of the church. The church, as the body of Christ, *lifts up* the world and so unites it with heaven. The direction is always heavenwards, *ascending* over *descending*. With this upward directionality, the church does not participate in history beyond acting as a passage out of history. Schmemann argues that "the Body of Christ can never be 'part' of this world, for Christ has ascended into heaven and his Kingdom is Heaven."[200] Thus, the church is only herself (i.e., the body of Christ) when she is lifted out of the world by the Spirit, and here the church is the kingdom (her static reality). This is why Schmemann argues that the church is not a means to an end but is the end.[201]

Can Schmemann distinguish between the kingdom and the church? Schmemann was certainly aware of corruption in the Orthodox Church,[202] but how can he reconcile the corruption of the church with the kingdom, which is her reality? Essentially, he must make a clear distinction between the church as institution and the church as the body of Christ. As institution, the church constantly needs to *transcend* itself (upward directionality) in order to be the body of Christ. It is as if the church is less of a historical participant than a bystander who repeatedly attempts to leave history. Of course, for Schmemann, it is through leaving *and* returning that the church has anything to offer the world—anagogy. He maintains that the church does not abandon the world, but, rather, she sheds light on the world. Nevertheless, there is a relational gap between the old and the new and between the church and the world.

In contrast with Schmemann, Ratzinger's conception of history means that the church is anything but a bystander. The church is in the thick of history. She does not reach back from a static point of non-history, but, rather, she represents salvation history—God's working in the midst of history. The *Logos* continues to act in the world, wooing it to return home. Thus, the church gets her hands dirty as she crawls through the muck of history, dragging the world with her as she heads

---

200. Schmemann, *Liturgy and Tradition*, 78.
201. Schmemann, *Liturgy and Tradition*, 80.
202. Schmemann, "Church Is Hierarchal."

home. In this sense, Ratzinger does not need to divide the church in two in order to preserve her purity, for she is not beyond history. With the *Logos*, she moves in the midst of history toward her future, and, "if the Church means the journey of mankind together with its God, if it is essentially incomplete and always short of its goal, then it is still the sinful Church continually in need of renovation.... It is a Church in continual need of God's forgiving kindness."[203] With Ratzinger's view of history, the church is not conflated with the fullness of the kingdom, and therefore, he does not need to, metaphorically speaking, jump through so many hoops in order to explain the nature of the church, as Schmemann must. Furthermore, he provides an image of the church that shares in the historical challenges of human life; whereas Schmemann's image is one of a church that is set far away from the ins and outs of human contingencies.

Conclusion: The Eternal Reality of Today

> When human life is lived with Jesus it steps into the "time of Jesus": that is, into love, which transforms time and opens up eternity.[204]

It is worth noting that, in Ratzinger's corpus, questions of time are often found within the existential context of death[205] or liturgy.[206] The assumption in all of his writings on time is that to speak about time is to immediately be drawn into the question of God, and such a question cannot exist merely in the abstract. For "the way we are able to understand time depends on the way we see God, on a 'yes' or 'no' to God."[207] The context of death (the last things) highlights God's relationality and how this is mirrored by time's relation to eternity.

There are three senses of time—cosmic, biological, and historical—and humans live in the midst of all three. Temporality involves two forms

---

203. Ratzinger, *Theological Highlights*, 77. Ratzinger writes that "the Church, precisely as a sinful society, is the expression of the Divine Mercy, of God's solidarity with sinners.... The Church is by nature 'paradoxical,' dimorphic, a mixture of failings and blessings" (Ratzinger, *Dogma and Preaching*, 223).

204. Ratzinger, *Eschatology*, 160.

205. For example, Ratzinger, "Beyond Death," in *Joseph Ratzinger in Communio*, 2:1–16; "My Joy Is to Be in Thy Presence," in Ratzinger, *God Is Near Us*, 130–48; Ratzinger, *Eschatology*.

206. For example, part 2 of Ratzinger, *Spirit of the Liturgy*; "What Corpus Christi Means to Me," in Ratzinger, *Feast of Faith*, 127–37.

207. Ratzinger, "End of Time," 25.

of movement: physical movement and movement of the spirit. The cosmos and *bios* are time's physical movement. History, on the other hand, takes place within the sphere of physical time and can be dated; yet, at the same time, it involves movement of the spirit, since it is centered on the eternal (Christ) and involves humans. Primarily, all time is in relation to eternity, as physical time finds its meaning in what is eternal.

Since God is love and therefore relational, eternity is not conceived as timelessness but as dominion over time, in which the fragmentation of the three tenses of time come together in the presentness of God. Eternity does not simply concern time in the abstract. It has to do with a quality of existence, in which eternal life is experienced in the midst of time. The presence of eternity in time abolishes the isolated self and opens the door to authentic I-Thou relationships. Where eternal life enters time, we encounter justice, truth, and love.

Eternity is anthropological, in that our natural human experience of time speaks of the reality of eternity. The human experience of the present involves one's mental attention, in which one chooses which section of reality to be the present—*memoria*-time. Here, we see the overcoming of the fragmentation of past, present, and future; thus, *memoria*-time is a glimpse of eternity. With *memoria*-time, the irrevocability and unrepeatability of physical time is overcome. Therefore, time lingers; it perdures and creates a relational web of connection that carries on into the hereafter.

Behind all of Ratzinger's musings on eternity, time, and history are two interwoven concerns: history and relationship. History cannot be overshadowed by an easy eschatological triumphalism nor by a conception of eternity in which history is already over (eternity as timelessness). Time as history is important because it is where relationships are developed, either for good or for bad. The *we* of human existence gathered in God's all in all means that relationships bind us to history, either in love or in guilt. Eternity will continue to pervade history until history comes to its fulfillment. With the end of history, time as physical movement will end and *memoria*-time will be made complete. In other words, eternity makes time definite, for the human experience of the temporal in memory comes to fruition in eternity: the eternal reality of *today*.

Conclusion

It is clear from the outset that Ratzinger desires to preserve the whole breadth of Christian teaching on eschatology. The kingdom of God and the last things are natural bedfellows, with the latter growing out of the former; the last things grew out of the same hope that undergirded the early church's emphasis on the kingdom of God. Both are held together in Christ and his personal engagement with the world; eschatology must be understood in light of Christ. What this means is that relationality informs Ratzinger's eschatology and not the inverse; relationality precedes eschatology. Perhaps this is most apparent when seen in contrast with Schmemann. Eschatology is the engine that drives Schmemann's theology,[208] and this creates problems for his account of temporality: the Christian must constantly leave the old and ascend to the new. Consequently, he has a static view of the church, in which it remains outside of history; whereas, for Ratzinger, relationality or dialogical theology[209] is the key for understanding eschatology. This preserves the import of this world and allows for a dynamic relational ecclesiology.

In Ratzinger's doctrine of creation, the concepts *exitus et reditus* and creation and covenant are also imbued with a relational emphasis. Humankind was created for relationship, and the underlying structure of the cosmos—the *Logos*—is love. We fell out of relationship and were unable to return on our own (our side of the relationship/dialogue). On that account, the Son came as the Good Shepherd and carried us back into relationship with God, the end we were created for. But *end* does not refer merely to the furthermost part of chronology. In the deepest sense, end refers to fulfillment, and we reach our fulfillment in relationship with Christ. Eschatology does not rupture creation but is the movement of return (*reditus*). Eschatology and creation are two aspects of the unbroken movement from *exitus* to *reditus*.

Ratzinger grounds his Christology in the resurrection, and this enables him to balance ontology with salvation history and eschatology. By holding these together, he preserves the ethical, historical, and personal dimension of faith and avoids falling into a theology of glory, gnosticism, or existentialism (faith as *pro me*). Furthermore, this safeguards relationality and the import of history, which go hand in hand. This is reiterated

---

208. "While rereading my articles, I realized that 'theologically,' I have one idea—the eschatological content of Christianity" (Schmemann, *Journals*, 174).

209. Collins, *Word Made Love*, 55.

with Ratzinger's depiction of time and eternity. Since temporality is where relationships are developed, time is of great importance. Eternity, like time, is relational and must therefore take account of history; if it did not, it would belittle relationality. Thus, eternity is not non-time. Eternity is the dominion over time, in which time and relationships are no longer fragmented by past, present, and future. Eternity makes definite the human experience of time as *memoria*-time, where past and future are held together in the present. Here, we participate in God's eternal gaze and are no longer separated by the isolation of our own present, for we are in God's present. To put it differently, eternal life is a quality of existence, in which true relationality is present.

Since eschatology is all about Christ—he is the kingdom—Ratzinger concludes that eschatology folds into ontology. As a result, in Ratzinger's theology, eschatology per se is often eclipsed by Christology: eschatology is the shadow cast by Christ. In Ratzinger's *Eschatology*, every aspect of eschatology takes shape in relation to Christ and his inherent relationality (Father, Son, and Holy Ghost), in which we partake. In the next chapter, we shall continue to look at eschatology, particularly Ratzinger's notion of purgatory and the immortality of the soul, and how these are based on an anthropology that is rooted firmly in Christology and its relationality. The analysis of the human person as a historical person in chapter 4 will confirm the relational reading of eschatology that has been established in this chapter.

4

Ratzinger and Personhood: "Beyond the Self"

God has become man so that men might become like God. In the last analysis, following Christ is nothing other than man's becoming man by integration into the humanity of God.

—JOSEPH RATZINGER

To understand just one life, you have to swallow the world.

—SALMAN RUSHDIE

THE PREVIOUS CHAPTER EXPLORED the thoroughly relational nature of eschatology and time. In this chapter, we shall continue to explore this theme but in regard to personhood. Christology is the cornerstone of Ratzinger's theological notion of person. This provides the relational basis for understanding identity, enabling Ratzinger's conception to go beyond Buber's I-Thou to an I-Thou-We relationship. In light of this relational identity, and in continuity with how death was perceived in the Old Testament and Christian antiquity, Ratzinger argues for the traditional understanding of the soul and its immortality. In other words, the soul is the Christian outworking of a personal understanding of reality given to us in and by Christ, and it enables Ratzinger to preserve the importance of temporality. Finally, according to Ratzinger, ontology and history run through the center of the human person, and we see this in the human conscience. As both ontological and historical, Ratzinger's vision of the person goes beyond essentialism and anti-essentialism.

The True Adam: Fully Man and Fully God

Ratzinger's view of the human person is christological, and there are three parts to his Christology that highlight the relational focus of his work: (1) Christ as *Logos*, (2) Christ as Son, and (3) Christ incarnate. Each part touches on a different aspect. Christ as *Logos* provides the cosmic context for relationship. Christ as Son is, so to speak, the metaphysical underpinning, the deepest mystery of reality that holds together the context along with the meaning of person. Lastly, Christ's incarnation reveals the human person as she is meant to be: the human person who relationally fits within both the cosmic context and the triune mystery.

Christ as *Logos*

With the proclamation of the gospel, the early church sought points of contact with philosophy and not religion.[1] It saw in Greek philosophy a self-criticalness of its own culture, a prioritizing of truth over established tradition, and a metaphysics of being that could fit with the Old Testament recognition of God as the ground of all being. The early church opted for *logos* over mythical religion.[2] Nevertheless, the God of the philosophers needed "baptizing" in order to represent the God who is Trinity. Ratzinger summarizes the differences with two points.

First, the God of philosophy is "essentially self-centred";[3] it simply contemplates itself. In contrast, the Christian God is best understood as relational. He is not locked within himself but is "involvement, creative power, which creates and bears and loves other things."[4] Second, the

---

1. Ratzinger, *Truth and Tolerance*, 197–202; Ratzinger, *Introduction to Christianity*, 137–50.
2. Ratzinger, *Introduction to Christianity*, 138.
3. Ratzinger, *Introduction to Christianity*, 147.
4. Ratzinger, *Introduction to Christianity*, 148.

God of philosophy is pure thought, whereas the Christian God is also love. Therefore, Christianity affirmed that thought and love are divine, and the two are identical in God.

The "I believe in God" of the Creed implies that the objective mind of the universe is the product of a subjective mind. The *Logos* that undergirds all reality is personal and loving. Consequently, it is

> an option for the primacy of the particular as against the universal. The highest is not the most universal but, precisely, the particular, and the Christian faith is thus above all also the option for man as the irreducible, infinity-oriented being. And here once again it is the option for the primacy of freedom as against the primacy of some cosmic necessity or natural law.[5]

Reflecting on the nature of prayer, Ratzinger makes similar claims. He writes, "To pray is put oneself on the side of this love-causality, this causality of freedom, in opposition to the power of necessity."[6] Ratzinger's method of knowing—prayer—highlights another aspect: Christianity is the true philosophy. Why? It asks the deepest questions, and, even more importantly, it involves a true encounter with the *Logos* himself.[7] In prayer, one participates and encounters the *Logos* and, in so doing, goes beyond what Plato ever imagined was possible.

In summary, the early church sided with Greek philosophy's language of truth over and against religion and culture. At the same time, it redefined the Greek notion of *logos*, in which the ground of all being is person and love. In light of this, Ratzinger concludes that the personal fabric of reality elevates both the particular above the universal and freedom over necessity. Lawrence Cunningham expresses this aspect of Ratzinger's theology (the mystery of Christ) as the creative tension between "the truth of the Eternal Logos and the Logos made flesh."[8] In Jesus Christ, the particular and the universal and the historic and the eternal come together. In other words, Christ, as *Logos*, reveals the deeply personal reality that is the context of the cosmos.

---

5. Ratzinger, *Introduction to Christianity*, 158.
6. Ratzinger, *Feast of Faith*, 32.
7. See Ratzinger, *Nature and Mission*, 13–29.
8. Cunningham, "Reflections," 150.

Christ as Son

Only Christ can hold together and unify the whole; when we speak of Christ, we must, of course, always see the trinitarian mystery in the background....

The Christocentric emphasis, is as such, always a trinitarian emphasis.[9]

Recognition of the Trinitarian mystery in the early church occurred through familiarity with Christ.[10] It is a mystery of relations, a mystery revealed in prayer. This section focuses on sonship, but to speak of sonship, one must speak of the Father and the Holy Spirit. We shall begin with Ratzinger's engagement with the definition of God as one being in three persons. Subsequently, we shall move to Christology proper and look at three aspects of Ratzinger's "spiritual Christology."[11]

Tertullian gave the West its formula for expressing the Trinity: one being in three persons (*una substantia—tres personae*). Ratzinger claims that "it was here that the word 'person' entered intellectual history for the first time with its full weight,"[12] even though the implications of this formulation took centuries to ripen. Ratzinger unpacks the meaning of the word *person* by looking at the Greek word *prosopon* (the Latin equivalent of *persona*). His explanation is similar to Zizioulas's description in *Being as Communion*,[13] except that Ratzinger follows what he calls "prosopographic exegesis"[14] through Western thinkers, beginning with Justin Martyr. In brief, Ratzinger avers that *prosopon* originally meant *role*; it referred to an actor's mask, and "prosopographic exegesis" is

> a form of interpretation developed already by the literary scholars of Antiquity. The ancient scholars noticed that in order to give dramatic life to events, the great poets of Antiquity did not simply narrate these events, but allowed persons to make their appearance and to speak. For example, they placed words in the mouths of divine figures and the drama progresses through

---

9. Ratzinger, *On the Way*, 132.
10. Ratzinger and Seewald, *God and the World*, 267.
11 Ratzinger, *Behold the Pierced One*, 9.
12. Ratzinger, *Joseph Ratzinger in Communio*, 2:104.
13. See ch. 1, §1, "From Mask to Person: The Birth of an Ontology of Personhood," in Zizioulas, *Being as Communion*.
14. Ratzinger gets this term from the Göttingen historian Carl Anderson (Ratzinger, *Joseph Ratzinger in Communio*, 2:104-5).

these words. In other words, the poet creates the artistic device of roles through which the action can be depicted in dialogue.[15]

The fathers engaged with the various scriptural dialogues utilizing this method:

> In their reading of Scripture, the Christian writers came upon something quite similar. They found that, here too, events progress in dialogue. They found, above all, the peculiar fact that God speaks in the plural or speaks with himself (e.g., "Let us make man in our image and likeness," or God's statement in Genesis 3, "Adam has become like one of us," or Psalm 110, "The Lord said to my Lord," which the Greek Fathers take to be a conversation between God and his Son). The Fathers approach this fact, namely, that God is introduced in the plural as speaking with himself, by means of prosopographic exegesis, which thereby takes on new meaning.[16]

Justin records that "'the sacred writer introduces different *prosopa*, different roles.'"[17] However, since potentiality does not exist in God, only pure act (*actus purus*), it means that, in the life of God, roles take on a new reality, dialogical realities. Justin argues that "'when you hear that the prophets make statements as if a person were speaking (*hos apo prosopou*), then do not suppose that they were spoken immediately by those filled with the spirit (i.e., the prophets), but rather by the *Logos* who moves them.'" Ratzinger points out that, for Justin, the *role* exists. It is "the face, the person of the *Logos* who truly speaks here and *joins* in dialogue with the prophet."[18]

Ratzinger returns to Tertullian's later works and quotes him at length to demonstrate that Tertullian came to realize the intra-relational aspect of personhood. Tertullian noted the oddity of the plural form that God gives himself, along with the seeming self-talk. With this, Tertullian apprehended the dialogical distinctions within the Trinity. Following from this, Ratzinger concludes that the concept of person came out of biblical reflection and that it came to be understood in light of divine dialogue.

---

15. Ratzinger, *Joseph Ratzinger in Communio*, 2:105.

16. Ratzinger, *Joseph Ratzinger in Communio*, 2:105.

17. Ratzinger, *Joseph Ratzinger in Communio*, 2:105. The quotations from Justin Martyr Ratzinger takes from Andresen, "Zur Entstehung."

18. Ratzinger, *Joseph Ratzinger in Communio*, 2:106.

By the time of Augustine and the late patristic period, Ratzinger notes, the notion of person reaches its maturity, and the divine persons are understood as pure relations: "In God, person is the pure relativity of being turned toward the other; it does not lie on the level of substance—the substance is *one*—but on the level of dialogical reality, of relationality toward the other."[19] Augustine recognizes that there is nothing accidental in God, only substance and relation. Unfortunately, Augustine poorly translates his insights on the divine persons into the human realm. Augustine "projected the divine persons into the interior life of the human person and affirmed that intra-psychic processes correspond to these persons. The person as a whole, by contrast, corresponds to the divine substance."[20] Thus, for Augustine, humans remain at the level of substance rather than relations.[21] The notion of person as relation remained, in large part, dormant, and the Greek philosophical category of substance persisted as the dominant approach for understanding person. Yet, the seed of person as relation was planted, and it is this that Ratzinger seeks to water.

There are three important principles that Ratzinger extracts from Tertullian's formula. First, God is beyond the division of unity and plurality. He encompasses both. God is three persons who are perfectly united in love. The unity of love is stronger and truer than a unity of substance (e.g., the atom). Second, the profession of God as person includes God as relation, since there is no person in the singular. Ratzinger contends that "the Greek word *prosopon* means literally 'look toward'; with the prefix *pros* (toward), it includes the notion of relatedness as an integral part of itself. It is the same with the Latin *persona* = 'sounding through'; again, the *per* = 'through . . . to' expresses relatedness, this time in the form of communication through speech."[22] The Latin definition, with the notion of "*sounding* through" is particularly expressive of Ratzinger's argument that God is not simply *logos* but "*dia-logos*." That is, God is "not only idea and meaning but speech and word in the reciprocal exchanges of

---

19. Ratzinger, *Joseph Ratzinger in Communio*, 2:108.

20. Ratzinger, *Joseph Ratzinger in Communio*, 2:111.

21. Matthew Drever makes some interesting arguments about Augustine's understanding of the relational dependence of humans on God by turning to the distinction of *de nihilo* and *ex nihilo*—a sort of ontological prioritizing of subsistence before substance. See ch. 3 in Drever, *Image, Identity, and Forming*.

22. Ratzinger, *Introduction to Christianity*, 180.

partners in conversation."[23] The Son is literally Word, in the sense of speech that expresses his relationship with the Father and with us. One caveat: Ratzinger makes clear that such divine relatedness takes us way beyond the anthropomorphic vision of God. "God infinitely exceeds the human kind of personality."[24] Third, Tertullian's formula emphasizes the primacy of relation, the absoluteness of the relative. Ratzinger describes the Trinitarian unity as "a unity that takes its being from the dialogue of love."[25] This Christian understanding of *dia-logos* rent the Greek category of substance and accident: relation is substance and not accident, and thus relation is equally a primordial form of being.[26] Therefore, Ratzinger argues,

> In its nature, the person does not generate in the sense that the act of generating a Son is added to the already complete person, but the person is the deed of generating, of giving itself, of streaming itself forth. The person is identical with this act of self-donation.
>
> One could thus define the first person as self-donation in fruitful knowledge and love; it is not the one who gives himself, in whom the act of self-donation is found, but is this self-donation, pure reality of act.... In God, person is the pure relativity of being turned toward the other, it does not lie on the level of substance—the substance is one—but on the level of dialogical reality, of relationality toward the other.[27]

We can see two important aspects to which we shall return: the priority of the personal over the natural and freedom over determinacy. That is, God as three persons freely exists and freely acts. He is not a necessary substance that is internally and eternally imprisoned within himself; he is free and freely gives himself. These Trinitarian realities are, so to speak, the Image that our image reflects, the *imago Dei*.[28]

---

23. Ratzinger, *Introduction to Christianity*, 183.

24. Ratzinger, *Introduction to Christianity*, 183. Walter Kasper succinctly states this as "the divine persons are not less dialogical but infinitely more dialogical than human persons are" (Kasper, *God of Jesus Christ*, 290).

25. Ratzinger and Seewald, *God and the World*, 267.

26. Ratzinger, *Introduction to Christianity*, 183.

27. Ratzinger, *Joseph Ratzinger in Communio*, 2:108.

28. See Ratzinger, *God of Jesus Christ*, 30–31; Ratzinger, *Called to Communion*, 115–16.

Having explored the definition of God as one being in three persons, let us turn to Christology proper. Ratzinger's spiritual Christology was inspired by his reading of the Third Council of Constantinople (681), the Council that completes the Christology of Chalcedon. In light of the Third Council of Constantinople, Ratzinger sets out seven christological theses.[29] For the purpose of this chapter, we shall look at only three of the theses. Peter John McGregor helpfully denominates the theses by subject rather than number.[30] The three theses at which we shall look he calls filial, personal, and volitional. We shall look at the volitional thesis in the following section ("Christ Incarnate"), since it specifically concerns the nature of the incarnation.

The filial thesis is the foundation of Ratzinger's Christology. Ratzinger claims that the center and life of Jesus is his communication (as Son) with the Father. Over *Christ* and *Lord*, *Son* is the comprehensive Christian title of who Jesus is: "It both comprises and interprets everything else."[31] Christ is used in the context of Jesus's death (emphasizing the human side), and "'Lord' designates Jesus as Ruler of the Universe and, in particular, as the Lord who gathers his Church about him."[32] Fundamentally, it concerns Jesus's cultic and eschatological manifestations. What these two titles fail to encapsulate is the unity of God—"There is *one* Lord" (1 Cor 8:6). The death of Christ has no meaning without the resurrection, so the two come together and are subsumed under the title Son. Why does Son take priority? Simply because it brings everything back to God and, ultimately, the Trinity. Ratzinger bases his conclusion on Heb 10:5, in which the incarnation takes place in dialogue/prayer between the Father and the Son: "Consequently, when Christ came into the world, he said, 'Sacrifices and offerings thou hast not desired, but a body hast thou prepared for me'" (Heb 10:5). Ratzinger avers that "Incarnation is acceptance by Father and Son in word—in a dialogue in the Spirit—of the body 'prepared' for the Cross."[33] In the statement of sonship, Lord and Christ coalesce.

The sonship of Jesus does not undo the historical emphasis and fall into the metaphysical errors of later Christianity, as Oscar Cullmann

---

29. Ratzinger, *Behold the Pierced One*, 13–46.
30. McGregor, "Spiritual Christology," 65.
31. Ratzinger, *Behold the Pierced One*, 16.
32. Ratzinger, *Principles of Catholic Theology*, 19.
33. Ratzinger, *Principles of Catholic Theology*, 20.

claims.³⁴ In contradistinction, Ratzinger argues that Son represents the historical eyewitness of Jesus's followers (e.g., "You are the Christ, the Son of the living God" [Matt 16:16]). His followers witness that the root of Jesus's life is prayer. We see this particularly in Luke's Gospel. Luke "shows that the essential events of Jesus' activity proceeded from the core of his personality and that this core was his dialogue with the Father."³⁵ Ratzinger provides three examples.³⁶ First, the calling of the twelve (Luke 6:12–17), in which Jesus "inaugurates the 'People of God' in a new way, i.e., their calling is to be seen theologically as the beginning of all that is 'Church,'" and occurs chronologically after Jesus's nocturnal prayer to the Father. Ratzinger concludes, "The Church is born in that prayer in which Jesus gives himself back into the Father's hands and the Father commits everything to the Son."³⁷

Second, the origin of the Christian confession pronounced by Peter—"'But who do you say that I am?' And Peter answered, 'The Christ of God'" (Luke 9:20)—is set in the context of prayer: "Now it happened that as he was *praying* alone, the disciples were with him" (Luke 9:18).³⁸ Ratzinger points out the connection of Peter's confession with the Petrine office: "The confession of faith in Jesus and the unity of the Church, are inseparably linked together with Peter and centered on him."³⁹ Most importantly, Peter recognizes who Jesus is in the context of prayer. By witnessing Jesus's communication with the Father, Peter perceives Jesus's sonship. Ratzinger claims that Jesus's identity is seen only in his communication with the Father.

Third, the transfiguration reveals Jesus's identity in the midst of prayer. Peter, John, and James witness that Jesus shares in the radiance of the Father. In the transfiguration, what occurs in prayer between the Father and the Son is made visible. This reveals the meaning of the Old

---

34. Ratzinger, *Principles of Catholic Theology*, 20–21.

35. Ratzinger, *Behold the Pierced One*, 17–18.

36. Ratzinger first developed this in *The God of Jesus Christ* (1976), but he provides only two examples from Luke. Written eight years later, *Behold the Pierced One* sets out three Lukan examples.

37. Ratzinger, *Behold the Pierced One*, 18.

38. Ratzinger points out that the oddity of this sentence (the disciples were with him while he was alone) reveals that Luke was not writing history but theology. "Those who do not know the solitude of Jesus take him to be this or that; but the profession of faith translates into human language what Jesus really is, since it sees what truly 'drives' him, namely, his solitary speaking with the Father" (Ratzinger, *God of Jesus Christ*, 82).

39. Ratzinger, *Behold the Pierced One*, 18.

Testament and, for that matter, all of history. Turning to the Gospel of Mark (9:1), Ratzinger points out that "the Transfiguration is a kind of anticipation of Resurrection and parousia."[40] In the transfiguration, we see that Jesus could not be overcome by death because of his communication with the Father. Hoping to denigrate the transfiguration, some scholars have claimed that the resurrection narrative is written retrospectively into the earthly life of Jesus. Ratzinger creatively turns this on its head and claims,

> It is possible for the Father to permit an appearance in the glory that radiates forth from himself even before the Resurrection, since the inner foundation of the Resurrection is already present in the earthly Jesus, that is, the immersion of the core of his existence in his dialogue with the Father, an immersion that is also the glory of the Son and is indeed the very form his sonship takes. His Passion and death would then mean that his entire earthly existence, too, is poured out into the total dialogue of love, where the fire of love transforms it.[41]

Once again, the emphasis on the Son concerns dialogue and highlights the centrality of relations in Ratzinger's work.

Ratzinger's emphasis on relations comes into even greater focus when put in contrast with Schmemann's account of how Christ overcame death. For Schmemann, death could not swallow Christ, for he is life itself. In the victory of the resurrection, the true end, i.e., life, replaced the false end, death. Christ, by entering into our end (beings toward death), became our new end. Biological death is transformed into a passage that leads to Christ. It is clear that Schmemann works from within the language of ends and is grounded in a thoroughly teleological framework; *logos*, as in meaning, requires an end, whereas *logos*, for Ratzinger, is primarily understood as *dia-logos*. While time overshadows Schmemann's approach, relations grounds Ratzinger's. To be clear, Schmemann has a relational ontology, as we saw in his depiction of Christ's obedience, but he does not ground it in divine dialogue. Ratzinger emphasizes something akin to Schmemann's notion of obedience, but he uses dialogical terminology: "Jesus Christ is Yes."[42] "Act of obedience," in this sense, is ontological. Both theologians insist that Christ is his actions. For

---

40. Ratzinger, *Behold the Pierced One*, 20.
41. Ratzinger, *God of Jesus Christ*, 81–82.
42. Ratzinger, *Feast of Faith*, 27.

Schmemann, this means Christ is obedience, just like "Jesus Christ is Yes" for Ratzinger. The difference here is that obedience is unidirectional, whereas *yes*, a word, implies conversation/dialogue, which is bidirectional.[43] Broadly speaking, we could say that the unidirectional flow of obedience fits within Schmemann's teleological framework. Schmemann's priority of ends is distinct from Ratzinger's thoroughly relational vision.[44]

The personal thesis concerns epistemology, and the claim is that there must be similarities between the knower and the known—only like can know like (know *of*, not simply *about*). Ratzinger applies this to Christology. If the center of the Son's existence is prayer, then we can know the Son only in prayer. As already noted, this is prayer in the body of Christ, for only in the body can we say "*our* Father." Christ's prayer reveals two other principles: prayer is an act of self-surrender, and prayer is an act of love. Both principles are directed to God and fellow humans. Thus, when Ratzinger writes about prayer connecting us with the Son and the Father, it involves more than simply spending time on our knees. In summary, only in prayer (an act of love and self-surrender)—a deeply relational act—does one know Christ and the Father. By praying in fellowship with Christ we can say Abba, but "apart from the Son, the Father remains ambivalent and strange."[45] Likewise, as our understanding of *our* Father grows, so does our understanding of the Son. Prayer provides a foundation for a theological epistemology; "the person who prays begins to see; praying and seeing go together because—as Richard of St. Victor says—'Love is the faculty of seeing.'"[46] The personal thesis underscores relationality. Even human knowledge is relational; knowing involves loving.

Christ Incarnate

Christ is *the* human: *Ecce homo*. Pilate's pronouncement was far truer than he imagined. What was said in irony was taken up by the church in earnest. To conclude what was initiated in the previous section, we

43. See Ratzinger, *Christian Brotherhood*, 46.

44. For an article that emphasizes the similarities between Ratzinger's and Schmemann's relational ontology, see Kaethler, "Freedom in Relationship." In this article, I conclude that Schmemann and Ratzinger have remarkably similar views of human freedom because both of them have a relational ontology that enables them to ground freedom ontologically.

45. Ratzinger, *Feast of Faith*, 28.

46. Ratzinger, *Behold the Pierced One*, 27.

shall look at Ratzinger's volitional thesis. Inspired by the Third Council of Constantinople, this thesis gets at the heart of human and divine unity. It reveals that true union is communion, and such union is what makes us fully human.

In particular, it is the volitional thesis that grew out of Ratzinger's study of the Third Council of Constantinople. With Chalcedon, one is left with what Ratzinger calls "a certain parallelism of the two natures in Christ."[47] The unity in Christ was simply and insufficiently expressed as "one person." The Third Council of Constantinople addresses this more fully:

> On the one hand it teaches that the unity of God and man in Christ involves no amputation or reduction in any way of human nature. In conjoining himself to man, his creature, God does not violate or diminish him; in doing so, he brings him for the first time to his real fullness. On the other hand (and this is no less important), it abolishes all dualism or parallelism of the two natures, such as had always seemed necessary to safeguard Jesus' human freedom.[48]

In brief, the Council, according to Ratzinger, asserts that Jesus's human will is not absorbed into the divine will, but, rather, the human will follows the divine will. Ratzinger makes an important distinction concerning the notion of following. The human will of Jesus does not *naturally* follow the divine will; it *freely* follows the divine will. This stresses *personal* unity, over and above *natural* unity. Ratzinger argues that "this free unity—a form of unity created by love—is higher and more interior than a merely natural unity. It corresponds to the highest unity there is, namely, trinitarian unity."[49] Therefore, there is only one I in Christ. The human I completely surrenders and becomes one with the will of the *Logos*.

Maximus the Confessor illuminates this by referring to Jesus's prayer on the Mount of Olives: "not what I will, but what thou wilt" (Mark 14:36). Following Maximus's lead, Ratzinger explicates the prayer:

> Jesus' human will assimilates itself to the will of the Son. In doing this, he receives the Son's identity, i.e., the complete subordination of the I to the Thou, the self-giving and self-expropriation of the I to the Thou. This is the very essence of him who is pure relation and pure act. Wherever the I gives itself to the Thou,

---

47. Ratzinger, *Behold the Pierced One*, 37.
48. Ratzinger, *Behold the Pierced One*, 38.
49. Ratzinger, *Behold the Pierced One*, 39.

there is freedom because this involves the reception of the "form of God."[50]

Ratzinger also describes this coming from the other side. The *Logos* places his own I in this man and takes this man's human speech into the eternal Word, allowing man to join in his yes. This is not imprisoning for the human will but liberating. By joining with man, the *Logos* makes him divine. In Christ, "being with the other is realized radically."[51]

Anthropologically, this means that the more the human person transcends himself, the more he is himself.[52] By the joining of Jesus's human will with that of the *Logos*, we have the complete human person, Jesus Christ. Likewise, we, too, become complete by submitting and joining our yes with God's yes. This takes us back to the notion of *exitus et reditus*, in which we are called to step beyond the self and freely return home to God. The human person is called "to surpass himself and, thus, to come into his true authenticity."[53] By joining our yes with the Son's yes, we become, so to speak, part of the family as sons and daughters of God.

Ratzinger's engagement with the Third Council of Constantinople shows how the union of the incarnation is a union of freedom and love. It is not a natural union. If it were natural, it would not truly be a union but a subsuming, because it would be void of choice. This *personal* christological union mirrors the Trinitarian union: "The highest unity there is—the unity of God—is not the unity of unstructured, amorphous substance but unity by communion, a unity which both creates and is love."[54] This, too, is the union, analogically, into which we are called. We are called to participate in the life of God. Christ takes humanity into a new depth of union that goes beyond the Old Testament notion of covenant. In Christ, "the words of Sinai are heightened to a staggering realism, and at the same time we begin to see a totally unsuspected depth in them."[55] In God become man, the covenant is deepened. A new relationship is created, "a sacramental relationship."[56] Humans now, in the deepest sense, com-

---

50. Ratzinger, *Behold the Pierced One*, 41.

51. Ratzinger, *Joseph Ratzinger in Communio*, 2:116.

52. Ratzinger, *Joseph Ratzinger in Communio*, 2:115–16; Ratzinger, *Principles of Catholic Theology*, 345; Ratzinger, *In the Beginning*, 47–48.

53. Ratzinger, *Dogma and Preaching*, 155.

54. Ratzinger, *Behold the Pierced One*, 92.

55. Ratzinger, *Many Religions, One Covenant*, 60.

56. Ratzinger, *Many Religions, One Covenant*, 61.

mune with God. In addition, union as communion reflects the personal nature of freedom.[57] We are more than matter ("that which is thrown upon itself").[58] The human spirit is that which *is* and knows and has itself. It is its nature to put itself in relation. Thus, it knowingly and freely throws itself forward into relation and is never more itself.[59]

Identity

Where is one's identity located? Or, to put it differently, what is the self? Ratzinger's account of personhood could be misread as a dissolution of the self. After all, Ratzinger is opposed to the isolated self. In fact, according to his logic, the isolated self is a contradiction in terms, and there are three reasons for this. First, as a creature, the human self is contingent. The human person is the result of one's parents (biologically) and, fundamentally, is the result of God's original creative act. Second, in the day-to-day of life, we cannot subsist on our own; we depend upon a network of human relations. Even more elementally, the human person is sustained by God. Third, there is no instance, either on earth or in heaven, of the isolated self. God himself is in relation; God is not a purely egotistical being, for "the true God is, of his own nature, being-for (Father), being-from (Son), and being-with (Holy Spirit)."[60] Even death does not bring about an isolated self. "Death," argues Ratzinger, "is absolute loneliness. But the loneliness into which love can no longer advance is—hell."[61] It is only hell, the antithesis of life, in which an isolated self exists (mere existence).[62] Hell is the rejection of otherness. The Scottish writer George MacDonald worded this well: "The one principle of hell is—'I am my own!'"[63] From another angle, "eternal life steadily withdraws from a person whose attention is fixed on himself. In turning toward God it becomes obvious that anyone upon whom God has looked, and whom

---

57. Ratzinger, *Pilgrim Fellowship of Faith*, 81.

58. Ratzinger, *Joseph Ratzinger in Communio*, 2:115.

59. There are beautiful literary parallels to this found in George Bernanos's novels. See Kaethler, "I Become Thousand Men."

60. Ratzinger, *Truth and Tolerance*, 248.

61. Ratzinger, *Introduction to Christianity*, 301.

62. Even in this state of being, the shell of a human subsists by the mercy of God.

63. Lewis, *George MacDonald*, 103.

he loves, shares in his eternity."[64] One does not protect or increase the self by turning inward and closing off to otherness. The opposite is true. As we saw in the *Logos*, the Son, and the incarnation, relationality goes all the way down.

Therefore, self-growth and self-identity occur only by moving out from the self. I love myself and am myself when I love another (ultimately, God). While the one who only looks inward is caught in the destructive "anthropological circle,"[65] the one who affirms the other enters into a "healing circle, a circle of salvation."[66] This is most fully seen in Christ who gives to us the greatest affirmatory yes. In return, I am enabled to respond with a yes, Christ's yes and yet distinctly my own. For, in him, I have truly come to myself, my homecoming. While the anthropological circle ends in a flight from self, the circle of salvation expands and sets free the self. Christ's yes takes me out of myself and, in so doing, returns me to myself, for myself is found in Christ. Thus, my limited self (self without Christ) is set free and is greatly expanded in Christ, as it participates in his infinity. In short, human identity is found in Christ.

There are eschatological implications to our Christ-based identity, which Ratzinger highlights in an article titled "On Hope." At the outset of the article, Ratzinger claims that hope "is the very definition of Christian existence";[67] in fact, the opposite, the absence of hope, defines the atheist. This leads Ratzinger into confrontation with Ernst Bloch and Marx. Ratzinger out-narrates both thinkers by revealing the shortcomings of their definitions of hope, which he then counters with the Christian vision. We shall skip the details of the argument and move to the conclusion. For both Bloch and Marx, hope is the product of human activity.[68] Ratzinger finds this problematic, for doing and hoping are different activities, and, in the end, no matter what we accomplish, doing does not satisfy our hopes. Hope, so maintains Ratzinger, goes beyond human ability. He calls this the "anthropological problem of hope."[69]

What is hope—not just hopes but the one conclusive hope that lies beneath all other hopes? First, hope is part of our existence as persons in

64. Ratzinger, *God Is Near Us*, 132.
65. Ratzinger, *Yes of Jesus Christ*, 99.
66. Ratzinger, *Yes of Jesus Christ*, 104.
67. Ratzinger, *Joseph Ratzinger in Communio*, 2:28.
68. Ratzinger argues that such hope is based on the dynamic of progress. In contrast, Christian hope is a gift (Ratzinger, *Yes of Jesus Christ*, 47).
69. Ratzinger, *Joseph Ratzinger in Communio*, 2:32.

time: "It [hope] signifies that man expects of the future some joy, some happiness that he does not now have. Hope therefore rests on the experience of temporality according to which *man never totally possesses his own being. He is himself only within the tension between the past and the future as he passes through the present.*"[70] Ratzinger does not unpack the depths of this quotation, but the previous chapter, along with what has already been examined in this chapter, provide the necessary backdrop to make sense of it. The unknown future is an essential aspect of the human person. The present is the experience of the past or the future decided upon by the person (*memoria*-time). While we can be present in either the future or the past, the presentness of each tense is different. The past has happened, and thus we can hold to the past in a way that we cannot hold to the future, for the future remains a possibility. That is, part of my identity rests in what may be, in the possible.[71] Nevertheless, we are caught in the tension between both times. Even though my identity is based upon who I *was*, I cannot remain in what *was*. Similarly, my identity is caught up in what I *will* become, yet what *will* be is also beyond my grasp. I think this is the quandary at which Ratzinger is getting with the statement "man never totally possesses his own being." Since I cannot remain in any tense or, more accurately, I cannot *be*, my identity always remains beyond me. In addition to this quandary is the "anthropological problem of hope." Namely, the tense of hope (the future) remains temporally out of hand, and hope itself remains out of reach, in that it is disconnected from my own doing—I cannot achieve it. To adumbrate, hope is an essential aspect of our human reality as temporal beings. It is key to our identity and yet eludes us. Hope also highlights what was touched upon earlier, i.e., the human person finds herself by transcending herself. Second, hope is intimately connected to love. Ratzinger illustrates this by examining the opposite of hope, fear. We experience numerous fears in life, but there is one fear that undergirds all other fears. The greatest fear is losing love: "fear of an existence in which the little daily disturbances fill everything, without anything large and reassuring coming along to

---

70. Ratzinger, *Joseph Ratzinger in Communio*, 2:29 (italics added).

71. The possible is where Heidegger grounds the human person. His perceptions on the possible are insightful, and there are certainly points of contact between Ratzinger's and Heidegger's conception of becoming. However, Ratzinger's view of *memoria*-time essentially means that his conclusions are not simply based on the possibilities of the future.

keep the balance."[72] Ratzinger concludes that life without love is hopeless, and such a life is unbearable. Therefore, "if the fear that transcends all fears is in the last resort fear of losing love, then the hope which transcends all hopes is the assurance of being showered with the gift of a great love. One could then say that simple objects become hopes by taking on the coloration of love, by more or less resembling it, each according to its uniqueness."[73] The great gift of love is Christ. Ratzinger writes, "The goal of Christian hope is the kingdom of God, that is the union of world and man with God through an act of divine power and love."[74] If the opposite of hope is fear, and hope is the assurance of love, then it is clear, Ratzinger avers, why, anthropologically, "perfect love casts out fear" (1 John 4:18).

In summary, hope is based on something missing in the human condition; it highlights the provisional. Furthermore, hope is based on this human longing having a response and on the anticipation of what is to come. Ratzinger also maintains that "through hope, what is 'not yet' is already realized in our life [*dass durch die Hoffnung das, was 'noch nicht' ist, doch 'schon' in unser Leben hereinleuchtet*]. Only a certain kind of present can create the absolute confidence which is hope."[75] The kind of present to which he refers is that which is experienced in faith, the world known in relationship with Christ. Through "faith, hope has gotten a footing. The cry of waiting wrung from our being is not lost in the void. It finds a point of solid support to which we for our part must hold fast."[76] In other words, Christ is the substance of hope, and Christ is not only with us; he is also the one who comes to us. Or, to use kingdom language, the kingdom that awaits those hid with Christ in God also breaks into the present.

Let us return to the futurity of hope in order to highlight the eschatological element of hope. Ratzinger argues that the feast of the ascension best expresses our hope, for

> with Christ our substance abides in God. It is now going to be our concern to ground our daily life in our substance, not ignoring the substance of our very selves, not leaving our life outside

---

72. Ratzinger, *Joseph Ratzinger in Communio*, 2:30.
73. Ratzinger, *Joseph Ratzinger in Communio*, 2:30.
74. Ratzinger, *Yes of Jesus Christ*, 46.
75. Ratzinger, *Joseph Ratzinger in Communio*, 2:34. The English translation loses the potency of the German. See "Über die Hoffnung: Ihre spirituellen Grundlagen aus der Sicht Franziskanischer Theologie," in Ratzinger, *Auferstehung and ewiges Leben*, 418.
76. Ratzinger, *Joseph Ratzinger in Communio*, 2:34.

> its substance, not letting it sink into nothingness, chance, the accidental.... The hope that sustains us is that our substance is already in paradise. To live like someone who hopes is to have our life enter into reality itself, to live in and by the body of Christ.[77]

My identity is in Christ and with God; I am an eschatological being. But this is not the whole story, for I am still one who hopes. I move in the midst of history toward eschatological fulfillment, where, in a sense, I am already. I can hope for eschatological fulfillment because I already, albeit limitedly, experience the reality of it now.

Does this mean that my identity is bifurcated, with part of me "up there" and the other part "down here"? It could be construed this way, but not if we follow Ratzinger's logic. Accordingly, in Christ, my being begins to become more my own, for the future and the present have moments of coalescence. How does this work? To answer this, we need to return to the problem of temporality: "man never totally possesses his own being." The problem is that the past and the future always escape me. Thus, my identity is never really in my grasp. In contrast, if I am "hid with Christ in God," then my future (the kingdom, being united with God) is tied with my present, including the past, for I can *be* in Christ who *is being*. In other words, the Son *is*. He is not a *was* (past) nor a *will be* (future). He is eternal; past and future come together in his present. Hid with Christ, time no longer separates my being. There is one caveat: this life is a journey, and we are pilgrims. The good work that Christ began must be made complete.[78] Temporality still affects us and divides us, while eternity awaits us. We still participate in the physical movement of time, as well as the movement of the heart. Finally, there is an irony about the aforementioned quotation ("man never totally possesses his own being"). On the one hand, the quotation is concerned with the effects of time on the human person and can be seen as a negative statement. On the other hand, it is a positive claim: the human person only comes to *be* when she gives herself away. Truly, "man never totally possesses his own being," for possession and being are opposites. Being is in communion.

---

77. Ratzinger, *Joseph Ratzinger in Communio*, 2:36–37.
78. See Ratzinger and Seewald, *Salt of the Earth*, 100.

I-Thou-We

As a seminarian, Ratzinger was introduced to personalism by Theodor Steinbüchel, and, he narrates, it was "reiterated with renewed conviction in the great Jewish thinker Martin Buber. This encounter with personalism was for me a spiritual exercise that left an essential mark, especially since I spontaneously associated such personalism with the thought of Saint Augustine."[79] Buber's I-Thou (*Ich-Du*) notion entered and shaped Ratzinger's theology, but Ratzinger found it problematic and in need of conceptual baptism.

There are two basic and interrelated problems with the I-Thou concept. First, Ratzinger argues that it misconstrues God. God as pure Thou "conflicts with his nature as the ground of all being."[80] God becomes self-enclosed and is set too far away. This is particularly noticeable when we look at the I of the I-Thou concept. Ratzinger would ask, can there even be an I without God's Thou? The I-Thou concept "deprives God of his infinity and excludes each individual 'I' from the unity of being. By comparison with God, man's identity is not simply in himself but outside himself, which is why he can only attain it by 'transcendence.'"[81] Not only does this bring us back to the issue of identity and where it is located, but it also brings us back to the volitional thesis. If my identity is in Christ—in Thou—then the I-Thou dialectic breaks down: the I is not self-encapsulated. Likewise, the volitional thesis revealed to us the true union of communion: in the union of free love and obedience (communion), the man Jesus united his will with the *Logos*. Here the twoness remains (Chalcedon), yet within a profound unity, a profound oneness (Trinitarian logic). Such profound communion is also given to us in the nuptial mystery of the church. Ratzinger argues that Christ is so identified with the church that she is called his body. This mystery is embedded in the biblical concept of man and woman becoming one flesh in marriage, a beautiful example of both union in communion and twoness in oneness.[82]

79. Ratzinger, *Milestones*, 44.
80. Ratzinger, *Feast of Faith*, 30.
81. Ratzinger, *Feast of Faith*, 29. See Ratzinger, *Joseph Ratzinger in Communio*, 2:102.
82. Fergus Kerr is critical of the nuptial mystery, particularly since it reflects the "amnesic tendency" of the church. Those promoting nuptiality as the image of God seem to have forgotten all about Thomas's teachings, which underpinned the church for the last century. See Kerr, *Twentieth-Century Catholic Theologians*, 193–201. Kerr's

Second, according to Ratzinger, "it is impossible to start a conversation with Christ alone, cutting out the Church. A christological form of prayer which excludes the Church also excludes the Spirit and the human being himself."[83] To put it simply, the I-Thou notion is problematic because there is no *we*. As we have seen, reality is relational, God is relation, and we as the *imago Dei* are relational (*Sein-mit-anderen*). Human sin and brokenness sever relationships with both God and fellow humans.[84] Conversion, on the other hand, is the mending of our broken relationships. Ratzinger argues that, for St. Paul, conversion is the death of the I; it is an exchange of the old subject for another. The I ceases to be an autonomous subject standing in itself. It is snatched away from itself and fitted into a new subject. The I is not simply submerged, but it must really release its grip on itself in order then to receive itself anew, in and together with a greater I.[85] The "greater 'I'" is an I no longer imprisoned in subjectivity, in the Cartesian self.[86] Subjectivity is broken open with the breaking of bread. To participate in Christ is to be open to all and to be for the other (*Sein-für-die-Anderen*).[87] Ratzinger argues that Christ "is not only an example that is followed, but he is the integrating space in which the 'we' of human beings gathers itself toward the 'you' of God."[88] Therefore, Ratzinger concludes that "'the Body of Christ' means that all human beings are one organism, the destiny of the whole the proper destiny of each."[89] That is not to say there is no I but that the I is always known and judged in relation to the whole, to the we. Or, we could say,

---

comments and criticisms concerning the nuptial mystery are, in large part, based on *Letter of the Collaboration of Men and Women in the Church and in the World*, which was issued by the CDF in 2004 and signed by Cardinal Ratzinger. Interestingly, Ratzinger's nonofficial works have very little to say on the subject. For more on the nuptial image, ecclesiology, and the person, see Kaethler, "God Who Draws Near."

83. Ratzinger, *Feast of Faith*, 30.

84. *Catechism of Catholic Church*, 1849.

85. Ratzinger, *Nature and Mission*, 51.

86. Inspired by Xaver von Baader, Ratzinger rephrases Descartes's "I think, therefore I am" to "I am thought, therefore I am" (Ratzinger, *Introduction to Chrisianity*, 247).

87. Ratzinger, "Was ist der Mensch?," 48. Ratzinger writes, "Er [Christ] ist der, der seine Hoheit nicht dazu benützt, um für sich selbst dazusein, sondern um von sich wegzugehen und auf die anderen zuzugehen. Und darin kommt der Mensch in seine eigentliche Möglichkeit" (Ratzinger, "Was ist der Mensch?," 48).

88. Ratzinger, *Joseph Ratzinger in Communio*, 2:117.

89. Ratzinger, *Eschatology*, 190.

there is an I because there is a we. By being myself, I am in fellowship.[90] Desmond Tutu worded this beautifully: "My humanity is caught up, is inextricably bound up, in yours."[91] Like Tutu's *Ubuntu* theology, Ratzinger's personalism is not an I-Thou dichotomy, but an I-Thou-We relationship in which the hyphens unite rather than separate.

Immortality of the Soul: History, Resurrection, and Relationality

The most individual element in us—the only thing that belongs to us in the last analysis—our own "I," is at the same time the least individual element of all, for it is precisely our "I" that we have neither from ourselves nor for ourselves. The "I" is simultaneously what I have completely and what least of all belongs to me.[92]

The concept of the immortality of the soul plays an important role in Ratzinger's theology. Fully aware of the contemporary disdain for dualism, the context in which the soul has not fared well,[93] Ratzinger defends the traditional notion of the soul (not dualism per se). He claims that the immortality of the soul is a biblical concept that is based upon the dialogical character of existence and is not the residue of Greek metaphysics within Christianity. It is the underlying reasons motivating Ratzinger's defense of the immortality of the soul that are of particular interest to this project. Primarily, Ratzinger's argument for the immortality of the soul is christologically based and is formed in light of his high view of history. That is, the immortality of the soul is where we encounter Ratzinger's response to Heidegger's question of what it means to be a being in time or, in Christian terms, how eschatology shapes our personhood. In what follows, we will look at what happens in death prior to the last judgment, including purgatory.[94] This will lead us into other avenues of Ratzinger's

---

90. See Ratzinger, *Joseph Ratzinger in Communio*, 1:192; Ratzinger, *God Is Near Us*, 82.

91. Tutu, *No Future without Forgiveness*, 31.

92. Ratzinger, *Introduction to Christianity*, 190.

93. See Murphy, *Bodies and Souls*; Cullmann, *Immortality of the Soul*.

94. David H. Kelsey convincingly argues, "Hardly any other moment in life besides death provides a subject for theological reflection that brings to such clear focus the precise force of a theologian's anthropological proposals" (Kelsey, "Two Theologies of Death," 347).

thought, such as the relationship between body and soul, remembrance and personhood, temporality and relationality, and being and becoming.

The Soul

The immortality of the soul is often dismissed as an idea that arose out of Greek philosophy and is in contrast with the teachings of the New Testament. For example, Oscar Cullmann writes, "The concept of death and resurrection is anchored in the Christ-event . . . , and hence is incompatible with the Greek belief in immortality."[95] N. T. Wright provides an anecdote that reveals a similar attitude. He humorously recounts writing a letter to another professor, explaining that the soul obviously has nothing to do with the Old and New Testaments.[96] In such circles of thought, the immortality of the soul is passed over in favor of the resurrection of the body, as if the two are opposed. Beyond the all-too-often allergic reaction to anything Greek, there is concern that the account of the immortality of the soul suggests that immortality belongs naturally to humans "as opposed to the raising from the dead, which can only be effected by God, in other words, by sheer grace."[97] Is the immortal soul counter to the biblical witness? Does the immortality of the soul imply human self-sufficiency? Must belief in the resurrection of the body oppose belief in the immortal soul? Ratzinger does not see the two ideas as binary opposites, nor does he see the immortality of the soul as a Greek construct imposed upon the Bible. To make sense of this, we must comprehend how death is understood in both the Old and New Testament. In light of this understanding, Ratzinger argues that the concept of the soul is necessary to preserve the relational aspect of reality that is reflected in the biblical development of death and life hereafter. This touches upon the necessity of the soul to preserve identity after death and to retain the import of history.

Ratzinger highlights a number of Old Testament developments concerning death and sees a steady progression toward the Christian conception. He asserts that, in the early period of Jewish thought, the fullness of life consisted of a healthy, long life and progeny. It was through one's children that the Jews hoped to participate in the future of Israel and her promises. The bad events in life, such as premature death, were seen

---

95. Cullmann, *Immortality of the Soul*, 15.
96. Wright, "'Mind, Spirit, Soul.'"
97. Ratzinger, *Joseph Ratzinger in Communio*, 2:3.

as the result of one's actions, i.e., sin. Even though life concerned one's earthly reality, death was not the end of one's existence:

> The dead man goes down into Sheol, where he leads a kind of un-life among the shades. As a shade, he can make an appearance in the world above, and is thus perceived as dreadful and dangerous. Nonetheless, he is essentially cut off from the land of the living, from dear life, banished into a noncommunication zone where life is destroyed precisely because relationship is impossible. The full extent of Sheol's abyss of nothingness is seen from the fact that Yahweh is not there, nor is he praised there. In relation to him too, there is a complete lack of communication in Sheol. Death is thus an unending imprisonment. It is simultaneously being and nonbeing, somehow still existence and yet no longer life [Noch-Sein und doch Nicht-mehr-leben].[98]

Communication, relation, and praise are the key concepts in this quotation. Without these three central elements of life, the dead exist in a form of nonbeing, mere existence. Following this logic, it eventually became clear to the Jews that death cannot simply be a natural event (biological), although it is that as well: communication, relation (personal relationship), and praise do not fit in the category of biology. In consequence, "Israel developed a phenomenology of sickness and death wherein these things were interpreted as spiritual phenomena."[99]

The logic of this realization is twofold: death reaches into life, and life reaches into death. One can be the living dead, physically alive and yet relationally dead. He who cuts himself off from otherness, particularly divine Otherness, is hardly alive. The inverse is also true. A person who is dying (or, for that matter, already biologically dead) but is rich in relationships is more fully alive than the inverse. Divine communion is stronger than physical dying—so developed Jewish thought. Ratzinger traces the ups and downs of this development. In adumbration, wisdom literature remained uncertain about suffering and death (Job and Qoheleth), whereas exile literature recognized suffering and death as "areas" where God is present and concluded that Yahweh is stronger than Sheol.[100] It is clear that "communion with God [Gottesgemeinschaft] is true reality, and by comparison with it everything, no matter how massively it asserts itself, is a phantom, a nothing. . . . Communication is life, and its

---

98. Ratzinger, *Eschatology*, 80–81.
99. Ratzinger, *Eschatology*, 81.
100. Ratzinger cites Ps 16:7–11 and Ps 73.

absence is death. . . . Communication with God *is* reality. It is true reality, the really real, more real, even, than death itself."[101] Accordingly, as a result of this spiritual reflection, Israel's understanding of God grew, and, with this growth, Sheol could no longer be seen as a place beyond God's grasp. Likewise, death is not simply a physical event but a phenomenon that creeps into life, a reality based upon "non-communication" (*Kommunikationslosigkeit*) and "non-relation."

The resurrection is the central hub in which all notions of death in the New Testament coalesce. It pronounces that love is stronger than death; death does not have the last word. Thus, Ratzinger maintains that the New Testament does not bring anything new to what was developed in the Old Testament theology of death, but, rather, it pulls together and completes what was already laid out. In regard to the resurrection, Ratzinger writes,

> it is proof of what only immortality can create: being in the other who still stands when I have fallen apart. Man is a being who himself does not live forever but is necessarily delivered up to death. For him, since he has no continuance in himself, survival, from a purely human point of view, can only become possible through his continuing to exist in another.[102]

The Old Testament already highlighted the dependence humans have upon God and that it is divine communication that sustains us. In Christ (*dia-logos*), we have the God-man "who still stands" and sustains us. He conquers death, which "signifies the definitive and exclusive rule of God, the victory of life invincible, where the shadow of death cannot fall."[103] Christ extends communion that we may participate in the life of God, where death has no sting. Christ gives himself over to death and puts himself in complete obedience to the Father, a loving response in which love and obedience overcome death.

There are three dimensions to death:

1. Death is "the physical process of disintegration which accompanies life."[104]

2. Death is experienced as an empty existence, a sort of nonbeing that is distinct from nothingness.

---

101. Ratzinger, *Eschatology*, 89.
102. Ratzinger, *Introduction to Christianity*, 302.
103. Ratzinger, *Eschatology*, 92–93.
104. Ratzinger, *Eschatology*, 95.

3. Death is the end of the isolated self, in which one will move beyond the self in obedience and love to God.[105]

In *Dogma and Preaching*, Ratzinger highlights the ethical implications of death by describing death as a breakdown (*Zusammenbrüchen*), and this helps tie together the three dimensions. Life involves a series of breakdowns that eventually culminate in bodily death. These breakdowns, "which together make up our *one* death, are, therefore, not just random annoyances and not just blind biological occurrences; rather, they are ultimately God's action upon us, through which he tears away from us our selfish, self-seeking, egotistical existence so as to reshape us according to his image."[106] What this brings to the fore is that, in the final analysis, death is spiritual. To put it differently, death is physical, but physical death is based on a judgment by God (the fall).[107] Christ's death and resurrection reveal that one must die (to this world) before one can rise again; the cross precedes resurrection. The breakdowns in life can be recognized as the working out of this, the working out of our baptism, in which one is brought out of *self*-existence to existence-*with* (*Sein-mit-anderen*).[108] In Christ, the moral content (the meaning) of death is far clearer than it is in the Old Testament. Redemption can be seen behind the sad face of death, for "death is the beginning of resurrection; the frightful aspects of death—the birth pangs of new life."[109]

Before we consider more specifically what Ratzinger means by the immortality of the soul and how and why it functions, it is beneficial to return to Schmemann's conception of death. Schmemann is clear that death is the enemy of God. Death is the very denial of God. Like Ratzinger, he recognizes the three dimensions of death, and he clearly parses the first two dimensions. Schmemann argues that, according to Christianity, "death is above all a *spiritual reality*, of which one can partake while being alive, from which one can be free while lying in the grave. Death here is man's *separation from life*, and this means from God Who is the

---

105. Ratzinger makes this list in *Eschatology*, but he orders it differently. He switches around the first two points I set out. I think, with all due respect, that my ordering better expresses the narrative that Ratzinger set out.

106. Ratzinger, *Dogma and Preaching*, 250.

107. Ratzinger, *Dogma and Preaching*, 248–49.

108. Ratzinger, *Dogma and Preaching*, 251; Ratzinger approvingly sees this in Rahner's theology of death (Ratzinger, *Auferstehung and ewiges Leben*, 294–95).

109. Ratzinger, *Dogma and Preaching*, 249.

only giver of life, Who Himself *is* Life."[110] It is the spiritual reality of death that makes the physical reality of death truly death (e.g., Sheol). The third dimension of death Schmemann describes "as 'being with Christ.'"[111]

Schmemann concludes that Christ has destroyed *spiritual* death, but "He does not 'abolish' or 'destroy' the physical death because He does not 'abolish' *this world* of which physical death is not only a 'part' but the principle of life and even growth."[112] On one level, this quotation resonates with Ratzinger who writes that "dying is inherent to life, the *processus* [progression] of living is per se also the *processus* of dying into that life, so that that whole life is imbued, as it were, by death and in its movement is both a movement of living and a movement of dying."[113] However, there is a difference between the two approaches, which stems back to their respective interpretations of the fall. In Schmemann's portrayal, God remains passive in the human struggle with death. Adam and Eve simply walk away from God, but there is literally nothing (nothingness) that is away from God. Thus, they progress toward nothingness (death). Death does not come from God in the same way that evil does not originate in God. Ratzinger, on the other hand, maintains that Adam and Eve are punished. God is active; death "comes from God's hand. . . . God breaks something that has to be broken."[114] Here, death refers to physical death. It is physical life that must be broken for the sake of spiritual life. According to both theologians, death is the result of a spiritual choice, and spiritual death (broken communion with God) is the real crux of the matter that Christ remedies. Is the difference between the passive view of God and the active view of God important? Let us see how this shapes the way the theologians respectively understand suffering, as this helps bring greater clarity. In this regard, I follow Ratzinger's lead that suffering is the experience of the "breakdowns" of death, so suffering and death go hand in hand.

For Schmemann, suffering takes on significance by being offered up as Eucharist, a participation in *the* Eucharist. Everything that is offered to God in thanksgiving takes on meaning, for it is placed into meaning himself. In addition, Schmemann's sacramental account recognizes the

---

110. Schmemann, *Of Water and Spirit*, 62–63.
111. Schmemann, *Of Water and Spirit*, 64.
112. Schmemann, *Of Water and Spirit*, 64.
113. Ratzinger, *Dogma and Preaching*, 244.
114. Ratzinger, *Dogma and Preaching*, 249.

importance of suffering *with* the world so that we can participate in its redemption—redemptive co-suffering. He argues, "Through His [Christ's] own suffering, not only has all suffering acquired a meaning but it has been given the power to become itself the sign, the sacrament, the proclamation, the 'coming' of that victory; the defeat of man, his very dying has become a way of Life."[115] Unfortunately, Ratzinger's work on "the dying movement" focuses on the individual and does not touch on redemptive co-suffering; but such co-suffering, without contradiction, fits well with his emphasis on person as *Sein-mit-anderen* and as *Sein-für-die-Anderen*. Like Schmemann, Ratzinger argues that, in Christ, suffering takes on meaning: "Instead of blind fate, [the dying movement] can become a very practical sort of training in true freedom and can become the process through which someone becomes a 'new man'—which means precisely, a Christian."[116] Both have similar views on suffering, but are their respective views on suffering consistent with their respective notions of time and history?

According to Schmemann's logic, suffering remains as part of this world. The church and her parishioners are in the world ("this world") but not of the world. Of course, all Christians must affirm this biblical notion, but, with Schmemann, this must be read in line with his eschatological vision: Jesus is the end of history. Therefore, suffering is a throwback to what is of the past. We suffer, since the world rejected Christ and cut itself off from redemption. This world is no longer the place of redemption; hence, Schmemann emphasizes the ascension of the celebrant in the Divine Liturgy. The celebrant is taken out of the world to the place of redemption, the new eon. At the close of the Divine Liturgy, she returns to this world, full of the heavenly light, a type of transfiguration. Schmemann does not exactly describe it as transfiguration, but he comes close: "If there is meaning in Christian life, it lies precisely in always following Christ to Mount Tabor, so that at the end we can say, 'Lord, it is good for us to be here.'"[117] The transfiguration motif highlights the element of leaving/escaping the old—the land of shadows—and entering the new. Schmemann often accuses other theologians for having Platonic tendencies (a pejorative for Schmemann), but, ironically, he fails to see it in his own work. To be clear, I am not arguing, as Schmemann does,

---

115. Schmemann, *For Life of World*, 103–4.
116. Ratzinger, *Dogma and Preaching*, 251.
117. Schmemann, *Liturgy and Life*, 83.

that just because something is Platonic, it is non-Christian. I am arguing that Schmemann unintentionally creates a dualism that is problematic in regard to suffering.

Schmemann's eschatological focus on the end of history and the new eon means that suffering takes place in the old eon. Value is given to suffering by offering it to God in the same way that Christ did. Like Christ, we must participate in the suffering of the old eon; we must walk through the valley of death and offer it to God. For "glory and victory came only because of ultimate and complete sacrifice, ultimate emaciation, ultimate self-immolation so that nothing remained—everything was given away."[118] All of this is consistent with Schmemann's notion of the human person as priest. As priest, the human person is a sacrificial being.[119] How is she a sacrificial being? The answer is twofold. First, she is a sacrificial being, for she finds meaning and life in the other and offers meaning and life to the other (the sacrificial aspect). Second, the eucharistic movement of the Christian life is "a movement of adoration and praise in which all joy and suffering, all beauty and all frustration, all hunger and all satisfaction are referred to their ultimate End and become finally *meaningful*."[120] In other words, everything is offered to God. The crux of the problem concerns the word *End*. According to Schmemann, the end of history has occurred; we are not waiting for it. Keeping in mind the limitations of spatial description, perhaps we could imaginatively capture Schmemann's description of the end as hovering above the movement of time. The apparent struggles of history are, in one sense, only *apparent*, because history is finished and the end awaits us (hovers above us). In this sense, living in the midst of history is like attending a wedding ceremony in which the couple have long been wed or attending your grandmother's funeral for the second time. It seems that, with Schmemann's framework, suffering *could* easily be perceived as simply going through the motions, while the head and the heart are elsewhere.[121] If this is the case, can Schmemann truly speak of co-suffering?

Since Ratzinger does not divide history into a before and after Christ, and death is the result of God's judgment (for our own good), he

118. Schmemann, "Mystery of Easter," 17.
119. Schmemann, *For Life of World*, 35.
120. Schmemann, *For Life of World*, 35.
121. Bruce T. Morrill notes in his review of Schmemann's published journals the complete lack of awareness of the suffering of the poor. The poor seem to be outside his purview (Morrill, "Journals," 187–89). This confirms my criticism.

can consistently maintain that what occurs *in* time is in the process toward fulfillment. From within the framework of salvation history, all history is part of the Advent story. We still are waiting for Christ's coming, when God will be all in all. History is still a movement of hope: "No one can say of himself, 'I *am* completely saved.' In the era of this world, there is no redemption as a past action, already completed; nor does it exist as a complete and final present reality; redemption exists only in the mode of hope."[122] Ratzinger concurs with Schmemann that the human person is a sacrificial being. He avers, "There can be no love without suffering, because it always demands an element of self-sacrifice, because, given temperamental differences and the drama of situations, it will always bring with it renunciation and pain."[123] This brings us back to Ratzinger's claim that the human person is one who transcends himself: "When we know that the way of love—this exodus, this going out of oneself—is the true way by which man becomes human, then we also understand that suffering is the process through which we mature."[124] History as Advent and the human person as a transcending sacrificial being go together. The temporal is the realm in which we encounter Christ—he is in the midst of history—and, like salvation history, which leads temporality out of physical time to the fullness of time, the human person, as a being in history, is constantly jolted out of herself by the breakdowns of life. While called out of herself, the human person is not called out of time to the new eon (per Schmemann) but is called deeper into time, eternity (the fullness of time). Finally, Ratzinger argues that the before and after Christ "does not run through historical time, in an outward sense, and cannot be drawn on any map; it runs through our own hearts. Insofar as we are living on a basis of selfishness, of egoism, then even today we are 'before Christ.'"[125] If the before and after Christ ran through history, it would break apart the relationality of existence, Ratzinger's I-Thou-We. Previously in this chapter, we saw the following quotation: "'The Body of Christ' means that all human beings are one organism, the destiny of the whole the proper destiny of each."[126] With this in mind, suffering, both my own and the suffering of others, is very much part of the ongoing reality of history,

---

122. Ratzinger, *What It Means*, 84.
123. Ratzinger and Seewald, *God and the World*, 322.
124. Ratzinger and Seewald, *God and the World*, 322.
125. Ratzinger, *What It Means*, 40.
126. Ratzinger, *Eschatology*, 190.

so much so that, even in death, I am not completely separated from it. We shall look at this in greater depth in what follows.

Now that we have examined the concept of death, we are better positioned to define the immortal soul. By looking at Ratzinger's understanding of death, we were able to see the relational element. On the one hand, a person can cut himself off from communion with God and begin the steady descent into mere existence, a type of living dead. On the other hand, one can be on the steady decline toward bodily death, or even have died, yet be alive by communing with God. "Jesus is the Resurrection and eternal life; to the extent that we are united with Christ we have today 'passed from death to life', we are already living eternal life, which is not only a reality that comes after death but also begins today, in our communion with Christ."[127] Ratzinger's concept of the immortal soul is an outworking of this relational logic, and it concerns identity and temporality.

When Ratzinger uses the term *immortal soul*, he is not endorsing a Greek dualism of body and soul, nor is he arguing that the soul's *nature* is immortal.[128] In death, the soul is not freed from the imprisoned heaviness of the body (the accidental). The only human dualism, argues Ratzinger, is personalistic, not ontological. What this means is that "the decisive line of separation runs, not through man, but rather between Creator and creature."[129] He maintains that every other distinction is negligible in comparison. The entire person is God's creature. That is not to say that the human person does not have a soul, nor does it mean that existence ends for the human person in bodily death. What it emphasizes is that our existence both now and in the hereafter is contingent. I exist because God loves me "and *his* love, in turn, is man's eternity; in being loved by eternal Love, he is lifted up imperishably. He is lifted up, because he himself can love. For him, too, love is the only thing that gives eternity; the measure and manner of his eternity depend on the measure and manner of his loving."[130] Immortality is the consequence of being in relation with God, "'dialogic' immortality" (*"dialogische" Unsterblichkeit*).[131] This

---

127. Ratzinger, "Awake."

128. Nicholas Lash pithily expressed this, arguing that, in our future, "we die . . . into life, in God" (Lash, "Are We Born," 412).

129. Ratzinger, *Dogma and Preaching*, 268.

130. Ratzinger, *Dogma and Preaching*, 259. See Ratzinger, *Introduction to Christianity*, 306.

131. Ratzinger, *Introduction to Christianity*, 350.

is a two-way relationship. In other words, we must respond to God's love; "openness, not closure, is the end in which we find our beginning."[132] This is the first aspect of immortality that Ratzinger lays out.

The second aspect of immortality is based on creation. Ratzinger argues that a proper theology of creation entails that the entire creature is saved, "in the wholeness and unity of his personhood as that *appears* in embodied life."[133] This does not mean that I am not a transient being. As Schmemann made clear, the cells that make up my body are replaced every seven years. It means that what makes me who I am is retained. Matter is not what underpins continuity, and that is why we need the language of the soul. The soul is the form of the body, not a thing within the body. It is the identity of the human person that in this life is expressed in matter ("as that *appears* in embodied life"). Ratzinger argues that, in light of this, we can understood how one's body can waste away in disease and age in the movement toward eternity yet still remain the same person.

Lastly, "part of the Christian idea of immortality is fellowship with other human beings. Man is not engaged in a solitary dialogue with God."[134] Gifted by God, and through Christ, our immortality opens us to the dialogue that marks personal existence. In Christ, we come together and are led out of our isolation into the relational depth of humanity.[135]

Immortality, we can summarize, is founded on God, not humankind. It is a gift of grace,[136] in that we are brought out of our broken monologue into the dialogue of love. The immortal soul is that part of the human person that consistently retains the unity of one's personhood both in life and in death and opens us further into the fellowship of humanity.

Counter to Greek philosophical construals of the soul, Ratzinger posits that the soul[137] is what binds us to history.[138] As already outlined, the soul is dialogical, and relationality does not cease in death. For this

---

132. Ratzinger, *Eschatology*, 158.
133. Ratzinger, *Eschatology*, 158 (italics added).
134. Ratzinger, *Eschatology*, 159.
135. Ratzinger, *In the Beginning*, 72.
136. Ratzinger, *Dogma and Preaching*, 270.
137. From this point on, *soul* includes the notion of immortality as previously outlined.
138. Rejecting the importance of history seems to be a perennial concern, not just one found in Plato and his followers. Perhaps the contemporary view is worse, in that it also overlooks the future; Ratzinger writes, "Our age is unique in its narcissism in that it has cut itself off from the past and the future" (Ratzinger, *In the Beginning*, 34).

very reason, Ratzinger stands against theological arguments that claim bodily resurrection occurs immediately after death. If the end of history is the fruition of history (when God is all in all), it does not make sense to individualize history, in which my bodily resurrection occurs immediately following my death. Deification is not simply about me. Ratzinger argues that, "in the breakthrough from the world to God [the incarnation], everything that went before and everything that followed afterward is given its proper significance as the great movement of the cosmos is drawn into the process of deification, into a return to the state from which it originated."[139] The relational fabric of God's world, a world held together in love, necessitates a web of history that does not snap in my death. Previously, we saw that, for Ratzinger, love means to be always for someone, and, because of this, love cannot close itself off to time. I do not cease to love in death, nor do I remain unloved in death. Such love is not only directed to and received by God but also directed to and received by human persons in history (communion of the saints). Again, this brings us back to the relational reality of being a human person—all humans are one organism, humankind (there is no isolated human person). In death, I do not cease to be a human person; I remain a person, and thus I remain part of the organism of humanity.[140] Furthermore, eternity is not non-time, nor is eternity that in which God is, but is God himself. God is pure relations, a relationship of love that sustains our relations and thereby the web of history. Therefore, by entering into eternity (God himself), our relational ties are not cut, but, rather, we are opened to an even greater relationality. In consequence, there are only two logical conclusions. Either in bodily death there is an interval in which I cease to live as my being waits for the resurrection of the dead, or the human soul is real, and, in bodily death, it continues to live in Christ.

The first conclusion is problematic for two reasons. The first problem concerns relationships. If we are loved by God, how can we not exist?[141] Nonexistence is possible only if God is not person, is not relation, and *ipso facto* neither is the fabric of reality. The second problem concerns identity. If there is no soul, what sustains my identity? In bodily death,

---

139. Ratzinger, *What It Means*, 53.

140. See Ratzinger, *In the Beginning*, 72; Ratzinger, *Introduction to Christianity*, 245–47; Ratzinger, "Problem of Threats."

141. See Ratzinger, *Joseph Ratzinger in Communio*, 2:16. This fits well with Rom 8:38–39.

the body decomposes and eventually becomes another form of matter. Without a concept of the soul, my identity ends in bodily death.

The soul for Ratzinger is the logical conclusion of belief in a God who is person. Not only is God person, but, because of God, we are persons. In death, my identity as a person is preserved in like manner to how it is in life, by the love of God. "Soul is nothing other than man's capacity for relatedness with truth, with love eternal. The relationship to that which is eternal, viz., remaining in communion with Him, is partaking in His eternity. This theo-logical interpretation of eternal life incorporates the christological concretization of our faith in God."[142] Ratzinger's notion of the soul emphasizes the historicity and particularity of the human person.

The Body

What is the relation between the soul and the body? Is Ratzinger a dualist? Like his understanding of the soul, the body must be understood relationally and, as a result, historically. Ratzinger follows Thomas's trajectory and maintains that the soul is the form of the body, that our "physiology becomes truly 'body' through the heart of the personality."[143] Elsewhere, he writes that the soul "occupies the whole of man,"[144] and the "body itself is the person."[145] It is clear that, for Ratzinger, the human person is not human without the body.[146] It is a real part of the self, and "where man despises his body—whether as an ascetic or as a libertine—he also despises his own self.... When he despises his body, man quarrels on a radical level with Being itself, which he understands, no longer as God's creation, but as 'the existing order,' which must be destroyed."[147] The human creature is unique, in that he is a bridge between matter and spirit. In him, the two "meet and mingle."[148] As an embodied creature, man has a priestly function. Ratzinger does not specifically use the term *priest*, but he certainly describes this in priestly terms:

142. Ratzinger, *Eschatology*, xxi.
143. Ratzinger, *Eschatology*, 181.
144. Ratzinger and Seewald, *God and the World*, 90.
145. Ratzinger and Seewald, *God and the World*, 83.
146. Ratzinger is concerned about the divorcing of the biological from the personal in modern science, particularly in the realm of human reproduction (Ratzinger, *Joseph Ratzinger in Communio*, 2:73).
147. Ratzinger, *God of Jesus Christ*, 44.
148. Ratzinger and Seewald, *God and the World*, 89.

> Through man, the material world is lifted up into the spiritual realm, and through their combination in man we see that the two are compatible, each with the other. Material being is not a thing along side of which the spirit leads an unconnected and indivisible existence. The unity of creation is demonstrated at the point where the two are united in man. That gives him a quite special function: that is to say, sharing the responsibility for the unity of creation, incarnating spirit in himself and, conversely, lifting material being up to God—and thereby, all in all, making a contribution to the great symphony of creation.[149]

The quotation correlates with Schmemann's depiction of the human person as priest, and it reveals something important about bodily resurrection and the nature of physical bodies.

Let us first look at the nature of the physical body. Ratzinger's descriptions of bodily physicality are limited, in that he does not set aside sections of his writings for this particular topic. I think the reason for this is that, for Ratzinger, the term *body* refers to the whole person.[150] This corresponds to the Eucharist. When we partake of the Eucharist—"this is my body"—we do not digest Christ's physical body but his life, his person.[151] Nevertheless, as the block quotation implies, the physical body connects us with the world of matter. In this sense, we are part of the rhythms of the cosmos and fit within the logic of the cosmos.[152] It is also through our bodies that we embrace history and community.[153] At the very base level, we see this in biological progeny.[154] At the same time, the body is what separates us; it physically marks the boundary of the self. We can choose which direction to head, either toward greater communion or toward greater separation. It is interesting that Ratzinger

---

149. Ratzinger and Seewald, *God and the World*, 89.

150. Patrick Fletcher examines Ratzinger's use of the *Leib-Körper* distinction (body-flesh) and highlights the development in Ratzinger's thought: a move away from the distinction toward a unity (Fletcher, *Resurrection Realism*, 159–78). I maintain that, although there is development, it concerns emphasis, and Ratzinger's overarching approach remains consistent.

151. Ratzinger, *God Is Near Us*, 79.

152. Ratzinger, *In the Beginning*, 27.

153. Ratzinger, *God Is Near Us*, 80.

154. It is interesting that Ratzinger sees birth as "a self-transcending of man, in which there is more than he has and is: through the human action of begetting and birth, there occurs creation" (Ratzinger, *Joseph Ratzinger in Communio*, 2:80).

describes the movement toward greater separation as the direction of the body:

> Man can therefore live in the direction of "body"; he can so shut himself up in selfishness that the body is nothing more than a division, a limit, preventing any communion, and he no longer really encounters anyone in it, lets no one touch his closed-up inner self.
>
> But bodily existence can also be lived in the opposite way: as opening oneself up, as the developing freedom of a person who shares himself.[155]

The "direction of 'body'" connects with the previous block quotation's "matter." This brings us back to Ratzinger's article "Concerning the Notion of Person in Theology," where he distinguishes between matter and spirit. He argues, "Matter is what is '*das auf sich Geworfene*' (that which is thrown upon itself)," and "spirit is '*das sich selbst Entwerfende*' (that which throws itself forth, guides itself or designs itself) . . . is itself in transcending itself."[156] The direction of the body is the movement of matter, whereas it is the human person—fully united body and spirit—who lifts the world to God and, in so doing, participates in the process of deification. The human person moves in either the direction of the body or the direction of the spirit, either away from unity or toward unity.

Ratzinger more aptly describes the movement of unity with the term *resurrection*. He avers, "Resurrection means quite simply that the body ceases to be a limit and that its capacity for communion remains."[157] To rise from the dead literally means to be communicable, not cut off from the world. Resurrection also draws attention to the provisional nature of our current body.[158] Ratzinger turns to the apostle Paul (2 Cor 5:1–10) and points out that Paul does not want to abandon the body. In fact, Paul is anxious about being naked (being without the body), and "his hope is to be, not 'unclothed', but 'further clothed', to receive the 'heavenly house'—the definitive body—as a new garment. The Apostle does not want to discard his body, he does not want to be bodiless."[159]

155. Ratzinger, *God Is Near Us*, 80.

156. Ratzinger, *Joseph Ratzinger in Communio*, 2:115. It is interesting that with the concept of "thrownness" (*Geworfenheit*), Ratzinger does not mention Heidegger. Instead, he cites Hedwig Conrad-Martius.

157. Ratzinger, *God Is Near Us*, 81.

158. See Ratzinger, *Spirit of the Liturgy*, 218.

159. Ratzinger, *Spirit of the Liturgy*, 218.

Paul's hope is in resurrection. The earthly provisional body anticipates the definitive body. We are embodied creatures, and the resurrection confirms this truth. It does not confirm that I receive the same physical body that is presently me.

In one sense, Ratzinger is a dualist, for he speaks of the soul. A strict physicalist (monist) account would not use such language. In another sense, Ratzinger's conception of the soul is what enables him to speak of the human person as a relational and historical being. It also brings together the movement of salvation history with eternity. In fact, Ratzinger sets himself apart from modern dualisms:

> It should be noted here that western culture increasingly affirms a new dualism, where some of its characteristic traits converge: individualism, materialism, utilitarianism, and the hedonist ideology of self-fulfillment for oneself. In fact, the body is no longer perceived naturally by the subject as the concrete form of all of his relations with God, other persons and the world, i.e., as that datum which in the midst of a universe being built, a conversation in course, a history rich in meaning, one can participate in positively only by accepting its rules and its language.[160]

Ratzinger's conception of the soul avoids the strong distinction between matter and spirit as found in materialism, individualism, and utilitarianism.[161] Matter belongs to spirit. He insists that "what is purely spiritual is inappropriate to the nature of man."[162] But, as I explicated in the previous section, Ratzinger argues for an intermediate state between death and the general resurrection. Does this not mean that, for Ratzinger, the human person can exist in a disembodied state?

Ratzinger's response is based upon a literal reading of Col 3:3—"For you have died, and your life is hidden with Christ in God"—along with 2 Cor 5:1–10 and the parable of Lazarus in Luke 16:19–31. The intermediate state is to be clothed with Christ, to become part of his body. He writes, "The soul on its own would be a sad fragment. But even before the general resurrection, it enters into the Body of Christ, which in a sense becomes our body, just as we are supposed to become his Body."[163] In

---

160. Ratzinger, "Problem of Threats."

161. These modern dualisms wreak ethical havoc. See Ratzinger, "Abolition of Man"; and Ratzinger, *Turning Point for Europe?*, pt 1.

162. Ratzinger, *Spirit of the Liturgy*, 191.

163. Ratzinger, *Spirit of the Liturgy*, 219.

death, we rest in Christ's bosom (Abraham's bosom has been replaced by Christ's), until history is complete and we are given new bodies.

Ratzinger puts an interesting spin on purgatory, which is worth mentioning because of its relational basis and its connection with time. Purgatory is simply the purifying encounter that one has with Christ in death.[164] We could describe it as the summation of our baptism, the completion of our death to egoism. In this life, conversion does not occur in a vacuum but in the temporal reality of community. My continual dying to the self in Christ is affected by those around me, and, in the same way, I affect the lives of others. Even in death, the actions of my life continue to affect others. Ratzinger argues that this is part of the logic of purgatory, for "'purgatory' means still unresolved guilt, a suffering which continues to radiate out because of guilt. Purgatory means, then, suffering to the end what one has left behind on earth."[165] Guilt binds one to time, whereas love opens one to eternity. In this sense, guilt must be overcome by love, if one is to participate in eternity. Clearly, the import of history shapes Ratzinger's conception of purgatory.[166]

---

164. See Ratzinger, *Eschatology*, 229.

165. Ratzinger, *Eschatology*, 189.

166. Peter C. Phan claims that Ratzinger's conception of purgatory and temporality is inconsistent. He argues that it is "a clear instance of trying to have one's cake and eat it too" (Phan, "Contemporary Context," 520n49). Phan points out that Ratzinger maintains that man does not have to have his temporality stripped away in order to become eternal. Yet, Ratzinger avers that the "transforming moment" of purgatory cannot be qualified as long or short according to the measurements derived from physics. In other words, Phan's contention is that, in describing purgatory as nonmeasurable, Ratzinger negates the temporal, and, in so doing, he nullifies the previous claim. It is clear that Phan misses the heart of Ratzinger's argument. Eternity is not "non-time" but dominion over time. The human person's experience of time is similar to eternity, in that the human experience of the present is one that involves either the future or the past. Eternity makes definite this experience of human time. Therefore, according to Ratzinger, an encounter with the Eternal One does not abolish but heightens human time. Furthermore, *memoria*-time, like eternity, is not physical time, and, as such, it is not measurable according to physics. Ratzinger is clear that, in death, the human person shakes off physical time but retains *memoria*-time. Hence, the purgatorial encounter with Christ does not involve the ticking clock. Physical time does not measure *Existenzzeit* (Ratzinger, *Eschatology*, 230). The next argument that Phan rallies against Ratzinger is worth quoting at length since his argument rests on the omission of a key phrase: "Ratzinger argues that time must be understood not only physically but also anthropologically. He calls this time '*memoria*-time' which, he claims, separates itself from physical time, yet does not for all that become eternity (ibid. 184). Granted that this time exists (and I think it does), still the question remains whether there is a difference within this time before and after death (and I think that there is; otherwise, death

In short, purgatory is "the inwardly necessary process of transformation in which a person becomes capable of Christ, capable of God and thus capable of unity with the whole communion of saints."[167] The inward fires of purgatory—the fires of Christ—remove the impurities of the ego and preserve the full ascent of faith. In so doing, the subjective enclosed I is fully opened in and for communion.

Re-Membering

As we have seen, the human person is a relational being (*Sein-mit-anderen*) whose identity is found in Christ and Christ's body. Purgatory completes the work of Christ. It burns off the subjective I and opens us to the we of his body. Ratzinger argues that "whether others curse us or bless us, forgive us and turn our guilt into love—this is part of our *own* destiny. The fact that the saints will judge means that encounter with Christ is encounter with his whole body."[168] The underlying reality of love that undergirds reality—the *Logos*—binds us together. As G. K. Chesterton pithily claims, "Love is not blind; that is the last thing that it is. Love is bound; and the more it is bound the less it is blind."[169] Christ opens our eyes so that we see each other, and we are bound together in his love. Love not only binds us together but is bound to our very being; we are created in love—we are lovable.[170] To be is to love and be loved. This connects to the remembering of *memoria*-time, as explicated in the previous chapter. The *to be* of the human present is the act of re-membering, of putting together time, binding it (in eternity, past and future are not

---

causes no rupture at all). Ratzinger does not seem to be aware of this question and only speaks of this time as different from physical time and eternity" (Phan, "Contemporary Context," 520n49). What Ratzinger actually writes is (Phan's omission is the phrase in italics): "When a human being steps out of the world of *bios*, *memoria*-time separates itself from physical time, *yet, though left sheerly to its own devices* does not for all that become eternity" (Ratzinger, *Eschatology*, 184). With Phan's omission, it appears that Ratzinger is inconsistent. Without the omission, it is clear that Ratzinger maintains that in death there is, to use Phan's term, a rupture. However, the rupture, like purgatory, does not just happen but involves the transformative encounter with Christ, the eternal one. We become eternal only in Christ.

167. Ratzinger, *Eschatology*, 230.
168. Ratzinger, *Eschatology*, 232 (italics added).
169. Chesterton, *Orthodoxy*, 70.
170. Ratzinger's understanding of love is shaped considerably by Josef Pieper. See Pieper, *Faith, Hope, Love*.

separated). Likewise, Christ reunited us with God and put together what was sundered. We could say that to live in Christ's love and to follow in his path is to reunite what was separated, both time itself and human relations. To love is to re-member.

The Ontological and Historical Person

> Conscience—the secret core of one's being where one is face to face with God—is the place of true freedom.[171]

In an article on relational ontologies, C. C. Pecknold insightfully points out that Ratzinger's concept of the person goes beyond the traditional essentialist and anti-essentialist divide. In particular, Pecknold suggests that Ratzinger's book *Eschatology* is "an attempt to overcome these de-hellenizing, anti-essentialist tendencies."[172] Indeed, Ratzinger claims that,

> ultimately, the tension between ontology and history has its foundation in the tension within human nature itself, which must go out of itself in order to find itself; it has its foundation in the mystery of God, which is freedom and which, therefore, calls each individual by a name that is known to no other. Thus, the whole is communicated to him in the particular.[173]

Here, we see the coming together of the particular (anti-essentialist) and the universal (essentialist), the historical and the ontological in the human person. What this means is that Ratzinger does not shy away from claiming that there is a human nature, that essence precedes existence, nor does he ignore the particular for the sake of the universal. In what follows, we shall look at Ratzinger's conception of the conscience. The conscience in Ratzinger's work is arguably understood as that which bridges the divide between ontology and history in the human person. Lastly, we shall consider how Ratzinger's approach to personhood avoids the pitfalls of essentialism and anti-essentialism.

---

171. Twomey, *Theology*, 88.

172. Pecknold, "Man Is by Nature," 2. Although I wholeheartedly agree with Pecknold's helpful and astute observation, his argumentation could be further elaborated.

173. Ratzinger, *Principles of Catholic Theology*, 171.

Conscience

> "Shall I ever be able to read that story again; the one I couldn't remember? Will you tell it to me, Aslan? Oh do, do, do." "Indeed, yes, I will tell it to you for years and years."[174]

The concern of this section is not to provide an exhaustive exposition of Ratzinger's formulation of conscience but to look at it in light of history and ontology.[175] In his homilies on creation, Ratzinger makes three important statements concerning ontology. First, the Ten Commandments are an echo of creation.[176] Second, the human person is directly related to God through creation.[177] Third, as the *imago Dei*, the human person has the capacity for relationship with God. In fact, human persons "are most profoundly themselves when they discover their relation to their Creator."[178] All three statements connect with the conscience; Ratzinger argues that "belief in the Creator God is also belief in the God of our conscience."[179] This is a clear ontological statement in regard to conscience, but how does this work? Before this question can be answered, we must see how Ratzinger defines the conscience.

Ratzinger describes the conscience in several ways:

1. Conscience means acknowledgement of oneself, others, and the world as created. This acts as both a limit and as a guide to power.[180]

2. Conscience is a window to see reality, an openness to the ground of reality.[181]

3. Conscience is a type of co-knowledge of human persons and God.[182]

4. "Conscience is an organ, not an oracle."[183]

---

174. Lewis, *Voyage of Dawn Treader*, 137.
175. For a clear and helpful overview of Ratzinger's notion of conscience see Twomey, *Theology*, 80–104.
176. Ratzinger, *In the Beginning*, 26.
177. Ratzinger, *In the Beginning*, 45.
178. Ratzinger, *In the Beginning*, 48.
179. Ratzinger, *God of Jesus Christ*, 47.
180. Ratzinger, *Joseph Ratzinger in Communio*, 2:19.
181. Ratzinger, *On Conscience*, 16.
182. Ratzinger, *On Conscience*, 51–52.
183. Ratzinger, *On Conscience*, 61.

The first three descriptions concern epistemology. The conscience has to do with a type of seeing, recognizing, or understanding. What it recognizes is being and reality or, ultimately, the Truth. Ratzinger argues that being bears the language of the *Logos*, and the language of being (or nature) is identical with the language of conscience.[184] Ratzinger rejects the Kantian subject-object distinction, in which objective moral knowledge is impossible. In a way, we could say that the conscience is a bridge between subject and object. *Object* is not to be understood in the Kantian sense (locked within human constructs), but, rather, it concerns reality, which is grounded in the *Logos*. Conscience, for Ratzinger, enables one to perceive reality, reality subsisting in the *Logos*. The way this works is connected with the fourth description. Ratzinger uses the term *organ* to denote that the conscience is intrinsic to the person and is not externally imposed. Like a part of the body, the conscience belongs to us and requires growth. He provides a helpful illustration, likening the conscience to human speech. A child needs a family to teach her to speak, and, as she grows, she continues to refine and develop this capability. Although speech depends on a community of teachers, speech is an innate gift. In the same way, conscience needs to be fostered by the church, and it is something that can develop beautifully or be hampered. Nevertheless, it is innate. To be clear, innate, in this sense, means gifted by God in creation. This brings us to *anamnesis*.

Ratzinger argues that there are two levels of conscience: *anamnesis* and *conscientia*. Twomey helpfully parses the two levels of conscience as primal conscience and conscience as judgment.[185] Only the first level is applicable to the argument. *Anamnesis* concerns the innate primal aspect of conscience. We have the capacity and disposition inside us for observing divine commandments ("the spark of love").[186] It is a type of memory of the good and true, an "inner ontological tendency."[187] Thus, Ratzinger dissolves the tension that exists between a morality of conscience and a

---

184. Ratzinger, *On Conscience*, 67.
185. Twomey, *Theology*, 122–27.
186. Ratzinger, *On Conscience*, 31.
187. Ratzinger, *On Conscience*, 32. See Ratzinger and Seewald, *Salt of the Earth*, 41. Twomey writes, "All human beings long for the truth, since each one is *capax veritatis*, *capax Dei*—capable of knowing God (truth), capable of becoming one with God—and so since the dawn of human history all peoples have sought that truth. Another word for this capacity for truth is conscience. More precisely, conscience is that urge to know the truth that is at the root of our humanity" (Twomey, "Centrality of Truth").

morality of authority. The *within* of the conscience is not in contradiction with the *without*. The Ten Commandments, Christ, and the church are not authorities that speak against the self.[188] Instead, they confirm, guide, and grow the conscience. Ratzinger concludes, "My own 'I' is the site of the profoundest surpassing of self and contact with him from whom I came and toward whom I am going."[189] This fits with Ratzinger's notion that the human person is a being who needs the help of others to become herself,[190] or, as worded earlier, the human person is one who transcends herself. Hence, Ratzinger avers that "the revelation of God's will is the revelation of what our own being truly wishes—it is a gift."[191] And "faith in Christ simply renders the inmost part of our being, our conscience, once more articulate."[192] We could easily transpose this into the language of *exitus et reditus*. Man was created (*exitus*) to be in relationship with God (*reditus*). By freely responding in the movement of return, the human person moves toward the Other and, in so doing, comes home to herself. *Anamnesis* is the recognition of *exitus* (we are created contingent beings), but, unless one moves in return—a temporal event, the conscience is hampered.

The second level of conscience (*conscientia*) concerns judgment and is the level about which most theologians and philosophers have written. Ratzinger spends little time explicating this level, for it is the first level that is of the utmost importance. There are three aspects to *conscientia*: (1) recognizing, (2) bearing witness, and (3) judging.[193] Ratzinger is primarily concerned with recognizing, for it is here that the two levels of conscience connect. He argues, "Whether something is recognised or not depends too on the will, which can block the way to recognition or lead to it. It is dependent, that is to say, on an already formed moral character."[194] That is, it is dependent upon a past habit of listening to and perceiving being—*anamnesis*. Hence, moral fault does not lie at the second level of conscience (*conscientia*). One can do nothing other than listen and follow one's own judgments,

---

188. See Ratzinger, *On Conscience*, 35.
189. Ratzinger, *On Conscience*, 33.
190. Ratzinger, *On Conscience*, 62.
191. Ratzinger, *God Is Near Us*, 104.
192. Ratzinger, *God Is Near Us*, 105.
193. Ratzinger, *On Conscience*, 37.
194. Ratzinger, *On Conscience*, 37.

> but it can very well be wrong to have come to such askew convictions in the first place, by having stifled the protest of the anamnesis of being. The guilt lies then in a different place, much deeper—not in the present act, not in the present judgment of conscience, but in the neglect of my being that made me deaf to the internal promptings of truth.[195]

One must be attuned to creation, to our created nature. Christ leads the way, but the *Logos* is more than the truth to which we must be attuned. The *Logos* is love and forgiveness, and he transforms us from within. Not only does Christ point the way, but he also makes it possible. He takes us beyond our capabilities and incapabilities. Thus, in the end, *anamnesis* calls us to the Son (*reditus*) who is both *within* and *without*.

In summary, the human person is both ontological and historical. The conscience is the ontological organ that shows who we are: beings who must transcend themselves. The transcending of the self is a temporal act (historical).[196] In history, the human person is on the way to fulfilling that for which she was created, ontological becoming. Christ makes this possible:

> The Cross is not the "crucifixion of man" at all, as Nietzsche thought, but rather his true healing, which saves him from the deceptive self-sufficiency in which he can only lose himself and miss out on the endless promise that lies within him for the sake of the bourgeois mush of his supposed naturalness. Then the Paschal way of the Cross, this breaking down of all earthly assurances and their false satisfactions, is man's true homecoming, the true cosmic harmony in which God will be "everything to everyone" (1 Cor 15:28), in which the whole world is a song of praise to God and to the Paschal Lamb who was slain (Rev 5).[197]

Beyond Essentialism and Anti-Essentialism

There are four main criticisms of essentialism: (1) it falsely assumes that it can get "below the surface" to an undergirding substance, (2) it depersonalizes and devalues persons that do not fit within its category, (3) it demarcates humanity from the created world, and (4) it assumes

---

195. Ratzinger, *On Conscience*, 38.
196. See Ratzinger, *Truth and Tolerance*, 173.
197. Ratzinger, *Dogma and Preaching*, 161.

the priority of the universal over the particular (antihistorical).[198] The main criticism leveled against anti-essentialism is that it cannot define what it is to be a human person. Furthermore, it is arguable that the anti-essentialist over-prioritization of the particular easily separates persons into Leibnizian monads, in which absolute otherness makes fellowship impossible.

Along with Pecknold, it is my contention that Ratzinger's conception of the human person avoids all these pitfalls by recognizing both the ontological and the historical reality of the person. First, Ratzinger thinks that he can get "below the surface" but not by external means. Our ontological openness for relationship with the Creator means that we can have true relationship with the ground of all being (the *Logos*). By participating in the life of God, we are internally (both *within* and *without*), so to speak, part of reality. Schmemann expresses this well when he admits that, without Christ, we are enframed (*Gestell*)[199] within Kant's distinction, and our knowledge is only *about* the world. But, through thanksgiving in Christ, we have knowledge *of* the world. When one is hid with Christ, there is no digging below the surface, for one has struck the rock and is part of the very ground of all being. Second, Ratzinger's relational understanding of reality enables him to say what it means to be a human person (one in relationship) without depersonalizing; relationships involve others. Third, Ratzinger recognizes that the human person is part of the rhythms of the cosmos and, at the same time, is more than the cosmos. Through human deification, the cosmos is spiritualized. I think Schmemann's approach is particularly beneficial in this regard. His emphasis on the human person as priest offers a helpful corrective to the image of steward: thankfulness rather than domination (an oft-misconceived view of stewardship). Nevertheless, both Ratzinger and Schmemann maintain a hierarchy, in which the human person plays a special role as one made in God's image. There is still demarcation but for the sake of the world—not an antithesis.[200]

---

198. Horan, "Beyond Essentialism and Complementarity," 98–100. Horan highlights the first three issues, but I think the fourth point is the most significant.

199. Schmemann does not use this Heideggerian term, but it encapsulates the idea better than any other word. Heidegger writes, "Enframing, as a challenging-forth into ordering, sends into a way of revealing. Enframing is an ordaining of destining" (Heidegger, *Question Concerning Technology*, 24).

200. Certainly, this would not appease the critics of an anthropocentric position, such as Catherine Keller, who calls for a social ontology that makes all creatures equidependent. For Keller, a relational ontology demands such a perspective (Keller, "Seeking and Sucking," 59–60). It makes one wonder how she perceives the incarnation.

Fourth, Ratzinger does not move from the universal to the particular but from the particular to the universal. He maintains that this is the way in which God has always revealed himself (e.g., Abraham, Moses, the prophets, Jesus and the church). In a personal reality, the universal comes through the particular. Therefore, history (given vast import by the incarnation) cannot be skirted. It is through the historical that we encounter what is beyond history. As we saw with Ratzinger's conception of time and the soul, one of the strengths of his position is the value he places on history. In contrast with the anti-essentialist positions, Ratzinger clearly articulates what it is to be a human person. The image of the human person is given to us in Christ.[201] To be a full human person is to be like Christ or, for that matter, to be in Christ. Christ is the place in which humanity unites, and the subjective encapsulated I is no more. He avers, "The Bible establishes a definitive standard for the being *man*, which, it is true, looks to man's future, but to a future that is also fulfillment because it restores him to his essential nature."[202]

Conclusion

And only where God rules, only where God is acknowledged in the world, is man also held in honour; only there can the world be set right. The primacy of worship is the fundamental prerequisite for the redemption of mankind.[203]

There are three aspects of Christology that significantly shape Ratzinger's conception of the person: (1) Christ as *Logos*, (2) Christ as Son, and (3) Christ incarnate. These three aspects are under the umbrella of Ratzinger's spiritual Christology, which is based on relationship; the Son's identity is

---

201. See Ratzinger, *Faith and the Future*, 98.

202. Ratzinger, *Principles of Catholic Theology*, 160. In defending the use of the language of substance in theological anthropology, John Webster summarizes what Ratzinger's anthropology is able to maintain: "That is, its use [the language of substance] does not prescribe the kind of being that humankind is, by, for example, placing humankind in the category of immobile presences. It identifies the subject who is in the history or drama of fellowship with God and the relations in which that subject stands; and so it is entirely possible to respond to deconstructive criticism of onto-theology by developing an historical and social ontology of the human. Theological talk of human nature and destiny does not refer to abstract, a-historical entities but to the identity acquired by subjects as they act and are acted upon in the reciprocities of relation to God and others" (Webster, "Human Person," 226–27).

203. Ratzinger, *On the Way*, 99.

founded on his prayer with the Father. Christ as *Logos* reveals that the fabric of reality is relational. Christ as Son discloses that true unity is in plurality, relation is not an accidental property of substance, and person is primarily revealed to us in the Trinity. Christ incarnate unveils what it means to be a *human* person. As put forth in Ratzinger's volitional thesis, the apogee of our human personhood is found in giving ourselves to God. In more abstract terms, "a being is the more itself the more it is open, the more it is in relationship. And that in turn will lead us to realize that it is the man who makes himself open to all being, in its wholeness and in its Ground, and becomes thereby a 'self,' who is truly a person."[204] The volitional thesis follows the Trinitarian logic of unity as communion. Ratzinger clearly distinguishes between natural unity and communion. The human person is not naturally united with God, as this would mean absorption, and the self would no longer be. Instead, Ratzinger posits that, by freely giving herself to God in communion, the human person remains herself yet is united with God. This naturally connects to temporality.

The arena of history is where God woos us to himself and where we are given the freedom to return home to God (the freedom to *be*).[205] My identity is developed in temporality, in which I must journey toward him who came into the midst of time as Jesus Christ. In a sense, this is an eschatological movement, for humans are creatures who hope. Nevertheless, our hope is in Christ, and so are we (hid with Christ in God). Christ is not simply to be understood as our end; he is also the center of history. In him past, present, and future hold together, so that we already live in him for whom we hope; the promise is already a present reality, a foretaste.

The major differences between Ratzinger and Schmemann concern temporality. There are three major points of divergence. First, Ratzinger's description of history as Advent matches his relational vision. Schmemann, on the other hand, divides history into two and breaks apart the relationality of history. Both in the Eucharist and in bodily death, one

---

204. Ratzinger, *Eschatology*, 155.

205. James Corkery argues that Ratzinger's anthropology is over-spiritualized and world-weary. Furthermore, he avers that Ratzinger's account accentuates discontinuity, so that the emphasis is on grace healing and transforming nature, rather than on grace elevating and perfecting nature (Corkery, *Joseph Ratzinger's Theological Ideas*, 37–51). Corkery clearly overlooks Ratzinger's conception of *exitus et reditus* and the importance of freedom in his theological vision, not to mention the vital role that temporality plays in Ratzinger's relationality. It is true that Ratzinger asserts that we need healing and transforming. However, this is in order that we may continue the return journey home, which is our process of elevation and perfection.

leaves the old eon (history) behind and enters into the new eon. With Schmemann's construal, one must ask, how important is history if its end (the new eon) does not occur and manifest within history? Second, with Schmemann's divided history, it is easily construed that one is called out of time, and, if this is the case, suffering can be conceived of as simply going through the motions. Ratzinger's understanding of time places Christ in the midst of our suffering. Thus, suffering does not take us out of time, but pulls us deeper into the heart of time, into the one who is eternal. Third, Schmemann's emphasis on Christ as the end of history (it is already over) seems to affect his vision of relationship that is based on the act of obedience, an act done toward an end (unidirectional). Similarly, obedience is central for Ratzinger's understanding of Christ, but he highlights this act with the word *yes*. In so doing, he calls attention to the dialogical nature that emphasizes the bidirectional nature of relationship.

Ratzinger's construal of the last things is based on the relational reality he envisages. Thus, his notion of the soul, purgatory, and last judgment is shaped by his relational vision rather than the inverse. In other words, eschatology is the conclusion that follows from a personal God. As a result, Ratzinger does not fall prey to Schmemann's claim that the immortality of the soul is based upon an escapist ideology found in Plato. It is the exact opposite. Ratzinger's argument for the immortality of the soul is based upon the need to preserve the import of history and the relational grounding of identity.

Finally, Ratzinger's notion of conscience reveals the ontological and historical nature of the human person. The primary element of conscience, *anamnesis*, reveals that the human person was made to be in relation with the Truth. At the same time, it reveals that this internal reality is dependent upon an external reality, i.e., God. What is *within* correlates and finds its being in what is *without*. The Creator has made us to be in communion with him, and we need him as Redeemer to realign and remind us and, even more importantly, to renew and transform us through his forgiveness and love. We were made (*exitus*) to return (*reditus*) to the loving arms of God. Thus, we are pilgrims who must die to the self (martyrs) in order to be oneself: a being in communion (Eucharist). With this in mind, Ratzinger's construal of the human person goes beyond the essentialist and anti-essentialist divide, for the human person is grounded in a relational historical existence in the being of God who is pure relation. In God's being, from *within* and *without*, we *are*.

5

Conclusion: A Matter of Time

> It is the dull eventless times that have no duration whatever. A time splashed with interest, wounded with tragedy, crevassed with joy—that's the time that seems long in the memory. And this is right when you think about it. Eventlessness has no posts to drape duration on. From nothing to nothing is no time at all.
>
> —JOHN STEINBECK

How we approach theological anthropology is essential to the well-being of the church. *Gaudium et Spes* makes clear that the church is entrusted "to reveal the mystery of God, Who is the ultimate goal of man, she opens up to man at the same time the meaning of his own existence, that is, the innermost truth about himself. . . . Whoever follows after Christ, the perfect man, becomes himself more of a man."[1] In this sense, the good news of the gospel reveals what it means to be a human person. But, as soon as we look into the question of personhood, we find ourselves obliged to engage in eschatology. Eschatology is a fundamental component in our interpretation of personhood for three reasons. First, it concerns our new identity in Christ, which begins with the death of the old self and the rising in Christ of the new self. Second, it provides the

---

1. Vatican Council II, *Gaudium et Spes*, 41.

telos for human existence (*theosis*).² Third, it informs our understanding of temporality and the human person as a being in time. It is these notions concerning eschatology and personhood that Schmemann and Ratzinger have both helped to define and cast in a new light.

There are, in sum, two main questions that I have sought to address in this monograph. First, how do Schmemann's and Ratzinger's interpretations of eschatology inform their respective conceptions of human temporality? Second, what are their resulting interpretations of what it means to be a person? In short, what does it mean to be a person in time?

Schmemann is more enigmatic than Ratzinger, particularly on this topic. There are two main reasons for this: (1) Schmemann is not a systematic theologian, and (2) theological anthropology is a secondary concern that arises only in relation to his essential concern, i.e., liturgical theology. In order to make sense of Schmemann's view of eschatology and personhood, I had to form connections between various notions that Schmemann himself did not always succeed in integrating. Ratzinger, on the other hand, writes with great clarity and focus, and his analysis of the relationship between personhood and eschatology has received a significant amount of his attention in both article and monograph form.

References to relationality are found throughout most of Ratzinger's works, which verify the centrality it plays in his theological vision (e.g., his spiritual Christology). Similarly, one would be hard-pressed to find a single work of Schmemann's that does not somehow touch on eschatology or the kingdom. It is arguable that this difference of focus in Ratzinger's and Schmemann's work is apparent in their divergent conceptions of temporality. At the heart of the matter, the difference between the two theologians is a matter of time.

A Person in Time

What does it mean to be a person in time? We have come at this question from a number of angles. Here, I would like to summarize as briefly as possible Schmemann's and Ratzinger's answers to this question. For Schmemann, it is possible to collapse all the distinctions about what it means to be a person in time with one simple phrase from Schmemann's book *For the Life of the World*: "The basic definition of man is that he is

---

2. Webster highlights these two aspects of why theological anthropology is eschatological. See Webster, "Eschatology, Anthropology and Postmodernity," 14.

the priest."³ Time is the space within which the human person lovingly and freely offers all back to God. This means that, in Christ, we offer not only ourselves but the world and time back to him. What has been given as gift, we give back in thanksgiving as gift. In so doing, we fulfill the relational element and our existence as Eucharist. Here, temporality (the old eon) is offered *up* and opened to eternity, to the new eon, and is made meaningful. Thus, for Schmemann, our priestly identity is anagogical. As priests, we also participate in this meaning. Through our priestly participation, we move anagogically into deeper communion with God, always climbing further up and further in to everlasting love. Since this journey begins here in this world, Schmemann suggests that we can embrace this life and echo St. Peter: "Lord, it is good for us to be here."[4]

For Ratzinger, we find our identity in the homeward movement of *reditus*, in which we are transformed into persons in the fullest sense. In the constant death of self that begins with baptism and continues into the rest of life, we move deeper into union with Christ and are drawn into his act of sacrifice.[5] This is not something we do on our own, but, rather, it takes place in the body of Christ. As the body, we are to suffer vicariously for the world with Christ. Thus, what it means to be a person (truly Christian) is to live for the other, a dying to the self for the life of the world: "Election is always at bottom election for others."[6] This life, our temporality, is relational. As pilgrims, we move through temporality, deepening relations as we wait for and, at the same time, already partake in the definiteness of temporality, in which time is transformed into eternity. Personhood, as such, is not counter to the human person as a creature, but, rather, it is in her very nature to transcend herself. All who participate in God participate in his all in all, and "that is why the purely private existence of the isolated self no longer exists, but 'all that is mine is yours.'"[7] Truly, in Christ, "I become a thousand men and yet remain myself."[8]

---

3. Schmemann, *For Life of World*, 15.

4. Schmemann, *Liturgy and Life*, 88. Most of this paragraph comes from the conclusion I offer in Kaethler, "Eucharistic Anthropology."

5. Ratzinger, *Pilgrim Fellowship of Faith*, 116.

6. Ratzinger, *Christian Brotherhood*, 80.

7. Ratzinger, *God Is Near Us*, 145.

8. Lewis, *Experiment in Criticism*, 141. Lewis uses this phrase to talk about the effect that reading good literature has on one's life. I used the phrase because it poetically highlights life in Christ, but I also think it is arguable that there is a connection between literature and theology and that they, at times, act upon us in similar ways.

Shared Affinities

As this project began with ecumenical hopes, it is only fitting to highlight the points of contact before recapitulating the differences. The relational nature of the human person is the most significant similarity. The human person has identity in God, and, through God, she is put in relation with all of reality. Relationships are not an addition to personhood but constitute the very nature of the person. Schmemann describes this by positing that the role of the church is to transform individuals into persons.[9] Ratzinger expresses the same point by saying, "It is because the human being is capable of the absolute Thou that he is an I who can become a Thou for another I. The capacity for the absolute Thou is the ground of the possibility and necessity of the human partner."[10] The relational grounding for both theologians is found in Christology.

Both theologians see the Son's relationship with the Father as key to understanding personhood. Schmemann focuses on Christ's obedience to the Father and claims that this is not merely an external act but is the fiber of Christ's being. He is obedience. This marks his sonship and is the basis for our sonship. In Christ's obedience, my obedience finds traction and becomes my identity. Ratzinger also highlights Christ's obedience but primarily through the lens of dialogue, through Christ's yes. The communication between the Father and Son is the center of the Son's being. Christ's yes is part of the ongoing dialogue. Accordingly, the divine prepositions of the Trinity are *for* (Father), *from*, (Son) and *with* (Holy Spirit), an interdependent relationship of persons. By becoming man, Christ took human speech and made it his own, and, in so doing, his yes has opened the doors for all human affirmative responses. Our yes is the yes of God. Ratzinger fleshes out the implications of sonship for anthropology to a much greater degree than Schmemann. The central claim he makes is that the human person is never more herself than when she transcends herself. She is called to give herself away in love, and it is here that she finds herself (*is* herself). The breaking down of the isolated ego not only enables us to recognize the truth about ourselves (we are contingent beings) but also opens us to the relational fabric of reality. By being myself, I am in fellowship. What is clear for both theologians is that human personhood is fulfilled only through participation in Christ.

---

9. Schmemann, *Of Water and Spirit*, 143.

10. Ratzinger, "Dignity of Human Person," 122. See Ratzinger, *Chritian Brotherhood*, 50.

Sonship and Trinitarian relations are absolutely central for Ratzinger's concept of person, whereas, beyond the Son's relational obedience, Schmemann says very little about Trinitarian relations. In his journal and in "Towards a Theology of Councils,"[11] Schmemann reflects on the Trinitarian hierarchy as a relationship of love and equality, but, in large measure, the depths of personhood remain unplumbed. Nevertheless, this is not to suggest that Schmemann would have problems with Ratzinger's account of the Trinity as *true persons*, in which "person is the pure relativity of being turned toward each other."[12] Likewise, there is nothing in Ratzinger's spiritual Christology that is in stark tension with Schmemann's approach. The personal, epistemological, and volitional theses all fit within Schmemann's broad canvas of thanksgiving.

Divergences: Temporal Problems

Schmemann's and Ratzinger's different accounts of eschatology and temporality can be broadly summarized in two ways. First, relationality is what shapes Ratzinger's eschatology, and eschatology is what shapes Schmemann's relational vision. Second, Ratzinger understands history as a continual Advent—*fulfillment* is the key term—whereas Schmemann argues that history is divided into a before and after Christ; the key term is *end*.

There is no doubt that Ratzinger provides a more comprehensive vision of what it means to be a person in time than Schmemann. But this does not necessarily entail that his account is superior. We must ask, who offers a more cogent and consistent vision of what it means to be a person in time? And, of particular concern in this work, who provides a consistent image of relationality and temporality? Whose vision of eschatology and temporality is unfailingly relational?

My conclusion is that, as a result of an inconsistent relational vision, Schmemann's perspective dangerously teeters toward denigrating both temporality and relationality. Ratzinger, on the other hand, has a relationally consistent perspective. His vision of relationality goes all the way down, so to speak, and we see this in his view of history, time, and the immortality of the soul. We shall look at each of these in turn and highlight Schmemann's shortcomings in contrast with Ratzinger's consistent account.

---

11. Schmemann, *Church, World, Mission*, 165–66.
12. Ratzinger, *Joseph Ratzinger in Communio*, 2:108.

History

Schmemann has a divided view of history that can be linearly charted, in which there is a before and after Christ or, as he would put it, the old and new aeons. Accordingly, he argues that history came to its completion in Christ. He is the end of history. In contrast, Ratzinger argues that history is indivisible. As those who lived before us, we live in the Advent of time, and "it is characterized as a whole by the weakness and wretchedness of man, and as a whole it stands beneath the merciful love of God, who constantly surrounds and supports this history."[13] History will end with the fullness of time, when Christ returns. The last judgment will mark the end of history, and then God will have completed what he started and be all in all.

The problem with Schmemann's depiction of history concerns his focus on the end. The end has happened, and everything that follows has meaning only in reference to it. Beyond the problems this raises in regard to why, post-Christ, there is still evil and corruption in the world is the problem of relationality. Schmemann's focus on the end, on that which is outside of time, means that relationships with God are unidirectional. To embroider my criticism, we could turn to St. Patrick's famous prayer and make bold what Schmemann's view of history highlights at the expense of the other senses of Christ's presence:

> Christ with me, Christ before me, Christ behind me,
> Christ in me, Christ beneath me, Christ above me,
> Christ on my right, Christ on my left,
> Christ when I lie down, Christ when I sit down,
> Christ in the heart of every man who thinks of me,
> Christ in the mouth of every man who speaks of me,
> Christ in the eye that sees me,
> Christ in the ear that hears me.[14]

Schmemann's view *risks* taking Christ out of the world.[15] Yes, Christ is *accessible* through the world (anagogy), but he is *encountered* beyond this world in the new eon. It is only in the new eon that we experience the fullness of Christ's presence, "Christ before me" and "Christ above me," as presented in St. Patrick's prayer. Ratzinger's vision of history, on the other hand, takes up all of St. Patrick's prayer. Christ is not simply the

---

13. Ratzinger, *What It Means*, 35.
14. Patrick, "Lorica of St Patrick."
15. It is clear that this is not Schmemann's intent. For a helpful discussion of this, see Plekon, "World as Sacrament."

end toward whom we move. As Ratzinger makes clear, Christ surrounds and supports us in the midst of history, in this temporal existence (and in the intermediate state). Ratzinger's relationality goes all the way down.

Time

Schmemann has a compelling yet problematic view of time. It is compelling because it resonates with one aspect of our experience of time: time unceasingly moves us toward death. It is problematic for three reasons. First, it is incomplete and is severed from our experience of time as movement of the heart/spirit. Second, like his view of history, it is unidirectional. Third, it is dualistic, and, consequently, it means that a barrier has been erected between God and the world. The problem underlying all three points is that Schmemann's perspective denigrates time. We shall look at each point in turn.

As expounded in chapter 1, Schmemann argues that there are two experiences of time: time as cyclical and time as death. The first experience is cosmic and concerns the seasons. This cyclical experience seems to reveal an endless cycle of life and death. While both life and death revolve around each other in cyclical time, in the second experience of time, death looms before us. Time is experienced as a road ending in death. Schmemann argues that the second experience dominates the first. Death presides over life. As compelling and, in many ways, as true to experience as this account of time is, it is incomplete. It recognizes only one mode of time, i.e., physical time. The cyclical account of time is based upon cosmic movement, and the second account of time is founded on biological movement. As both accounts are based on time as physical movement, the emphasis is placed on the end. The cyclical account is, in large part, free from this critique,[16] but Schmemann's emphasis is on the latter view. Time as death is his anthropological view of time, a view of time that is teleologically focused. This understanding of time does not take into account the nonlinear and nonprogressive experience of time as *memoria*-time, in which the past, present, and future have porous boundaries—movement of the heart/spirit. Schmemann's limited account of time is reflected in his unidirectionalism and dualism.

---

16. The human experience of cyclical time does not include an end; but, unless the cosmos is eternal, which is not the conclusion of modern science, it ultimately has a physical end.

CONCLUSION: A MATTER OF TIME

According to Schmemann's logic, as beings in time, humans are inevitably swept down the river of time toward death. If we are to be saved from time's death-inducing grip, time itself must be transformed. Thus, the Son entered into our temporality, including its conclusion, death. But death could not overcome life himself, and, as a result, Christ is the new *telos* of time. Accordingly, time is still experienced as a linear progression. The difference simply concerns the end. Inevitably, Schmemann's unidirectional conception of time means that anyone who desires to be with Christ desires *ipso facto* to transcend time. This is reflected in Schmemann's understanding of sacrament as passage. Death itself is sacramental and therefore can be transformed into a passage into life. Passage, for Schmemann, involves an upward movement, a lifting out of the old into the new. Consequently the unidirectional emphasis easily lends itself to a denigration of the present.

To be fair, Schmemann argues that Christ is with us in the present (via the church), and the end is an event in the midst of human time. We gather on the first day of the old eon and, on this *statu die*, we enter into the new eon:

> From the very beginning, it was on the *first day* of the week (i.e., on the day following the seventh day) that Christians gathered as "Church" to celebrate the Eucharist. Thus, in terms of "this world," this was one of the seven days, fully belonging to the time of this world. Yet the whole meaning of that gathering, of that celebration, as we already have said, was that in it the Church experienced herself as ascending to heaven, and this means fulfilling herself beyond time, partaking at Christ's table of His eternal Kingdom. She experienced the first day of the time of "this world" as the *eighth day*—the one beyond time, beyond seven, beyond "this world"—as her participation in the "day without evening" of the Kingdom.[17]

In other words, Schmemann wants to maintain that our present intersects with our future, and, at this intersection, we encounter Christ. But, clearly, the present is only a point, albeit a specific point, of departure. Time acts as a barrier that must be transcended, but this can happen only from our side (the church ascends to the new). Schmemann argues that the new cannot enter into the old without subsuming it. Schmemann's

---

17. Schmemann, *Of Water and Spirit*, 122–23. Note especially "fulfilling herself beyond time."

old and new dualism must remain in tension in order to preserve the freedom and the distinction of the old.

Unfortunately, Schmemann's earnest intention to preserve the import of time ultimately fails, and his dualistic vision denigrates it. His antinomical tension/dualism is really about anagogical ascent. Our temporality is simply a means to enter the new eon. Time is a stairway to heaven. Paradoxically, temporality functions as a means to transcend temporality, so that we can encounter Christ. The Son entered our world and left. If we desire to have fellowship, we must also leave and ascend to the new eon.

It is true that, by having Christ as the end, our lives are instilled with purpose. In this regard, Schmemann successfully preserves the importance of this life. Yet, in the process, he denigrates temporality, for the purpose of this life is to get beyond this life: it is in the new eon that we truly have relationship with the Son.[18] Or, as he words it, the church fulfills "herself beyond time."[19]

18. Certainly, Schmemann did not intend to denigrate the temporal. The following quotation is a great example of his attempt to highlight the importance of this world: "We should concentrate upon this world lovingly because it is full of God, because by way of the Eucharist we find Him everywhere—in hideous disasters as well as in little flowers. In a way it is not supernatural at all; we return to our original nature, to the garden where Adam met God in the cool of the evening. No, we do not meet Him wholly and unconsciously: we are still fallen, still estranged, and our fallen nature could not at present survive that. A sacramental correspondence is not an identification. *It always points beyond.* But it creates also a present unity, making us contemporary witnesses of Christ's death but also of His coming again, and of the fulfillment of all things in Him. Thankfully we accept from God's hands His lovely garden, the world. We eat its fruits, transform its substance into life, offer that life to God on Christ's cross and our daily altars, and look forward to the possession of it, as a risen body, in the Kingdom. But it will be the same world, the same life. 'Behold, I make all things new.' These were God's last words to us, and they only say at the end, and eternally, what was in his mind at the very beginning, when he looked on the sacramental world of his creation and saw that it was good" (Schmemann, *Church, World, Mission*, 226–27 [italics added]). In this beautiful passage, we see the struggle Schmemann has with bringing together the two worlds. He inevitably returns to what is beyond. Furthermore, the Eucharist, according to Schmemann, allows us to see the world for what it *will be*. It is always a forward looking vision, or an eschatological vision of the new eon.

19. We must also asks where Schmemann's perspective leads in terms of nature. If we are always trying to get beyond the old eon, nature, too, is anagogical. Schmemann prefers to remain silent on the nature-grace question, which he sees as a Western concern. The East, he argues focuses instead on the old and the new. In this regard, he is clear that, with the coming of Christ, we are not given a new world but one made anew. Does this sufficiently engage with the question of nature? See Schmemann, *Church, World, Mission*, 225–26. He is certainly correct that the nature-grace question

Ratzinger avoids the problems to which Schmemann falls prey because Ratzinger has a consistent and well-developed view of temporality. As we saw in chapter 3, he recognizes that time involves movement but maintains that there are two types of movement: physical movement and movement of the heart/spirit (anthropological time). Ratzinger makes sense of the latter movement with Augustine's *memoria*-time. This enables Ratzinger to affirm relationality and temporality in three ways. First, *memoria*-time is relationally grounded and dialogical, rather than unidirectional. *Memoria*-time reflects a temporality that is shaped by the befores and afters of relationships. Both human and divine love, which are at the core of *memoria*-time, are not enslaved to the forward flow of physical time. Second, it avoids the old and new dualism. *Memoria*-time, so to speak, foreshadows eternity. Therefore, we do not need to leave behind our temporality (*memoria*-time) in order to enter eternity. Likewise, but in reverse, eternity can enter into time without subsuming it; eternity makes definite the human experience of time. Simply put, eternity can enter into the human realm of temporality without destroying it, for eternity is not counter to anthropological time/*memoria*-time. In Ratzinger's account, time is not a barrier between humanity and God.[20] Third, the relational element of *memoria*-time correlates with the relational movement of history. In death, the human person remains connected to history, both in the memories of others and in her own experience of *memoria*-time.

---

is important to the West. The typical Catholic position articulates that "grace builds on nature, working through it, elevating and perfecting it. Nature is not something to be transcended" (Rausch, "Catholic Anthropology," 37).

20. Time is a barrier only "if we deny ourselves an existence which allows itself to span these dimensions [yesterday, today, and eternity]" (Ratzinger, *Joseph Ratzinger in Communio*, 2:85). Ratzinger argues that, by cutting ourselves off from these dimensions, we cut ourselves off from Christ, "for only that which possesses roots in yesterday and the power of growth for tomorrow and for all time has true power over today and in today, and stands in contact with eternity" (Ratzinger, *Joseph Ratzinger in Communio*, 2:86). Elsewhere, in the context of the problems with pure monotheism, he argues that "if there cannot be a reciprocal influence between time and eternity, then eternity (if there is an eternity) can be of no significance to men" (Ratzinger, *Feast of Faith*, 21). The comment in parentheses concerns Ratzinger's rejection of eternity as timelessness: "Instead of the negative 'timelessness' of eternity, we need to work out a concept of the creativity which eternity exercises with regard to time" (Ratzinger, *Feast of Faith*, 21). It is worth noting that, in the section where the aforementioned quotation is found, Ratzinger uses the logic of prayer to argue against monotheism in its pure Aristotelian sense. Pure monotheism is problematic because it is non-relational.

In light of Ratzinger's conception of time, we can see where Schmemann errs and are given a hint as to where, within Schmemann's own thought, a solution can be sought: the memory of God and remembrance. Schmemann's account of memory and remembrance is similar to Ratzinger's *memoria*-time. If Schmemann had allowed his account of memory and remembrance to shape his conception of temporality, he may very well have avoided the aforementioned problems. But, unfortunately, Schmemann's view of memory and remembrance is subsumed by his teleological and eschatological theory of temporality. Memory and remembrance remain beyond the confines of the old eon. As a result, his view of time problematically remains dependent on the mode of physical movement.

The Last Things

Schmemann claims that an eschatology that is concerned with the last things is an eschatology that has no bearing on the present and is the result of a juridical and individualistic aberration. In order to preserve the import of this life, he repeatedly calls his readers to return to the eschatological vision of the fathers. Ironically, it is Schmemann's eschatologically informed temporality that inadvertently denigrates the present.

As a result of his intentional avoidance of the last things, Schmemann's account of the soul and the intermediate state suffer. His relational account of identity is inconsistent. Schmemann insists that the body is the most significant element of the human person—chiefly, the body is our means of communion. The soul simply functions as an identity placeholder. In other words, for the sake of avoiding the last things and the Platonism they supposedly entail, Schmemann elevates the role of the body and demotes the soul. What he fails to realize is that, by emphasizing the body, he creates a functional dualism. Not only is this the exact opposite of what he intends, it also contradicts his relational ontology. That is, Schmemann maintains that our identity is found in relation to God; but the problem with his account is that the soul is unable to commune, and therefore, bodily death extinguishes our identity. According to the logic of Schmemann's account, death separates us from God, from history, and from ourselves. In short, if Schmemann is to retain the Christian notion of life after death, he either must reject his relational ontology or must reformulate his conception of the soul.

Ratzinger's relational vision of reality, which is grounded in the Trinity, shapes the way he conceives of the kingdom and the last things. It is fascinating that Ratzinger's eschatological vision embraces what Schmemann criticizes yet falls prey to none of Schmemann's conclusive judgments. Ratzinger's vision of the last things is based on the import of temporality and the anti-individualistic I-Thou-We vision of personhood. Thus, his account of the immortality of the soul accentuates the relational fabric of reality. In death, the soul is with Christ—*in* his body— and its identity remains relational, related to God, the saints, and those within history.

Relationality and Thanksgiving

Ratzinger's theology is thoroughly relational, and Schmemann's is grounded in gratitude. The correlation of relationality and temporality in Ratzinger's approach has already been expounded, but how does thanksgiving correlate with Schmemann's view of temporality? For Schmemann, the image of thanksgiving is associated with our priestly calling. The priest is one who offers everything *up* to God in thanksgiving. To put it differently, our priestly activity is to gratefully lift the world out of the old and into the new eon. The act of thanksgiving for Schmemann is clearly anagogical. We have already looked at why this is problematic, yet a theology of thanksgiving is not necessarily dependent on Schmemann's perspective of temporality; it is not necessarily anagogical.

Schmemann's emphasis on thanksgiving can be maintained in Ratzinger's theological vision. Ratzinger writes about the eucharistic "transformation of existence into thanksgiving"[21] that occurs through participation in the words, worship, and sacrifice of Christ. Certainly, the grammar of thanksgiving has a place in his vision.[22] Nevertheless, Ratzinger is most often recognized as a theologian of truth, and for good reason. Truth is a reoccurring theme in his writing and an important

---

21. Ratzinger, *God Is Near Us*, 51.

22. "Corpus Christi is to counter man's forgetfulness, to elicit thankfulness.... Our relationship to time is marked by forgetting.... The only way to master time, in fact, is the way of forgiving and thankfulness whereby we receive time as a gift and, in a spirit of gratitude, transform it" (Ratzinger, *Feast of Faith*, 129). "And true priesthood is therefore the ministry of word and sacrament that transforms people into an offering to God and makes the cosmos into praise and thanksgiving to the Creator and Redeemer" (Ratzinger, *Jesus of Nazareth*, 238).

aspect of his life.²³ Unfortunately, what is sometimes overlooked is Ratzinger's argument that love is the counterpart to truth. As Twomey makes clear in his article on the centrality of truth in Ratzinger, "God Himself is the Truth. The truth is to know Christ Jesus, to be led by his Spirit into the fullness of Truth."²⁴ The truth is a person and is love himself. Regardless, we live in an era in which the notion of truth is more often than not deemed offensive. The language of thanksgiving, on the other hand, carries a certain appeal.²⁵ As a result of the damaging footprint we are leaving on the environment, an increasing number of people are beginning to recognize that we are not technological masters of this world but rather participants (perhaps a subtle awareness of our contingency). Such a recognition can elicit a sense of gratitude, and thus the grammar of gratitude can act as a segue to Christian dialogue. But as much as thanksgiving resonates with the (post)modern soul, truth cannot be avoided. Truth and thanksgiving are connected.

Properly understood, thanksgiving is based on truth, especially the truth about God and the love he has for us.²⁶ In this sense, Ratzinger and Schmemann complement each other. We can truly be thankful and celebrate because death has been overcome; death is no longer the truth about this life. Contra Nietzsche, Christianity affirms life by acknowledging its eternal quality.²⁷ We can celebrate because of the resurrection. Jesus is the truth, and he is life. We can celebrate and be grateful because of the truth: "The novel Christian reality is this: Christ's Resurrection enables man genuinely to rejoice."²⁸ The language of thanksgiving may

---

23. See Twomey, "Centrality of Truth."

24. Twomey, "Centrality of Truth."

25. Twomey acutely notes that "the theme of truth in Ratzinger's writings would be incomplete, if I did not mention another theme that runs through his writing: joy. It is the term that is most frequently repeated in his homilies and addresses since his election [as pope]. Truth is the source of joy, above all the truth that God is love, that creation is due to his loving design, that man's sin has been overcome by his incarnate love, that we can encounter him in Word and sacrament" (Twomey, "Centrality of Truth"). Joy seems to capture something similar to gratitude. The emphasis on joy highlights the pastoral wisdom of Ratzinger as Pope Benedict XVI. Ratzinger is well aware of the modern aversion to truth. See Ratzinger, *Joseph Ratzinger in Communio*, 2:88.

26. Ratzinger, *Feast of Faith*, 65.

27. See Nietzsche, *Birth of Tragedy*, 23.

28. Ratzinger, *Feast of Faith*, 65.

be a good place to begin dialogue in our contemporary setting, but a Christian theology of gratitude is a theology grounded in truth.[29]

Finally, gratitude emphasizes the gift of life, and, as a spiritual posture, it orients us toward the gift of the Eucharist. This liturgical posturing is where all theology must begin and end. It is here that I learn to perceive reality properly by recognizing the Thou of my reality, and am opened to the we of my identity. What Ratzinger offers to Schmemann's theology of gratitude is a refocusing, in which gratitude not only looks toward the future and the past but to the present. In gratitude, I can offer my yes in the midst of Christ's ongoing yes.[30] And in the celebration of the Eucharist, my gratitude partakes in the eternality of time, not taking me out of time but solidifying time as eternal, as relational.[31]

Conclusion

In order to provide a consistent account of how Schmemann conceives of what it means to be a person in time, I have brought together and organized various elements of his theology. By placing this in dialogue with Ratzinger's account of what it means to be a person in time, we have seen the shortcomings of Schmemann's approach. Schmemann's account of temporality and eschatology do not reflect the relationality of reality, a relationality that emanates from the Trinitarian relationship. His dualism of old and new, his division of history, and his exclusive focus on ends is problematic. Schmemann's eschatology appears to subsume Christ; in other words, for Schmemann, eschatology precedes Christology. As a result, Schmemann unintentionally degrades temporality and narrows the scope of human and divine relationship. This side of Schmemann's theology, arguably, would best be supplanted by Ratzinger's thoroughgoing relational theology. Ratzinger's conception of *exitus et reditus* avoids the antinomical tension of old and new, and it permits him to have an

---

29. I think Ratzinger's emphasis on truth is extremely important, especially in regard to theological anthropology. For example, in Susan Ross's recent book on Catholic anthropology, the trends of culture dictate her approach, particularly with gender, birth control, and sexuality. She repeatedly criticizes the church's position because it does not fit with the current perspectives, but she does not ask if such perspectives are true. As a result, her book lacks critical engagement and, in large part, is mere assertion. See ch. 5 in Ross, *Anthropology*, 85–107.

30. See Ratzinger, *God Is Near Us*, 19–20.

31. Ratzinger, *God Is Near Us*, 53.

undivided view of history—a continual Advent. Finally, Ratzinger's concept of *memoria*-time allows for the purpose that comes from having a teleology but evades the enslavement of the forward movement of time. In so doing, Ratzinger provides a vision of temporality that is relationally dialogical. By subsuming eschatology in Christology, Ratzinger's vision of temporality and the last things remains fundamentally relational.

Unfortunately, Schmemann's approach to the West is too often polemical.[32] As a result, many of his criticisms of the West miss their mark or are outdated.[33] And there is an irony in the fact that much of his polemics are actually inspired by Western thinkers, i.e., the *ressourcement* theologians.[34] This facet of his approach damages the ecumenical conversation, a vitally important conversation. Ratzinger's theology clearly demonstrates that Schmemann's claims about the vapidity of the West are ill founded. Chapters 3 and 4 reveal that Ratzinger's theology affirms life, temporality, and relationality. His theology of the last things is not the result of a juridical and individualized understanding of Christianity. In fact, as we saw, in terms of relationality, Ratzinger's theological vision extends further than Schmemann's, and, in this regard, Schmemann could only gain by turning westward to the work of Ratzinger.

---

32. A great example of this can be seen in his response to Andrew Sopko's reflection on Orthodox psychological negativism (Schmemann et al., "Debate on Western Rite"). There are exceptions, where Schmemann takes on a hopeful ecumenical tenor. For example, see Schmemann, "Rome, Ecumenical Council."

33. He seems to overlook the developments of Vatican II. Nevertheless, the West still can learn much from Schmemann. For example, see O'Donoghue, "Schmemann's Challenge"; Fagerberg, "Cost of Understanding Schmemann."

34. O'Donoghue, "Schmemann's Challenge," 141.

Bibliography

Andresen, C. "Zur Entstehung und Geschichte des trinitarischen Personenbegriffs." *Zeitschrift für die neutestamentliche Wissenschaft und die Kunde der ältern Kirche* 52 (1961) 1–38.

Aquinas, Thomas. *Summa Contra Gentiles*. Jacques Maritain Center, n.d. https://maritain.nd.edu/jmc/etext/gc.htm.

Ayres, Lewis, et al. "Benedict XVI: A Ressourcement Theologian?" In *Ressourcement: A Movement for Renewal in Twentieth-Century Catholic Theology*, edited by Gabriel Flynn and Paul D. Murray, 423–39. Oxford: Oxford University Press, 2012.

Barth, Karl. *Church Dogmatics* 4/2. Translated by G. W. Bromiley. London: T. & T. Clark, 2009.

———. *The Epistle to the Romans*. Translated by Edwyn C. Hoskyns. London: Oxford University Press, 1968.

Benedict XVI, Pope. *Tod und Ewiges Leben*. 6th ed. Regensburg, Germany: Pustet, 1990.

Boersma, Hans. *Embodiment and Virtue in Gregory of Nyssa: An Anagogical Approach*. Oxford: Oxford University Press, 2013.

———. *Heavenly Participation: The Weaving of a Sacramental Tapestry*. Grand Rapids: Eerdmans, 2011.

———. *Nouvelle Théologie and Sacramental Ontology: A Return to Mystery*. Oxford: Oxford University Press, 2009.

Boeve, Lieven. "Europe in Crisis: A Question of Belief or Unbelief? Perspectives from the Vatican." *Modern Theology* 23 (2007) 205–27.

———. "Revelation, Scripture and Tradition: Lessons from Vatican II's Constitution *Dei Verbum* for Contemporary Theology." *International Journal of Systematic Theology* 13 (2011) 416–33.

Bouyer, Louis. *Life and Liturgy*. London: Sheed and Ward, 1962.

Bulgakov, Sergius. *Icons and the Name of God*. Translated by Boris Jakim. Grand Rapids: Eerdmans, 2012.

Catechism of the Catholic Church. 2nd ed. Vatican City: Vatican, 2000.

Cavanaugh, William T. *Theopolitical Imagination: Discovering the Liturgy as a Political Act in an Age of Global Consumerism*. London: T. & T. Clark, 2002.

Cayley, David. *George Grant in Conversation*. Concord, ON: Anansi, 1995.

Chesterton, G. K. *Orthodoxy*. New York: Doubleday, 2001.

Chrysostom, John. "The Divine Liturgy of St John Chrysostom." St. Nicholas Russian Orthodox Church, n.d. http://www.orthodox.net/services/sluzebnic-chrysostom.pdf.

Collins, Christopher S. *The Word Made Love: The Dialogical Theology of Joseph Ratzinger / Benedict XVI*. Collegeville, MN: Liturgical, 2013.

Corkery, James. *Joseph Ratzinger's Theological Ideas: Wise Cautions and Legitimate Hopes*. Dublin: Dominican, 2009.

Cullmann, Oscar. *Immortality of the Soul or Resurrection of the Dead? The Witness of the New Testament*. London: Epworth, 1958.

Cunningham, Lawrence S. "Reflections on *Introduction to Christianity*." In *Explorations in the Theology of Benedict XVI*, edited by John C. Cavadini, 142–54. Notre Dame, IN: University of Notre Dame Press, 2012.

Daniélou, Jean. "The Conception of History in the Christian Tradition." *Journal of Religion* 3 (1950) 171–79.

Drever, Matthew. *Image, Identity, and the Forming of the Augustinian Soul*. Oxford: Oxford University Press, 2013.

Fagerberg, David W. "The Cost of Understanding Schmemann in the West." *St. Vladimir's Theological Quarterly* 53 (2009) 179–207.

———. *On Liturgical Asceticism*. Washington, DC: Catholic University of America Press, 2013.

———. *Theologia Prima: What Is Liturgical Theology?* Chicago: Hillenbrand, 2004.

Fletcher, Patrick J. *Resurrection Realism: Ratzinger the Augustinian*. Eugene, OR: Cascade, 2014.

Flynn, Gabriel, and Paul D. Murray, eds. *Ressourcement: A Movement for Renewal in Twentieth-Century Catholic Theology*. Oxford: Oxford University Press, 2012.

Gaál, Emery de. *The Theology of Pope Benedict XVI: The Christocentric Shift*. New York: Palgrave MacMillan, 2010.

Guerriero, Elio. *Benedict XVI: His Life and Thought*. Translated by William J. Melcher. San Francisco: Ignatius, 2018.

Hart, David Bentley. *Atheist Delusions: The Christian Revolution and Its Fashionable Enemies*. New Haven, CT: Yale University Press, 2009.

Hastetter, Michaela C. *Die Dynamik der Theologie Joseph Ratzingers: Quellen und Konsequenzen*. Regensburg, Germany: Schnell und Steiner, 2014.

Heidegger, Martin. *Being and Time*. Translated by Joan Stambaugh. New York: State University of New York Press, 1996.

———. *Discourse on Thinking*. Translated by John M. Anderson and E. Hans Freund. London: Harper & Row, 1966.

———. *The Question concerning Technology: And Other Essays*. Translated by William Lovitt. London: Garland, 1977.

Horan, Daniel P. "Beyond Essentialism and Complementarity: Toward a Theological Anthropology Rooted in *Haecceitas*." *Theological Studies* 75 (2014) 94–117.

Jenson, Robert W. "Eschatology." In *The Blackwell Companion to Political Theology*, edited by Peter Scott and William T. Cavanaugh, 407–20. Oxford: Blackwell, 2004.

John Paul II, Pope. *Redemptor Hominis*. Vatican, March 4, 1979. https://www.vatican.va/content/john-paul-ii/en/encyclicals/documents/hf_jp-ii_enc_04031979_redemptor-hominis.html.

Kadavil, Mathai. "Sacramental-Liturgical Theology: A Critical Appraisal of Alexander Schmemann's Sacramentology of 'Eschatological Symbolism.'" *Questions Liturgiques/Studies in Liturgy* 82 (2001) 112–27.

Kaethler, Andrew T. J. "Eucharistic Anthropology: Alexander Schmemann's Conception of Beings in Time." In *The Resounding Soul: Reflections on the Metaphysics and*

Vivacity of the Human Person, edited by Eric Austin Lee and Samuel Kimbriel, 60–77. Eugene, OR: Cascade, 2015.

———. "Freedom in Relationship: Joseph Ratzinger and Alexander Schmemann in Dialogue." *New Blackfriars* 95 (2014) 397–411.

———. "The God Who Draws Near to Us: A Ratzingerian Approach to Christology, Eschatology, and Protology." *Path: Pontificia Academia Theologica* 18 (2019) 403–22.

———. "'I Become a Thousand Men and Yet Remain Myself': Self-Love in Joseph Ratzinger and Georges Bernanos." *Logos: A Journal of Catholic Thought and Culture* 19 (Spring 2016) 150–67.

———. "Mary, Unity, and the Pathos for Equality: Alexander Schmemann's 'Scandalous' Embrace of Difference." *Logos* 22 (2019) 64–82.

Kasper, Walter. *The God of Jesus Christ*. Translated by Matthew J. O'Connell. London: SCM, 1983.

Keller, Catherine. "Seeking and Sucking: On Relation and Essence in Feminist Theology." In *Horizons in Feminist Theology: Identity, Tradition, and Norms*, edited by Rebecca S. Chopp and Sheila Greeve Davaney, 54–78. Minneapolis: Augsburg Fortress, 1997.

Kelsey, David H. "Two Theologies of Death: Anthropological Gleanings." *Modern Theology* 13 (1997) 347–70.

Kerr, Fergus. *Twentieth-Century Catholic Theologians: From Neoscholasticism to Nuptial Mysticism*. Oxford: Blackwell, 2007.

Knight, Douglas H. *The Eschatological Economy: Time and the Hospitality of God*. Cambridge, UK: Eerdmans, 2006.

Lash, Nicholas. "Are We Born and Do We Die?" *New Blackfriars* 90 (2009) 403–12.

Lewis, C. S. *An Experiment in Criticism*. Cambridge: Cambridge University Press, 2003.

———, ed. *George MacDonald: An Anthology: 365 Readings*. New York: HarperCollins, 2001.

———. *Mere Christianity*. New York: HarperCollins, 2001.

———. *The Voyage of the Dawn Treader*. Hammondsworth, UK: Puffin, 1975.

Loon, Hans van. "Karl Barth and the Early Church on Time: Liturgy and Time according to Alexander Schmemann." *Zeitschrift für Dialektische Theologie* 4 (2010) 209–22.

McGregor, Peter John. "The 'Spiritual Christology' of Joseph Ratzinger / Pope Benedict XVI: An Exposition and Analysis of Its Principles." *Radical Orthodoxy* 2 (2014) 51–89.

Metz, Johann Baptist, and Joseph Ratzinger. "God, Sin, and Suffering: A Conversation." In *The End of Time? The Provocation of Talking about God*, edited by Tiemo Raine Peters and Claus Urban, 47–53. New York: Paulist, 2004.

Meyendorff, John. "A Life Worth Living." In *Liturgy and Tradition: Theological Reflections of Alexander Schmemann*, edited by Thomas Fisch, 145–54. Crestwood, NY: St. Vladimir's Seminary Press, 2003.

Monge, Rico G. "Alexander Schmemann and 'the West': A Reexamination of Schmemann's Theological Vision in Light of His Engagement with Feuerbach and Nietzsche." *Questions Liturgiques/Studies in Liturgy* 93 (2012) 17–33.

Morrill, Bruce T. "The Journals of Father Alexander Schmemann, 1973–1983." *Worship* 76 (2002) 187–89.

"Most Cited Authors of Books in the Humanities, 2007." *Times Higher Education*, March 26, 2009. http://www.timeshighereducation.co.uk/405956.article.

Murphy, Nancey. *Bodies and Souls, or Spirited Bodies?* Cambridge: Cambridge University Press, 2006.

Nichols, Aidan. *The Thought of Benedict XVI: An Introduction to the Theology of Joseph Ratzinger.* London: Burns & Oates, 2005.

Nietzsche, Friedrich. *The Birth of Tragedy.* Translated by Walter Kaufmann. New York: Modern Library, 2000.

Noble, Ivana R. "From the Sacramentality of the Church to the Sacramentality of the World: An Exploration of the Theology of Alexander Schmemann and Louis-Marie Chauvet." In *Charting Churches in a Changing Europe: Charta Oecumenica and the Process of Ecumenical Encounter*, edited by Tim Noble et al., 165–200. Amsterdam: Rodopi, 2006.

O'Donoghue, Neil Xavier. "Schmemann's Challenge for Contemporary Roman Catholicism." *Irish Theological Quarterly* 73 (2008) 133–47.

Patrick. "Lorica of St Patrick." Ancient Texts, n.d. http://www.ancienttexts.org/library/celtic/ctexts/p03.html.

Pecknold, C. C. "'Man Is by Nature a Social and Political Animal': Essential and Anti-Essentialist Relational Ontologies Revisited." *Heythrop Journal* 57 (2016) 883–99.

Phan, Peter C. "Contemporary Context and Issues in Eschatology." *Theological Studies* 55 (1994) 507–36.

Pieper, Josef. *Faith, Hope, Love.* Translated by Richard Winston et al. San Francisco: Ignatius, 1997.

———. *Hope and History: Five Salzburg Lectures.* Translated by David Kipp. San Francisco: Ignatius, 1994.

Plekon, Michael. "'The World as Sacrament' in Alexander Schmemann's Vision." *Logos: A Journal of Eastern Christian Studies* 50 (2009) 429–39.

Ratzinger, Joseph. "The Abolition of Man." *Le Figaro*, n.d. Interview by Jean Sévilla. https://web.archive.org/web/20030619061907/http://www.traces-cl.com/dico1/theabol.htm.

———. *Auferstehung und ewiges Leben: Beiträge zur Eschatologie und zur Theologie der Hoffnung.* Edited by Gerhard Ludwig Müller et al. Vol. 10 of *Joseph Ratzinger Gesammelte Schriften.* Freiburg, Germany: Herder, 2012.

———. "Awake, and Christ Shall Give You Life." Catholic Culture, n.d. http://www.catholicculture.org/culture/library/view.cfm?recnum=6466.

———. *Behold the Pierced One: An Approach to a Spiritual Christology.* Translated by Graham Harrison. San Francisco: Ignatius, 1986.

———. "Biblical Interpretation in Crisis: On the Question of the Foundations and Approaches of Exegesis Today." Christendom Awake, April 19, 2004. http://www.christendom-awake.org/pages/ratzinger/biblical-crisis.htm.

———. *Called to Communion: Understanding the Church Today.* Translated by Adrian Walker. San Francisco: Ignatius, 1996.

———. "Catholicism after the Council." *Furrow* 18 (1967) 3–23.

———. *Christian Brotherhood.* Translated by W. A. Glen-Doepel. London: Burns & Oates, 1966.

———. *Church, Ecumenism, and Politics: New Endeavors in Ecclesiology.* Translated by Michael J. Miller et al. San Francisco: Ignatius, 2008.

———. "The Dignity of the Human Person." In *Commentary on the Documents of Vatican II*, edited by Herbert Vorgrimler, 115–63. New York: Herder and Herder, 1969.

———. *Dogma and Preaching: Applying Christian Doctrine to Daily Life*. Translated by Michael J. Miller and Matthew J. O'Connell. San Francisco: Ignatius, 2011.

———. "The End of Time." In *The End of Time? The Provocation of Talking About God*, edited by Tiemo Raine Peters and Claus Urban, 4–25. New York: Paulist, 2004.

———. *Eschatology: Death and Eternal Life*. Translated by Michael Waldstein. Washington, DC: Catholic University of America Press, 1988.

———. *Faith and the Future*. San Francisco: Ignatius, 1971.

———. *The Feast of Faith: Approaches to a Theology of the Liturgy*. Translated by Graham Harrison. San Francisco: Ignatius, 1986.

———. *God Is Near Us: The Eucharist, the Heart of Life*. Translated by Henry Taylor. San Francisco: Ignatius, 2003.

———. *The God of Jesus Christ: Meditations on God in the Trinity*. Translated by Brian McNeil. San Francisco: Ignatius, 2008.

———. *Gospel, Catechesis, Catechism: Sidelights on the Catechism of the Catholic Church*. Translated by Adrian Walker. San Francisco: Ignatius, 1997.

———. "Grußwort" (Greeting). In *Orthodoxie und Ökumene: Gesammelte Aufsätze von Damaskinos Papandreou*, by Damaskinos Papandreou, 10–11. Berlin: Schneemelcher, 1986.

———. *"In the Beginning": A Catholic Understanding of the Story of Creation and the Fall*. Translated by Boniface Ramsey. Grand Rapids: Eerdmans, 1995.

———. *Introduction to Christianity*. Translated by J. R. Foster. San Francisco: Ignatius, 2004.

———. *Jesus of Nazareth Part Two: Holy Week from the Entrance into Jerusalem to the Resurrection*. Translated by Vatican Secretariat of State. San Francisco: Ignatius, 2011.

———. *Joseph Ratzinger in Communio*. Edited by David L. Schindler and Nicholas J. Healy. 2 vols. Cambridge, UK: Eerdmans, 2010–2013.

———. "Konzilsaussagen über die Mission außerhalb des Missionsdekretes" (Conciliar Statements about the Mission outside the Missionary Decree). In *Mission nach dem Konzil*, edited by Johannes Schütte, page range unavailable. Mainz, Germany: Grünewald, 1967.

———. "Liturgy and Church Music." Musica Sacra, November 17, 1985. http://media.musicasacra.com/publications/sacredmusic/pdf/liturgy&music.pdf.

———. *Many Religions, One Covenant: Israel, the Church, and the World*. Translated by Graham Harrison. San Francisco: Ignatius, 1999.

———. *Milestones: Memoirs 1927–1977*. Translated by Erasmos Leiva-Merikakis. San Francisco: Ignatius, 1998.

———. "The Morality of Exile: Biblical Aspects of the Theme of Faith and Politics." *Letter & Spirit* 5 (2009) 265–68.

———. *The Nature and Mission of Theology: Essays to Orient Theology in Today's Debates*. Translated by Adrian Walker. San Francisco: Ignatius, 1995.

———. *Offenbarungsverständnis und Geschichtstheologie Bonaventuras*. Edited by Gerhard Ludwig Müller et al. Vol. 2 of *Joseph Ratzinger Gesammelte Schriften*. Habilitationsschrift und Bonaventura-Studien. Freiburg, Germany: Herder, 2009.

———. *On Conscience: Two Essays by Joseph Ratzinger*. Edited by Edward J. Furton. San Francisco: Ignatius, 2007.

———. "On the Meaning of Sacrament." *Fellowship of Catholic Scholars Quarterly* 34 (2011) 28–35.

———. *On the Way to Jesus Christ*. Translated by Michael J. Miller. San Francisco: Ignatius, 2005.

———. *Pilgrim Fellowship of Faith: The Church as Communion*. Translated by Henry Taylor. San Francisco: Ignatius, 2005.

———. *Principles of Catholic Theology: Building Stones for a Fundamental Theology*. Translated by Mary Frances McCarthy. San Francisco: Ignatius, 1987.

———. "The Problem of Threats to Human Life." Catholic Culture, April 8, 1991. https://www.catholicculture.org/culture/library/view.cfm?recnum=187.

———. *The Ratzinger Reader: Mapping a Theological Journey*. Edited by Gerard Mannion and Lieven Boeve. London: T. & T. Clark International, 2010.

———. *The Spirit of the Liturgy*. Translated by John Saward. San Francisco: Ignatius, 2000.

———. *Theological Highlights of Vatican II*. Translated by Henry Traub et al. New York: Paulist, 1966.

———. "The Theological Locus of Ecclesial Movements." *Communio* 25 (Fall 1998) 480–504.

———. *The Theology of History in St. Bonaventure*. Translated by Zachary Hayes. Chicago: Franciscan Herald, 1971.

———. "Truth and Freedom." *ICR* 23 (Spring 1996) 16–35.

———. *Truth and Tolerance: Christian and World Religions*. Translated by Henry Taylor. San Francisco: Ignatius, 2004.

———. *A Turning Point for Europe?* Translated by Brian McNeil. 2nd ed. San Francisco: Ignatius, 1994.

———. "Was ist der Mensch? (1966/1969)." *Mitteilungen des Institut Papst Benedikt XVI* (2008) 28–49.

———. *What It Means to Be a Christian: Three Sermons*. Translated by Henry Taylor. San Francisco: Ignatius, 2006.

———. *The Yes of Jesus Christ: Spiritual Exercises in Faith, Hope, and Love*. Translated by Robert Nowell. New York: Crossroad, 1991.

Ratzinger, Joseph, and Vittorio Messori. *The Ratzinger Report: An Exclusive Interview on the State of the Church*. Translated by Salvator Attanasio and Graham Harrison. San Francisco: Ignatius, 1985.

Ratzinger, Joseph, and Peter Seewald. *God and the World: A Conversation with Peter Seewald*. Translated by Henry Taylor. San Francisco: Ignatius, 2002.

———. *Salt of the Earth: Christianity and the Catholic Church at the End of the Millennium*. Translated by Adrian Walker. San Francisco: Ignatius, 1997.

Rausch, Thomas P. "Catholic Anthropology." In *Teaching the Tradition: Catholic Themes in Academic Disciplines*, edited by John J. Piderit and Melanie M. Morey, 31–45. Oxford: Oxford University Press, 2012.

———. *Eschatology, Liturgy, and Christology: Toward Recovering an Eschatological Imagination*. Collegeville, MN: Liturgical, 2012.

Ross, Susan A. *Anthropology: Seeking Light and Beauty*. Collegeville, MN: Liturgical, 2012.

Rowland, Tracey. *Benedict XVI: A Guide for the Perplexed*. London: T. & T. Clark, 2010.

———. *Ratzinger's Faith: The Theology of Pope Benedict XVI*. Oxford: Oxford University Press, 2008.

Rushdie, Salman. *Midnight's Children*. London: Folio Society, 2009.

BIBLIOGRAPHY

Sartre, Jean-Paul. *Existentialism and Humanism*. Translated by Philip Mairet. London: Methuen, 1989.

Schmemann, Alexander. "Appendix II: Four Previously Unpublished Talks on 'The Orthodox Liturgy of Death' by Father Alexander Schmemann." In "From Lamentation to Alleluia: An Interpretation of Theology of the Present-Day Byzantine-Rite Funeral Service Analyzed through Its Practical Relationship to Bereaved Persons," by Robert Alan Hutcheon, 310–60. PhD diss., Saint Paul University, 2003.

———. "The Christian Concept of Death." Schmemann, March 13–20, 1980. http://www.schmemann.org/byhim/thechristianconceptofdeath.html.

———. "The Church Is Hierarchical." *St. Vladimir's Seminary Quarterly* 3 (1959) 36–41.

———. *Church, World, Mission: Reflections on Orthodoxy in the West*. Crestwood, NY: St. Vladimir's Seminar Press, 1979.

———. *The Church Year*. Translated by John A. Jillions. Crestwood, NY: St. Vladimir's Seminary Press, 1994.

———. "Ecclesiological Notes." *St. Vladimir's Seminary Quarterly* 11 (1967) 35–39.

———. *The Eucharist: Sacrament of the Kingdom*. Translated by Paul Kachur. Crestwood, NY: St. Vladimir's Seminary Press, 1987.

———. "Fast and Liturgy." *St. Vladimir's Seminary Quarterly* 3 (1959) 2–9.

———. "Final Words." *The Orthodox Church* 20 (1984) 1.

———. *For the Life of the World: Sacraments and Orthodoxy*. Crestwood, NY: St. Vladimir's Seminary Press, 1973.

———. "Fr. Schmemann Addresses Antiochian Archdiocesan Convention in Toronto." Schmemann, November 1983. http://www.schmemann.org/byhim/addressesantiochian.html.

———. *Great Lent: Journey to Pascha*. Crestwood, NY: St. Vladimir's Seminary Press, 1969.

———. *The Historical Road of Eastern Orthodoxy*. Translated by Lydia W. Kesich. Crestwood, NY: St. Vladimir's Seminary Press, 2003.

———. *Introduction to Liturgical Theology*. Translated by Asheleigh E. Moorehouse. Crestwood, NY: St. Vladimir's Seminary Press, 1966.

———. *The Journals of Father Alexander Schmemann, 1973–1983*. Translated by Juliana Schmemann. Crestwood, NY: St. Vladimir's Seminary Press, 2002.

———. "A Liturgical Explanation of Holy Week." Orthodox Info, n.d. http://orthodoxinfo.com/general/a-liturgical-explanation-of-holy-week.pdf.

———. "Liturgical Theology: Its Task and Method." *St. Vladimir's Seminary Quarterly* 1 (1957) 16–27.

———. *Liturgy and Life: Christian Development through Liturgical Experience*. New York: Department of Religious Education, Orthodox Church in America, 1993.

———. *Liturgy and Tradition: Theological Reflections of Alexander Schmemann*. Edited by Thomas Fisch. Crestwood, NY: St. Vladimir's Seminary Press, 2003.

———. "The Mystery of Easter." *St. Vladimir's Seminary Quarterly* 2 (1954) 16–22.

———. *O Death, Where Is Thy Sting?* Translated by Alexis Vinogradov. Crestwood, NY: St. Vladimir's Seminary Press, 2003.

———. *Of Water and the Spirit: A Liturgical Study of Baptism*. Crestwood, NY: St. Vladimir's Seminary Press, 1974.

———. "The Problem of the Church's Presence in the World in Orthodox Consciousness." *St. Vladimir's Seminary Quarterly* 21 (1977) 3–17.

———. "Problems of Orthodoxy in America: The Canonical Problem." *St. Vladimir's Seminary Quarterly* 8 (1964) 67–85.

———. "Problems of Orthodoxy in America: The Liturgical Problem." *St. Vladimir's Seminary Quarterly* 8 (1964) 164–85.

———. "Problems of Orthodoxy in America: The Spiritual Problem." *St. Vladimir's Seminary Quarterly* 9 (1965) 171–93.

———. "Rome, the Ecumenical Council and the Orthodox Church." *St. Vladimir's Seminary Quarterly* 3 (1959) 2–5.

———. "St. Mark of Ephesus and the Theological Conflicts in Byzantium." *St. Vladimir's Seminary Quarterly* 1 (1957) 11–24.

———. "This Is the Blessed Sabbath." Schmemann, March 13, 1982. http://www.schmemann.org/byhim/matinsholysaturday.html.

———. "'Unity,' 'Division,' 'Reunion' in Light of Orthodox Ecclesiology." Θεολογία ΚΒ (1951) 242–54.

———. "Worship in a Secular Age." *St. Vladimir's Seminary Quarterly* 16 (1972) 3–16.

Schmemann, Alexander, et al. "A Debate on the Western Rite." *St. Vladimir's Seminary Quarterly* 24 (1980) 253–69.

Schmemann, Juliana. *My Journey with Father Alexander*. Montreal: Alexander, 2007.

Schmidt, Larry. *George Grant in Process: Essays and Conversations*. Toronto: Anansi, 1978.

Schumacher, Jared. "Mapping the Theo-Political: Metaphysics Prolegomenon for Political Theology." In *Between Being and Time: From Ontology to Eschatology*, edited by Andrew T. J. Kaethler and Sotiris Mitralexis, 221–46. London: Lexington/Fortress Academic, 2019.

Seewald, Peter. *Benedict XVI: A Life*. Translated by Dinah Livingstone. 2 vols. London: Bloomsbury Continuum, 2020–2021.

Steinbeck, John. *East of Eden*. New York: Penguin, 2002.

Tutu, Desmond. *No Future without Forgiveness*. New York: Doubleday, 1999.

Twomey, D. Vincent. "The Centrality of Truth in the Thought of Joseph Ratzinger." Catholic Culture, n.d. http://www.catholicculture.org/culture/library/view.cfm?recnum=8856.

———. *Pope Benedict XVI: The Conscience of Our Age: A Theological Portrait*. San Francisco: Ignatius, 2007.

Vatican Council II. *Gaudium et Spes*. Pastoral Constitution on the Church in the Modern World. Vatican, December 7, 1965. https://www.vatican.va/archive/hist_councils/ii_vatican_council/documents/vat-ii_const_19651207_gaudium-et-spes_en.html.

Vinogradov, Alexis. "Father Alexander Schmemann: Singing in the Right Key." Orthodox Research Institute, Fall 1996. http://www.orthodoxresearchinstitute.org/articles/dogmatics/vinogradov_schmemann_singing.html.

Voegelin, Eric. *The New Science of Politics: An Introduction*. Chicago: University of Chicago Press, 1952.

Ware, Kallistos. *The Inner Kingdom*. Vol. 1 of *The Collected Works*. Crestwood, NY: St. Vladimir's Seminary Press, 2000.

Webster, John. "Eschatology, Anthropology and Postmodernity." *International Journal of Systematic Theology* 2 (2000) 13–28.

———. "The Human Person." In *The Cambridge Companion to Postmodern Theology*, edited by Kevin J Vanhoozer, 219–34. Cambridge: Cambridge University Press, 2003.

White, David A. "On Historicism and Heidegger's Notion of Ontological Difference." *Monist* 64 (1981) 518–33.

Wilken, Robert Louis. *The Spirit of Early Christian Thought*. London: Yale University Press, 2003.

Wright, N. T. "'Mind, Spirit, Soul and Body: All for One and One for All. Reflections on Paul's Anthropology in His Complex Contexts." N. T. Wright, March 18, 2011. http://ntwrightpage.com/Wright_SCP_MindSpiritSoulBody.htm.

Yoder, John H. "Armaments and Eschatology." *Studies in Christian Ethics* 1 (1988) 43–61.

Zizioulas, John D. *Being as Communion: Studies in Personhood and the Church*. Trowbridge, UK: Cromwell, 1985.

Index

Abraham, 23, 105, 173, 181
Active aspect, 57, 61
Adam, xvii, 49, 57, 59, 61–62, 69, 86, 95, 99, 138, 141, 192; and Eve, xvii, 7, 13, 29, 44, 162
Adoration, 20, 34, 62–63, 76, 164
Advent, 127, 130–31, 165, 182, 188–89, 198
Aeon. *See* Dualism, old and new aeon.
Anamnesis, 177–79, 183
Anthropological time. *See* Time.
Anderson, Carl, 140n14
Andresen, C., 141n17
Anthropology, xx, 35, 68, 71, 85n30, 91, 136, 181n202, 182n205, 184–85, 187, 197n29
Antinomic, 34; antinomical tension, 42, 192, 197
Apocalyptic theology, 79n2
Aristotle, 109, 117–19; Aristotelian, 193n20
Ascension, 7–8, 77, 153, 163
Ascent, 5, 14, 16, 40, 84, 174, 192
Asceticism, 18n86, 48, 50, 77
Augustine, Saint, xxii, 51n150, 72, 89, 95n66, 122, 125n176, 142, 155, 193
Ayres, Lewis, 103n96

Baader, Xaver von, 156n86
Baptism, 8, 16, 20, 22, 38, 39n15, 50, 56–57, 59–61, 69, 77, 155, 161, 173, 186

Barth, Karl, 24n112, 78, 80n25, 85n25, 86–88, 98, 101
Bernanos, Georges, 150n59
Bernard of Clairvaux, Saint, 130n195
Biological time. *See* Time.
Bloch, Ernst, 151
Boersma, Hans, 24n114, 35n2, 101n85
Boeve, Lieven, 103n95
Bonaventure, Saint, 107, 126–27
Bouyer, Louis, 39n15
Buber, Martin, xix, 58, 137, 155
Buddhism, 92, 97
Bulgakov, Sergius, 58n100
Bultmann, Rudolf, 78–79, 87–88, 99, 101–02, 104, 114

Campbell, Douglas, 79n2
Cavanaugh, William, 92n56
Chalcedon, 144, 148, 155; Chalcedonian Christology, 104, 111
Chesterton, G. K., 174
Chrysostom, John, Saint, 4, 68
Church, xx, xxii, 2, 4–6, 8, 10–11, 13–16, 18–22, 24–26, 31–32, 35, 37n8, 38, 39n15, 40, 43, 46, 48–49, 57–59, 61, 63, 69, 73–74, 80–83, 85, 92, 95–99, 103–04, 106, 115, 128–33, 135, 138–40, 144–45, 147, 155–56, 163, 177–78, 181, 184, 187, 191–92, 197n29
City, 95, 98, 120, 125

209

Collins, Christopher S., 126
Commandments, 176–78
Communication, 14, 32, 142, 144–46, 159–60, 187
Communion, 11–13, 20, 29, 32, 36, 44, 53–56, 58–59, 62, 74–76, 90, 121, 140, 143, 148–50, 154–55, 159–60, 162, 166, 168–71, 174, 182–83, 186, 194
Community, 15, 22, 73, 82, 91, 95, 98n75, 170, 173, 177
Congar, Yves, 35n2
Conscience, 138, 175–79, 183
Conscientia, 177–78
Constantinople, Third Council of, 10, 144, 148–49
Continuity, 55, 60, 86, 88, 91, 96–99, 102–04, 110, 116, 124, 137, 167
Corkery, James, xxin18, 182n205
Cosmic time. *See* Time.
Cosmos, xxii, 3, 6, 17, 57, 90–91, 112, 117, 125–27, 135, 139, 168, 170, 180, 190n16, 195n22
Covenant, 7n23, 84, 86, 88–89, 103, 112, 118, 135, 149
Creation, 1–5, 8, 15, 17–18, 28–29, 37, 44, 46, 49, 53–55, 59, 61–62, 69–70, 72, 76, 79, 83–86, 88–91, 105–06, 108, 110, 113, 116, 128, 130, 135, 167, 169–70, 176–77, 179, 192n18
Creator, 48, 59, 66, 99, 105, 108, 110, 166, 176, 180, 183, 195
Crucifixion, 7n23, 111, 179
Cullmann, Oscar, 75n159, 78, 99, 103, 144, 157n93, 158
Cunningham, Lawrence, 139
Cycle, 21n96, 27, 190

Daniél, Jean, 101n86, 127n186
Da-sein, xviii, 27n121, 48
Death, xviiin3, xx–xxiii, 4, 7–9, 21–22, 24, 27–33, 37, 39, 42n24, 44–47, 51–56, 59, 62, 65, 69, 72, 79, 82, 92, 104, 111, 117–19, 124, 133, 137, 144, 146, 150, 156–62, 164, 166–69, 172–74, 182, 184, 186, 190–96

Deification, 20, 89, 127, 168, 171, 180
Descartes, René, 93, 156n86
Dia-logos, 142–43, 146, 160
Dialogue, xx–xxi, 80, 85, 111, 135, 141, 143–47, 167, 187, 196–97
Dies irae, 80–81
Dix, Gregory, 21, 23, 25–26
Docetism, 105
Dominic, Saint, 130n195
Drever, Matthew, 142n21
Dualism, 42n21; body and soul, 51, 75, 157, 166, 172, 194; liturgical, 20–26, 28, 32–34; of old and new aeon, xxii, 19n89, 26, 118, 164, 190, 192–93, 197; of two natures, 148

Eighth day, 58, 60–61, 69, 77, 191
ἐκκλησίαι, 95
Epiklesis, 15, 40
Epiphany, 6, 9, 58–59, 81
Equality, 66–68, 188
Eschatological symbolism, 9, 17n82, 24n113, 32–34, 90, 116
Eschatologically transparent time. *See* Time.
Eschatology, xviii, xx–xxiii, 1–9, 19n89, 20–26, 32, 34–35, 42, 64, 71, 78–83, 85, 90–91, 96, 100–01, 103–04, 107, 110–11, 113–116, 121, 125, 130, 135–37, 157, 183–85, 188, 194, 197, 198
Eschaton, 4, 24, 32n141, 56, 79, 96, 111, 114
Essence, xviii–xix, 5, 14, 19n89, 39n15, 40, 46n41, 51n59, 57–58, 62, 64–67, 73, 89, 123–24, 129, 148, 175
Essentialism (anti-), 138, 175, 179, 180; essentialist (anti-), xviii, 175, 180–81, 183
Eternal life, 2, 11, 55, 58, 61, 72, 77, 82, 116, 118, 120–21, 134, 136, 150, 166, 169
Eternal reality, 40, 133–34
Eternity, xxii, 38, 40, 54, 59, 62, 72, 77–79, 116–25, 128, 133–34,

INDEX 211

136, 151, 154, 165–69, 172–74, 186, 193
Eucharist, xxii, 1, 2, 4–9, 13–20, 22–26, 32n141, 34–39, 42–47, 56, 61, 63–65, 67, 70, 72–74, 76–77, 90–91, 114–15, 130n195, 162, 170, 182–83, 186, 191–92, 195, 197
Evil, xxii, 28, 37, 44n29, 54, 67, 130–31, 162, 189
Exegesis, 102–03, 113. *See also* Prosopographic exegesis.
Existence, xviii, 25, 27, 31, 34, 37, 44, 51n59, 55, 60, 68, 75–76, 84, 86, 91–92, 96, 104, 108–09, 111n126, 112–13, 115–16, 118–21, 123, 134, 136, 146–47, 150–52, 157, 159–61, 165–67, 170–71, 175, 183–86, 190, 193n20, 195
Exitus et reditus, 83–85, 88, 113, 126, 130, 135, 149, 178, 182n205, 183, 197
Fagerberg, David, 11, 18n86, 42n21, 198n33
the Fall, 2, 13, 29, 69, 84, 161–62
Family, xx, 67, 130n196, 149, 177
Father, xxii, 4, 11, 25, 29, 56, 63–65, 67–68, 76, 87, 107–08, 120, 136, 140, 143–47, 150, 160, 182, 187
Fear, 76, 152–53
Feuerbach, Ludwig, xvii, 52
Filial thesis, 144
Finitude, 84, 103
Fletcher, Patrick, 170n150
Forgiveness, 30, 179, 183
Francis, Saint, 130n195
Freedom, 12, 18, 29, 53, 66–67, 83–85, 90–92, 99–100, 113, 139, 143, 147n44, 149, 163, 171, 175, 182, 192
the Future, xxii, 8, 20, 24–26, 31–32, 35, 47, 56, 70, 82, 85, 88, 94, 102, 112, 116, 119–22, 133–34, 136, 152, 154, 158, 166n128, 167, 173n176, 174, 181–82, 190–91, 197

Gaál, Emery de, 83, 99, 103n96
Gaudium et Spes, xvii, 85n30, 184
Genealogy of the devil, 66, 68
Germanus of Constantinople, 10–11
Gnosticism, 12, 18, 135
Good Shepherd, 85, 89–90, 135
Grace, 9, 14–15, 86, 88, 115, 119, 158, 167, 182n205, 192n19–193n19
Grant, George, xviiin3, xixn7
Gratitude, xxii, 17, 32, 36, 62–63, 71, 74, 77, 195–97
Gregory of Nyssa, 17n114
Guardini, Romano, 106
Guerriero, Elio, xxin16
Guilt, 124, 134, 173–74, 179

Hart, David Bentley, 130
Hastetter, Michaela C., 111n126
Heaven, 1, 5, 15, 17, 55, 76, 78, 87, 96, 108, 115, 124, 132, 150, 191, 192
Hebrew, 20–23, 108
Hegel, Georg Wilhelm Friedrich, 88n39, 99
Heidegger, Martin, xviii–xix, 24n21, 27, 31, 33, 48–51, 152n71, 157, 171n156, 180n199
Hell, 78, 150
Hierarchy, 11n40, 64–66, 68, 180, 188
Historical being, 27, 172; historical church, 129, 131–32; historical event, 24, 31, 37, 39, 40–42, 91, 101–02, 111; historical paradigm, 88, 93–94; historical person, 136, 172, 175, 179–80, 183; historical reduction, 48; historical time. *See* Time.
Historicism, xviiin3, 49, 51, 106
History, xxii, 2, 8, 20–23, 25–27, 36, 38–41, 45, 49, 51, 86–108, 110–19, 122, 124–36, 138, 140, 145n38, 146, 154, 157–58, 163–65, 167–68, 170, 173, 175–76, 177n187, 179, 181–83, 188–90, 193–95, 197–98; as salvation, 91–92, 94, 96, 98, 102

INDEX

Holy Spirit, 4–5, 11, 15–16, 24, 59, 65, 68, 140, 150, 187; Holy Ghost, 136
Homo adorans, 13, 47–48, 52, 63, 73–74, 89
Hope, 52, 79, 81–82, 88n37, 95–96, 98, 112, 121, 135, 151–54, 165, 171–72
Horan, Daniel P., 180n198
Humanity, 7, 13, 28–29, 48, 85, 90, 93, 106, 123, 137, 149, 157, 167, 177n187, 179, 181, 193
Human nature, xix, 44, 49–51, 85, 100, 148, 175, 181n202

Identity, xvii, xix, xxii–xxiii, 69, 85–86, 91, 108, 110, 137, 155, 158, 166–67, 174, 182–84, 186–87, 197; and the body, 52–56, 194–95; filial, 76; Jesus's, 145–48, 181; and hope, 151–54; and naming, 57–63, 65, 77; self-identity, 151; and the soul, 168–69; without relationship, 74–75, 77
Imago Dei, 45, 143, 156, 176
Immortality, 51–52, 56, 75, 78, 136–37, 157–58, 160–61, 166–67, 183, 188, 195
Immortal Soul, 52, 158, 166–67
Impersonal nature, 48, 51
Incarnate Word, xvii
Incarnation, xviii, 11, 17, 25, 29, 43, 45, 53, 76, 94, 97, 104, 113, 118, 125, 129, 138, 144, 149, 151, 180
Individualism, xviiin3, 74, 82, 120, 172
Israel, 111, 127, 158–59; Israelites, 131–32
I-Thou, 59, 62, 68, 75, 134, 137, 155–57
I-Thou-We, xxiii, 137, 155, 157, 165, 195

Jenson, Robert W., 80
Jesus (Christ), xviii, 7n23, 11, 26, 28, 30–31, 45–46, 58, 60, 64, 79, 82, 85, 87, 90, 94–95, 99–100, 103n97, 104–05, 107–08, 111, 114, 118n147, 119, 124–25, 128, 131, 133, 139, 144–49, 155, 163, 166, 181–82, 196
John Paul II, Pope Saint, xx, 126
Joy, 5, 7–8, 17, 24, 27, 30, 40–41, 58, 115, 133, 152, 164, 184, 196n25
Judgment, 2, 78, 82, 119, 157, 161, 164, 178–79, 183, 189
Justice, xix, 12, 110, 120–21, 134
Justin Martyr, 140–41

Kadavil, Mathai, 17n82
Kaethler, Andrew T. J., 51n61, 66n129, 68n135, 74n157, 147n44, 150n59, 156n82, 186n4
Kant, 93n61, 180
Kasper, Walter, xixn11, 143n24
Keller, Catherine, 180n200
Kelsey, David H., 157n94
Kerr, Fergus, 101, 155n82
King, 49–50, 63, 68–70
Kingdom, xxi–xxii, 1, 3–6, 8–9, 14–16, 19–22, 24–26, 31–33, 35–42, 45, 47, 55–56, 59–61, 69–70, 72–73, 76, 81–83, 98, 114, 116, 121, 124, 130–33, 135–36, 153–54, 185, 191–92, 195

Lash, Nicholas, 166n128
Last Supper, xvii, 16, 36–42, 46–47, 76
Last things, xxii–xxiii, 7, 76, 78, 80, 82, 118, 133, 135, 183, 194–95, 198
Lazarus, 172; Saturday, 28–29, 39–41
Lewis, C. S., 56, 186n8
Lex orandi, 11
Liturgy, 3–6, 9–11, 14–16, 21, 23, 25–26, 28, 36–37, 40, 43, 46, 56, 59, 62n108, 64, 69–70, 77, 133, 163
Liturgical dualism. *See* Dualism.
Logos, 28, 83n17, 93–94, 106, 114, 125–26, 128–29, 132–33, 135, 138–39, 141–43, 146, 148–49, 151, 155, 174, 177, 179–82
Lombard, Peter, 106
Loon, Hans van, 24n112

Love, 5, 18–19, 29–30, 34, 37, 41,
　　44–47, 53–54, 55n86, 58, 62,
　　64, 66–67, 73, 83, 84–85, 87,
　　89, 107, 109–13, 115, 119–21,
　　123–29, 130n195, 133–35, 139,
　　142–43, 147–53, 155, 160–61,
　　165–69, 173–75, 177, 179, 183,
　　186–89, 193, 196
Luther, Martin, 86, 88, 92, 96–98, 104,
　　109, 113

MacDonald, George, 150
Mark of Ephesus, Saint, 47n41
Marriage, 155
Marten, J. Louis, 79n2
Martyria, 45, 50, 77
Marx, Karl, 88, 92, 109, 151; Marxism,
　　79–80, 94, 120
Mary, 64n118, 65
Materialism, 18–19, 172
Maximus the Confessor, 10–11, 15,
　　148
McGregor, Peter John, 144
Memoria-time. *See* Time.
Memory, 35–36, 39–47, 76, 118n147,
　　122, 134, 177, 184, 194
Messiah, 22, 24, 26, 33
Metaphysics, 91, 93–94, 97, 99n77,
　　102, 105, 107–08, 110, 138, 157
Metz, Johann Baptist, 98, 118n147,
　　128n198
Microcosm, 8, 49, 126
Moltmann, Jürgen, 88n37
Monge, Rico, 52n67
Morrill, Bruce T., 164n121
Moses, 107, 181
Mount Tabor, 56, 72, 77, 163
Munus triplex, 64, 68. *See also* Office,
　　threefold.
Murphy, Nancey, 51–52
Mysterion, 10, 15
Mystery, xvii–xviii, 10, 15, 28, 39, 44,
　　100, 115, 138–40, 155, 156n82,
　　175, 184

Naming, 48, 57–59, 61–62, 65, 77
Nietzsche, Friedrich, 52n66, 109, 179,
　　196

Noble, Ivan R., 14n60
Nonbeing, 28–29, 89, 92, 159–60
Nuptial mystery, 155, 156n82

Obedience, 7n23, 29, 64–68, 71–72,
　　76, 146–47, 155, 160–61, 183,
　　187–88
Obliviousness, 44–45, 71, 76
O'Donoghue, Neil Xavier, 198n33
Office, threefold, 51, 63–64, 68–69
Ontology, 10, 35–36, 48, 51, 63, 79,
　　86–88, 90–91, 97–98, 100,
　　102–105, 108, 110–11, 113–16,
　　135–36, 138, 175–76, 181n202;
　　relational, xix–xx, 76, 78, 146,
　　147n44, 180n200, 194
Orthopraxy, 107, 109
Otherness, 68, 150–51, 159, 180

Palamas, Gregory, 47n41
Paradigm, 93–94, 102
Paradise, 2, 6–7, 9, 76, 83, 154
Parousia, 22, 81, 127, 146
Participation, 8, 10, 12, 16, 18, 23, 36,
　　38–41, 47, 49, 62, 68, 114, 120–
　　21, 125, 162, 187, 191, 195
Pascha, 16, 24, 30–32, 37–38, 41, 61
Passage, xxii, 5–6, 8, 14–16, 30, 37, 56,
　　73, 76, 132, 146, 191, 192n18
Past, xxii, 25, 31–32, 35–39, 41–43, 45,
　　47, 49, 60, 79, 82, 85, 94–95,
　　102, 112, 119, 120–23, 127,
　　134, 136, 152, 154, 163, 165,
　　167n138, 173n166, 174, 178,
　　182, 190, 197
Patrick, Saint, 189
Paul, Saint, 94, 103n97, 156, 171–72
Pecknold, C. C., 175, 180
Persona, 140, 142
Personal thesis, 147
Personalism, xix, 155, 157
Personhood, xviii, xix–xxiii, 6, 35, 48,
　　50–51, 55, 57, 59–60, 75, 77,
　　137, 141, 157–158, 167, 175,
　　182, 184–88; body of Christ
　　and, 72–74; the priesthood of
　　Christ and, 63–72
Peter, Saint, 46, 145, 186

Phan, Peter C., 173n166–174n166
Philosophy, 99–100, 106, 114, 129, 138–139, 158
Physical time. *See* Time.
Pieper, Josef, 121n158, 174n170
Piety, 40
Pilate, Pontius, 38, 147
Plato, 75, 92, 139, 167n138, 183; Platonism, 52n67, 92, 194
Plekon, Michael, 189n15
Praise, 17n81, 22, 67, 159, 164, 179, 195n22
Prayer, 1, 12, 21n96, 22–23, 36, 43, 57–58, 81, 139–40, 144–45, 147–48, 156, 182, 189, 193n20
the Present, xxii, 9, 25, 28, 31–32, 35–36, 39–41, 47, 54, 79, 81, 85, 106, 116, 121–23, 130n195, 134, 136, 152–54, 173n166, 179, 191, 194, 197
Priest, xx, 13, 48, 50, 63–64, 68–70, 164, 169–170, 180, 186, 195; high priest, 47–48, 64; priesthood, 36, 50, 51n59, 63, 70–71, 195n22
Prophet, 63, 68–70, 141
Prosopographic exegesis, 140–41
Punishment, 30, 81
Purgatory, 78, 136, 157, 173–74, 183

Rahner, Karl, 98–100, 113, 161
Rausch, Thomas, 118n147
Realism, 80, 101, 149
Receptive Aspect, 57
Reconciliation, 98
Redeemer, 85n22, 108, 110, 125, 183, 195
Redemption, 17, 46, 76, 79, 86, 88, 91, 108, 110, 161, 163, 165, 181
Reentrance, 38, 39n15, 41
Relationality, xxii–xxiii, 59, 66, 75, 114–15, 118, 123–24, 128, 133, 135–36, 142–43, 147, 151, 157–58, 165, 167–68, 182, 185, 188–90, 193, 195, 197–98
Relations, 83, 90, 114, 119, 123, 140, 142, 146, 150, 168, 172, 175, 181n202, 186, 188

Remembrance, xxii, 16, 35–47, 76, 158, 194
Resurrection, xxii, 7, 22, 24, 28, 30–32, 37, 41, 51–55, 78, 81–82, 89, 91, 103–05, 111–13, 135, 144, 146, 157–58, 160–61, 166, 168, 171–72, 196
Revelation, 15, 17, 46, 107, 178
Richard of St Victor, 147
Ross, Susan A., 197n29
Rowland, Tracey, xxn14, 98n75, 103n96
Rushdie, Salman, 137

Sabbath, 23, 69, 89
Sacrament(s), 47, 56, 60, 61, 63, 68, 74, 90, 115, 130–131, 163, 191, 192n18, 195n22, 196n25; of assembly, 73; and eschatology, 2–8; of person, 58–60; and symbol, 9–23, 32
Sacrifice, 29, 63, 85, 89, 112, 144, 164–65, 186, 195
Salvation, 2, 8, 15, 17, 29, 45–46, 49, 63, 82, 87, 91–92, 94–95, 97, 100–01, 108, 112, 128–29, 131, 151
Salvation history, 2, 23, 33, 59, 79, 82, 87n37, 91–92, 96–98, 100–04, 106–07, 110–13, 124–25, 127–29, 132, 135, 165, 172
Sartre, Jean-Paul, xviii
Savior, 46, 59, 72
Schumacher, Jared, 91n54
Second Vatican Council. *See* Vatican II.
Secular, 12, 48, 60, 63, 97–98
Seewald, Peter, xxin16, 154n78, 177n187
Sein-für-die-Anderen, 156
Sein-mit-anderen, 112, 121, 123, 161, 163, 174
Separation, 29–31, 53, 65, 89, 95, 161, 166, 170–71
Sheol, 124, 159–60, 162
Sin, 8, 13, 17, 29, 37, 39, 44, 56, 65, 84, 86, 112, 156, 159, 196, 196n25
Socrates, 92
Söhngen, Gottlieb, 101n86

INDEX

Sojourner, 95–96, 98
Son, xvii, 4, 7, 18, 29, 36–37, 46, 58, 64, 68 76, 81, 86, 119, 124, 129, 135–36, 138, 140–41, 143–51, 154, 179, 182, 187–88, 191–92
Sons and daughters of God, 36, 66, 76, 149
Sonship, 65, 67–68, 140, 144–46, 187–88
Sopko, Andrew, 198n32
Spiritual body, 54–55
Statu die, 60–61, 191
Steinbeck, John, 184
Steinbüchel, Theodor, 155
Subordination, 64–65, 76
Substance, xviii, 105, 142–43, 149, 153–54, 179, 181n202, 182, 192n18
Suffering, 124, 159, 162–65, 173, 183; co-suffering, 30, 163–64

Telos, 8–9, 28, 30–31, 33–34, 37, 42, 62, 71, 112, 125, 185, 191; teleological framework, 146–47, 190, 194; teleology, 129, 198
Temple, 4, 7n23, 21, 23, 55, 59, 62, 78
Temporality, xviii, xxii–xxiii, 20, 27, 32–35, 42, 77, 79, 94–95, 99, 116–19, 123–24, 133, 135–36, 138, 152, 154, 158, 165–66, 173n166, 182, 185–86, 188, 191–95, 197–98
Tertullian, 140–43
Thanksgiving, xxii, 2, 4, 6–7, 9, 16–17, 32, 34–38, 42, 46–48, 56, 62–68, 70–72, 76, 83, 162, 180, 186, 188, 195–96
Theosis, 89, 185
Third Council of Constantinople. *See* Constantinople, Third Council of
Thomas Aquinas, Saint, 75n158, 106, 155n82, 169
Time, xviii–xix, xxi–xxii, 2–3, 7–8, 14, 18–33, 35, 38–42, 45–47, 49–51, 55, 60–62, 69, 71–72, 76–75, 79, 81, 83, 85–86, 99, 105, 107, 114, 116–31, 133, 137, 146, 152, 154, 157, 163–65, 168, 173–75, 181–83, 184–86, 188–94, 195n22, 197–98; anthropological, 118–19, 121, 124n176, 193; biological, 116–17; cosmic, 116–17, 122, 124–25; eschatologically transparent, 21, 23, 26, 33; historical, 36, 125, 133, 165; *Memoria*-time, 117, 122–24, 134, 136, 152, 173n166, 174, 190, 193–94, 198; physical, 118, 120–21, 123–24, 134, 165, 173, 174n166, 190, 193
Transfiguration, 17, 60, 77, 145–46, 163
Trinity, xix, 5, 59, 83n17, 138, 140–41, 144, 182, 187–88, 195
Tutu, Desmond, 157
Twomey, D. Vincent, 102, 177, 196

Union, 17, 54, 89, 125, 148–50, 153, 155, 186
Unity, 5, 16, 63, 67, 99, 103n96, 105, 107–08, 142–45, 148–49, 155, 167, 170–71, 174, 182, 192n18
Universe, 61, 90, 110, 125, 139, 144, 172

Vatican II, xxi, 101, 129, 198n33
Vico, Giambattista, 93n61
Vinogradov, Alexis, 43n25
Vocation, 48–49, 51, 64, 68–73, 77
Volitional thesis, 144, 148, 155, 182

Ware, Kallistos, 55n86
Webster, John, 181n202, 185n2
Wilken, Robert Louis, 3
Worship, xix, 5, 7n23, 8–9, 13, 18–23, 26, 32, 34, 40, 43, 48, 60, 63, 66, 69, 73, 89, 181, 195
Wright, N. T., 158

Yahweh, 108, 159
Yoder, John Howard, 90

Zizioulas, John, xx, 140n13

www.ingramcontent.com/pod-product-compliance
Lightning Source LLC
Chambersburg PA
CBHW020408230426
43664CB00009B/1231